Laurens County
South Carolina

Minutes of the County Court

1786-1789

Brent H. Holcomb

HERITAGE BOOKS
2017

HERITAGE BOOKS
AN IMPRINT OF HERITAGE BOOKS, INC.

Books, CDs, and more—Worldwide

For our listing of thousands of titles see our website
at
www.HeritageBooks.com

Published 2017 by
HERITAGE BOOKS, INC.
Publishing Division
5810 Ruatan Street
Berwyn Heights, Md. 20740

Copyright © 2004 Brent H. Holcomb
SCMAR
Columbia, South Carolina

All rights reserved. No part of this book may be reproduced or transmitted in any form or by any means, electronic or mechanical, including photocopying, recording or by any information storage and retrieval system without written permission from the author, except for the inclusion of brief quotations in a review.

International Standard Book Numbers
Paperbound: 978-0-7884-5754-8

INTRODUCTION

It is very unusual for a record such as these minutes of the county court for Laurens County to surface after being lost for so many years. While this volume is not complete, missing the first fifty-four pages, pages 103-126, and an unknown number of pages at the end of the volume, it is still an exciting and significant find. There was probably at least one other volume, still missing, which would cover the years 1790-1799. There are now twelve counties in South Carolina for which such minutes are extant.

Laurens County was formed in 1785 as a county of Ninety Six District. In that year justices of the peace were elected by the General Assembly to be administrators of the county courts. Within the pages of these court minutes are small court cases, lists of deeds presented to be recorded, applications for administrations on estates and wills proved (beginning in 1787), jury lists, petitions of various kinds, appointments for various offices, apprenticeships, estray animals tolled, and other items. The cases heard for debt or damages could not exceed £50, and cases heard for personal damages could not exceed £20. Criminal cases heard could not call for the loss of life or corporal punishment. Larger court cases were heard in the district courts, such as Ninety Six. Some deeds are listed in these minutes which deeds were not recorded for lack of proof. There are deeds listed which appear to have been recorded in Laurens County Deed Book B on the twenty pages of that deed book which are missing.

Occasionally, one can infer a relationship of a plaintiff or defendant to a juror, when a juror does not serve on a particular case. For example, in the case on page 73 (13 December 1787) William Young vs James McNees & Hugh Young, one can notice the absence on the jury of Robt McNees, William Young, and Joseph Young, who served on the jury in other cases heard at that same court. Of course, the plaintiff William Young could not serve on the jury for his own case.

Laurens County bordered on the counties of Spartanburg, Union, Newberry, Abbeville, Greenville, and Edgefield. Before the formation of Greenville County, the area below Pearis's wagon road was considered to be in Laurens County. A small portion of Laurens County was annexed to Greenville County in 1793, the part of Greenville County which was below the "ancient boundary," or the Indian line, run by North Carolina in 1767. The map included herein contributed by Mrs. Anne K. McCuen indicates these areas.

My thanks goes to Mr. Charles W. Hawkins, of Gray Court, South Carolina, and to the South Carolina Archives and History Center for making this document available. My thanks goes to Mr. James D. McKain for preparing the excellent index.

Brent H. Holcomb
May 10, 2004

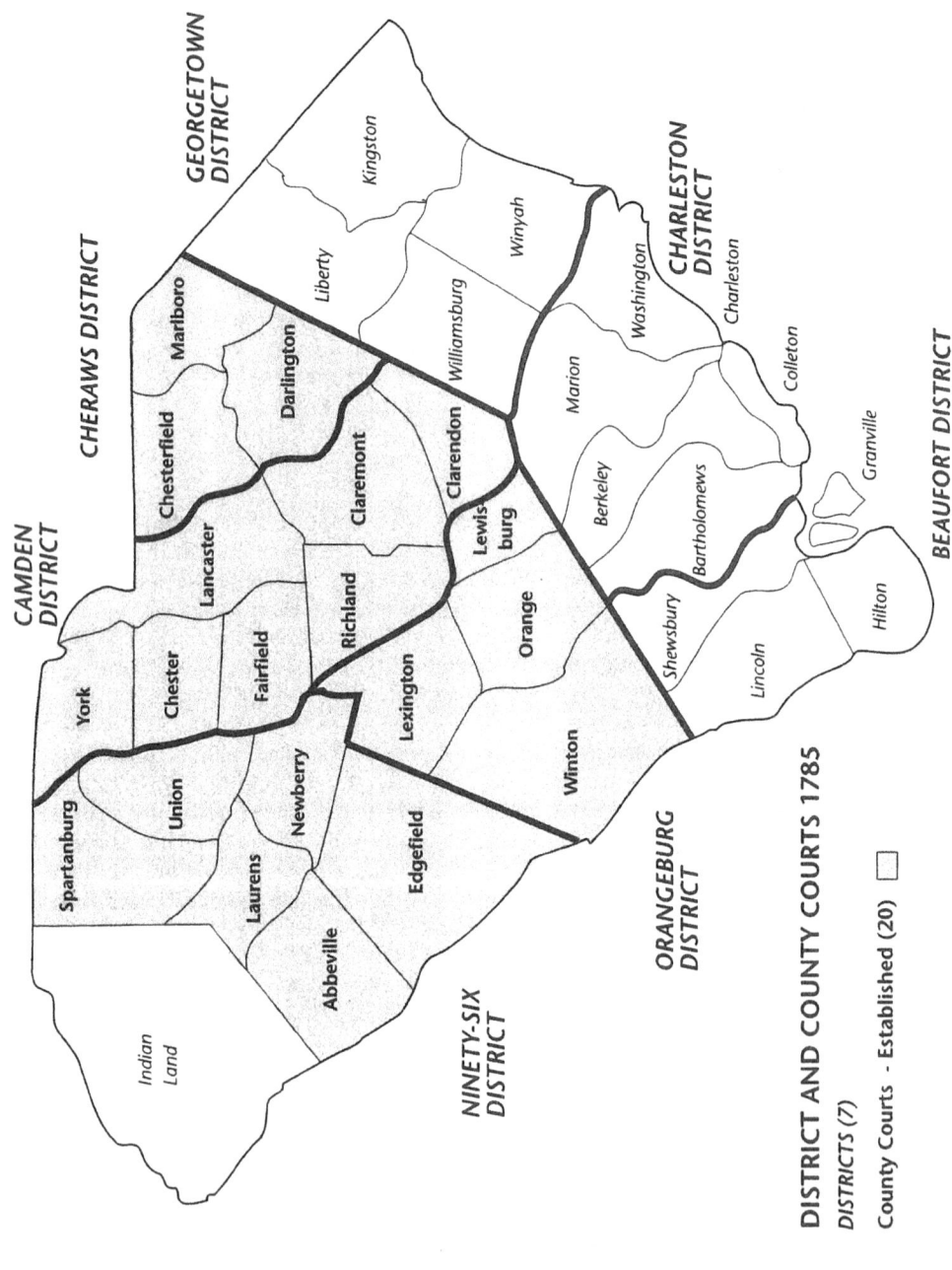

Map courtesy of the South Carolina Archives and History Center.

Map courtesy of Mrs. Anne K. McCuen, historian, Greenville, SC.

The following persons were Drawn to Serve as Grand Jurours at December Court next viz.

1 James Young	11 William Harris
2 Robert Cuningham	12 Arthur Dunham
3 John Brown Senr.	13 Wm Griffin
4 Reubin Pyles	14 Geo Aitchuson
5 John McClintock	15 Sandy Walker
6 James Craig	16 Lewis Banton
7 Thomas McCrary	17 George Hollingsworth
8 Thomas Vakes	18 George Young
9 Joshua Saxon	19 Richd. Pugh
10 Shadrach Martin	20 Nehemiah Franks

George Walker Esqr. Produced in Open Court a Credential Signed by the Honble. John Rutledge Edanus Burke and Henry Pendleton Esqrs. Judges of the Court of Common pleas of this State Admitting him the said George Walker to practice as an Attorney at Law in any of the Courts of Law or Equity in this State. Whereupon it was Ordered that he the said George Walker be enroled as such in this Court

The Last Will and Testament of James McCain Decd. was presented in Open Court by Elizabeth McCain the Executrix therein named & proven by John Hollingsworth one of the Witnesses thereunto and Ordered to be Recorded —

On motion of the said Elizabeth McCain Executrix aforesd. it was Ordered that Letters Testamentory Issue in form She being first Duly Qualified According to Law

Ordered that A Warrant of Appraisment Issue to four freehol=ders who being first Sworn before some one Justice of the peace of this County to praise the Estate of the d. Jas. McCain and Return a Copy of the d. Appraisment to the d. Exrx within forty Days &c

LAURENS COUNTY, SOUTH CAROLINA
MINUTES OF THE COUNTY COURT 1786-1789

[15 March 1786]

Page 55: Joseph Box Plf vs John[?] Ritchey Deft. Trespass. This day came the Deft by Chas Goodwin and Danl Brown his attorneys & the Pltf Tho solemly cald came not but made Default nor is his Suit further Prosecuted. Therefore on Motion of the Deft by his attorneys aforesaid it is Considered by the Court that the Deft Recover against the said Plf five shillings Damages besides his cost by him about his Defence in this behalf Expended, according to the Act of Assembly in that Case made & provided.

Clerks fees	£ 7	6
Sheriffs Fees	4	8
Attorney's fees	1 1	9.

Joseph Box Plt vs Saml Scott Deft. Trespass. Came the Deft by Chas Goodwin and Danl Brown his attorneys & the Pltf Tho solemly cald came not but made Default nor is his Suit further Prosecuted. Therefore on Motion of the Deft by his attorneys aforesaid it is Considered by the Court that the Deft Recover against the said Plf five shillings Damages besides his cost by him about his Defence in this behalf Expended, according to the Act of Assembly in that Case made & provided.

Clerks fees	£ 7	6
Sheriffs Fees	4	8
Attorney's fees	1 1	9
	£1 13	11.

Joseph Box Plf vs David Alexander Deft. Trespass. Came the Deft by Chas Goodwin and Danl Brown his attorneys & the Pltf Tho solemly cald came not but made Default nor is his Suit further Prosecuted. Therefore on Motion of the Deft by his attorneys aforesaid it is Considered by the Court that the Deft Recover against the said Plf five shillings Damages besides his cost by him about his Defence in this behalf Expended, according to the Act of Assembly in that Case made & provided.

Clerks fees	£ 7	6
Sheriffs Fees	4	8
Attorney's fees	1 1	9.

Page 56: Joseph Box Plt vs David Alexander Ju'r Deft. Trespass. This day came the Deft by Chas Goodwin and Danl Brown his attorneys & the Pltf Tho solemly cald came not but made Default nor is his Suit further Prosecuted. Therefore on Motion of the Deft by his attorneys aforesaid it is Considered by the Court that the Deft Recover against the said Plf five shillings Damages besides his cost by him about his Defence in this behalf Expended, according to the Act of Assembly in that Case made & provided.

Clerks fees	£ 7	6
Sheriffs Fees	4	8
Attorney's fees	1 1	9
	£1 13	11.

LAURENS COUNTY SC COURT MINUTES 1786-1789

[15 March 1786]
Joseph Box Plt vs John Moore Deft. Trespass. This day came the Deft by Chas Goodwin and Danl Brown his attorneys & the Pltf Tho solemly cald came not but made Default nor is his Suit further Prosecuted. Therefore on Motion of the Deft by his attorneys aforesaid it is Considered by the Court that the Deft Recover against the said Plf five shillings Damages besides his cost by him about his Defence in this behalf Expended, according to the Act of Assembly in that Case made & provided.

Clerks fees	£ 7 6
Sheriffs Fees	4 8
Attorney's fees	1 1 9
	£1 13 11.

Joseph Box Plt vs John Gocher Deft. Trespass. This day came the Deft by Chas Goodwin and Danl Brown his attorneys & the Pltf Tho solemly cald came not but made Default nor is his Suit further Prosecuted. Therefore on Motion of the Deft by his attorneys aforesaid it is Considered by the Court that the Deft Recover against the said Plf five shillings Damages besides his cost by him about his Defence in this behalf Expended, according to the Act of Assembly in that Case made & provided.

Clerks fees	£ 7 6
Sheriffs Fees	4 8
Attorney's fees	1 1 9
	£1 13 11.

Page 57: Edward Musgrove Plf vs Daniel Jackson Deft. On attachment. This day Came the Plt. by Wm. Shaw his attorney and the Deft in his proper Person and Sayeth that he cannot Gainsay the Plts action for £25 sterling with Intrest from the 10th day of December 1785 till the Levying the Execution and cost with Stay of Execution for Six Months. Therefore it is Considered by the Court that the Plt Recover against the said Deft the said £25 with Intrest with the Cost by him in this behalf Expended. and the said Deft in Mercy

Clerks fees	£ 8 6
Sheriffs Fees	
Attorney's fees	1 1 9.

Reubin Pyles & Con. Plf vs Shadrach Martin Deft. Case. This day came the Plt by J. Yancy and Jacob Brown his attorneys and the Deft. by Wm Shaw his attorney & the Plt failing to Produce or file his accounts when thereunto required on motion of the Deft by his attorney aforesaid it is considered by the Court that the Plt be non Suited, and that the Deft Recover against him five shillings Damages besides his costs by him about his Defence in this behalf Expended, according to the act of Assembly in that case made and Provided.

Clerks fees	£ 10 6
Sheriffs Fees	4 8
Attorney's fees	1 1 9
	£1 16 11.

LAURENS COUNTY SC COURT MINUTES 1786-1789

[15 March 1786]

An Indenture of a Bargain and Sale Between Wm Stewart and Alse Stewart his wife of the One Part, and Saml Eakins of the Other Part, was Proved this day in open court by the oaths of John Rainey and William Rainey the Subscribing Witnesses thereunto an ordered to be Recorded.

Page 58: George Anderson foreman. Saml Whorton, Jas Mcloklin, Benjn Rainey, Nehemiah Franks, Marshel Franks, James Abercrumbie, Charles Simms, John Ritchey, James Cook, Robt Ross, William Harris, Tully Choice, Where sworn Grand Jurors on inquest for the body of this County, and Haveing received their Charge Retired from the Bar, to Consult of their Verdict and after sum time Returned in to Court and present as follows to wit.

We Present Jean Berry for Haveing a Bastard Child and no Lawfull father for the same.
We further Present Lewis Devall and Elizabeth Duke for Living in Adultery &C.   George Anderson, foreman.
and the Grant Jury haveing Nothing further to present were Discharged.

Ordered that Process be Issued against the Several persons This day Presented by the Grand Jury to appear here at the next Court to answer to the presentments Exhibited against them Respectively.

Hugh McVay senr Plt vs Robert Maxwell Deft. In Trover and Convertion. Came the Plt by James Yancey & Jacob Brown his Attorneys & the Deft being Solemnly called but came not, and Thereupon came also a Jury to wit Samuel Eakins, James Underwood, Wm. Hunter, Mathew Hunter, Wm. Niel, John Manly, Saml Scott, Michael Waldrop, Wm. Martin, Joel Burges, Lewis Banton, Charles Allin, & Josiah East who being Sworn Diligently to Enquire of Damages in this Suit upon their oaths do say that the Plt. hath Sustaind Damages by Occation of the Convertion in the Declaration Mentioned to £19 s16 d 10 sterl'g besides his Cost by him in this behalf Expended.
Clerks fees   £ 16 2
Sheriffs Fees   12 8
Attorney's fees   1 1 9. But this Judgment to be Discharged by the Payment of Twelve pounds & cost of Suit.

Page 59: Alexander Harper Plt vs Nathaniel Austin Deft. Case. This day Came the Plt by Chas Goodwin his attorney and the Deft tho Solemnly calld came not but made Default. Therefore it is Considered by the Court that the Plt recover against the s'd Deft £2 s10 sterling & his cost by him about his Defence in this behalf Expended.
Clerks fees   £ 10 6
Sheriffs Fees   4 8
Attorney's fees   1 1 9
                    £1 16 11.

3

LAURENS COUNTY SC COURT MINUTES 1786-1789

Court Adjournd Till Tomorrow morning Nine Oclock. Minets sign'd after being publickly read by James Montgomery, John Rodgers, Wm. Mitchusson, Esquires.

Court Met according to adjournment the 16th March 1786. Present James Montgomery, Wm. Mitchusson, Charles Saxon, John Rodgers, Esquires.

On application of William Thomason he is Admitted To keep a Publick Tavern at his house where he now lives on Reaburns Creek for the Space of One Year from the Date hereof. Whereupon he the said William Thomason Together with Martin Williams and James Russel his Securities Entred into and Acknowledged their Bonds according to Law.

Page 60: John Rainey Plt vs Thomas Brandon Deft. Trespass, Assault and Battery. This day came the Plt by Wm. Shaw his Attorney and the Deft by J. Brown and James Yancey and Danl Brown his Attorneys Whereupon Came also a Jury to wit Samuel Eakins, James Underwood, William Hunter, Matthew Hunter, Wm. Niel, John Manly, Saml Scott, Michael Waldrop, William Martin, Joel Burges, Lewis Banton, Charles Allin, and Josiah East who being Sworn well and Truly to Trie the Issue Joined upon their oaths do Say that the Deft is Guilty of the assault and Battery in the Declaration Mentioned and they do assess the Plt Damages by Accation thereof to £2 sd besides his cost. Therefore it is Considerd by the Court that the Plt Recover against the said Deft his Damages aforesaid in form aforesaid assesst. and his cost by him in this Behalf Expended.

Clerks fees	£ 15	8
Sheriffs Fees	11	8
Attorney's fees	1 1	9
	£2 9	1.

Job Smith Plt vs Benjamin Evans & Charles Swillivant Defts. Debt. S. Process. This day came the Deft. by Danl Brown his Attorney and the Plf Tho Solemnly Calld Came not but made Default, Nor is his Suit further Prosecuted. Therefore on Motion of the Deft. by his Attorney aforesaid it is Considered by the Court, that the Deft recover against the said Plt five shillings Damages besides his cost by him in this Behalf Expended according to an act of Assembly in that Case made and Provided.

Clerks fees	£ 11	
Sheriffs Fees	3	6
Attorney's fees	14	9
	£1 8	6.

Page 61: Phillis Box Plt vs David Alexander Deft. Trespass. This day came the Deft. by Jacob Brown & James Yancey his Attorneys and the Plf Tho Solemnly Calld Came not nor is her Suit further Prosecuted. Therefore on Motion of the Deft. by his Attorneys aforesaid it is Considered by the Court, that the Deft recover against the said Plt five shillings Damages besides his

Costs by him in this Behalf Expended according to an act of Assembly in that Case made and Provided.

Clerks fees	£ 8 5
Sheriffs Fees	4 8
Attorney's fees	1 1 9
	£1 14 11.

[16 March 1786]

Robert Cooper Plt vs Charles Swillivant Deft. Debt. This day Came the Parties by their attys and the Deft Relinquishing his former Plea says he Cannot Gain say the Plts action for £16 s8 with Intrest thereon till paid, Therefore it is Considered by the Court that the Plt Recover against the said Deft the s'd Deft the said sum of £16 s8 with Intrest Thereon Besides his cost by him in this behalf Expended and the said Deft in Mercy &c.

Clerks fees	£ 10 6
Sheriffs Fees	4 8
Attorney's fees	1 1 9
	£1 16 11.

William Mitchusson Plt vs Edwerd Pugh Deft. This day came the Plt by J. Brown & J. Yancey his Attorneys and the Deft. by Charles Goodwin his Attorney whereupon came also a Jury to wit Samuel Eakins, James Underwood, Wm. Hunter, Matthew Hunter, Wm. Niel, John Manly, David McVay, Michael Waldroup, Wm. Martin, Joel Burges, Lewis Banton, and Charles Allin, who sworn well and truly to Try this Issue Joind, upon their oaths do say that the Plt. hath Sustaind [Page 62] Damages by Accation of the Defts Detaining the Debt in the Declaration Mentioned to one shilling sterling besides his Cost. Therefore it is Considerd by the court that the Plaintiff Recover against the said Deft his Debt amounting to £22 s5 d4 with Intrest and his cost by him in this behalf Expended and the s'd Deft. in Mercy &c.

Clerks fees	£ 18 2
Sheriffs Fees	14 2
Attorney's fees	1 1 9
	£2 14 1.

William Thomason Plt vs Henry White Deft. Trespass & Trover. This day came the Plt by Wm Shaw his Attorney and the Deft. by J. Brown, J. Yancey, & Charles Goodwin his Attorneys whereupon came also a Jury to wit, Samuel Eakins, James Underwood, William Hunter, Matthew Hunter, Wm. Niel, John Manly, David McVay, Michael Waldrop, Wm. Martin, Joel Burges, Lewis Banton, and Charles Allin, who sworn well and truly to Trie this Issue Joind, upon their oaths do say that the Deft. is not Guilty of the Trover & Convertion in the Declaration Mentioned in Manner & form as the Plt against him hath Declared. Therefore it is Considerd by the court that the Plt take nothing by his bill but for his false Clamour be in Mercy &c and that the Deft go hence without day & recover against the said Plt his cost by him about his Defence in this behalf Expended &c.

Clerks fees	£1 3 8	
Sheriffs Fees	14 2	
Attorney's fees	1 1 9	
	£2 19 7.	

Page 63: A Lease and Release for the Conveyance of 60 acres of Land from John Brotherton to James Adair Proven in open Court by the oath of Thomas Ewing & orderd to be Recorded.

A Lease and Release for the Conveyance of 139½ acres of Land from John Brotherton to James Cregg proved according to the former Act and Ordred to be Recorded.

A Lease and Release for the Conveyance of 200 acres of Land from Lewis Devall and Terry his wife to John Crumpton Proven in open court by the oaths of Thomas Word & John Powers and Ordred to be Recorded.

A copy of Daniel Ozburns oath Taken before William Mitchuson Esqr. the 16th March 1786 Present in open Court and ordred to be Recorded.

A Lease and Release for the Conveyance of 250 acres of Land from Joseph Adair Senr to Benj'a Adair proved according to the former Act & Ordred to be Recorded.

Elizabeth Tindsly Plt vs Robt McNees Deft. Trover and Convertion. Miss Trial and ordred to be Continued till the fourth day of Next June Court.

Court Adjournd Till Tomorrow morning 10 Oclock. The Minets after being publickly read in open Court were signed by James Montgomery, Wm. Mitchusson, John Rodgers, Esquires.

Page 64: Court Met According to Adjournment the 17 March 1786. Present the Worshipfulls James Montgomery, Charles Saxon, Wm. Mitchusson, Joseph Downs, Esquires.

Roger Brown Plt vs John Rogers Deft. Attachment. This day Came the Plt. and the Attach't being Returned Executed on a Bay horse the Property of the Deft. and the Deft not appearing to Replevy the same, it is considered by the Court that the Plt. recover against the said Deft. his Debt amounting to £2 s3 sterling and his cost by him in this behalf expended and the said Deft. in Mercy &C.

Ordred that the Sheriff Expose to publick the said horse by him attach't the property of the Deftt and pay the money arising from such sale to the Plt Towards Satisfaction of his Debt and Cost aforesaid and the overplus if any there be Return to the Deft.

Clerks fees	£ 6
Sheriffs Fees	5
	£ 11.

[17 March 1786]

Ordred that the following amendments be added to the Rates Established for the Regulation of the Publick Tavern keepers within this County to wit.

Good Pasturage P'r Night for one horse	/6d
Stableage and Plenty of Good fother for one horse Pr N't	/7
Corn P'r Gallon	/9
Ditto P'r pottle	/5
Oates P'r Gallon	/7
Ditto P'r pottle	/4
Good West Indian Rum Pr' ½ Pint	/10
Ditto P'r Gill	/6

Stephen Potter Plt vs Joseph Mayhon Deft. Trespass. By Consent of the Parties this Suit is Ordered to Continue Till June court next & c.

Page 65: John Martin Plt vs Robt McNees Deft. Case. This day came the Deft by J. Yancey his Attorney and the Plt failing to bring his Action Wright on motion of the Deft it is Considered by the court be non Suited & that the Deft Recover against the sid Plt five shillings Damages besides his costs by him about his Defence in this behalf Expended, according to the act of Assembly &c.

Lidia Shirley Plt vs John Obryan Deft. Detinue. By consent of the Parties by their Attorneys This Suit is ordred to be Continued to June Court next.

John Cargill Pl. vs James McNees Deft. Trover. This suit is ordred to be continued by consent of the Parties to June court next.

Andrew Rodgers Plf vs Daniel Wright Deft. Rover. Came the Deft. by Charles Goodwin his Attorney and the Plt. Tho Solemnly calld came not to Prosecute his suit, therefore on Motion of the Deft by his attorneys aforesaid it is Considerd by the Court that the Deft Recover against the said Plf five shillings Damages besides his cost by him about his Defence in this behalf Expended, according to the Act of Assembly in that Case made and provided.

Clerks fees	£ 8 6
Sheriffs Fees	4 8
Attorney's fees	1 1 9
	£1 14 11.

Page 66: Ann Madding Plf vs Clement Davis Deft. Trover & Convertion. Came the Deft by William Shaw his [sic] Attorney and the Plt tho Solemnly Calld came not but made Default nor is her suit further Prosecute, therefore, on Motion of the Deft by his atty aforesaid it is Considerd by the Court that

the s'd Det Recover against the said Plf five shillings Damages besides her Cost by him in this behalf Expended, according to the Act of Assembly in that Case made and provided.

Clerks fees	£ 18
Sheriffs Fees	1 9
Attorney's fees	1 1 9
	£2 18 11.

[17 March 1786]

Mary Williams Ex'r Plt vs Thomas Edgehill Ju'r Deft. Trover and Convertion. This day came the Plt by J. Brown, Y. Yancey and Wm. Shaw her attorneys, and the Deft by Charles Goodwin his Attorney, and thereupon Came also a Jury to wit William Neil, David McVay, Martin Williams John Manly Junr, Charles Allin, Robert Culbertson, Lewis Banton, Edwerd Mitchusson, William Dunlap, Joel Burges, James Downen, and John McElroy who being Sworn the Truth to Speak upon the Issue Joind upon their Oaths do say, that the Defendant is Guilty of the Trover and Convertion in the Declaration Mentioned, and they do Assess the Plt Damages by Accation thereof to £50 besides her cost. Therefore it is Considered by the Court that the Plt Recover against the said Deft her Damages aforesaid in form aforesaid assest, and her cost by her in This behalf Expended and the Deft in Mercy &c.

Clerks fees	£2 2 8
Sheriffs Fees	11 8
Attorney's fees	1 1 9
	£2 16 1.

Page 67: Jean Kellet Plf vs Wm Martin Deft. On attachment. This day came the Plt and the attachment being Returned Executed in Part and the Deft not appearing to Replevy &C it is Considered by the Court that the Plt Recover against the s'd Deft her Debt amounting to £3 s18 sterling and her cost by her in this behalf Expended, ordred that the Goods and Chattels attacht the Property of the Defts be Exposed to publick Sale, and the moneys arising from such sale Pay to the Plt towards Satisfaction of her Debt & Cost aforesaid and the overplus if any there be return to the Deft and if not Sufficient to discharge the Debt & Cost aforesaid, it is ordered that an Execution Issue against the Defts goods and Chattels for the Residue when Requird by the Plt.

Court adjourned to morrow morning Ten Oclock. Minets sign'd by Charles Saxon, Wm. Mitchusson, Joseph Downs, Jas Montgomery, Esquires.

Court Met according to adjournment the 18th March 1786. Present James Montgomery, Joseph Downs, Charles Saxon, John Rodgers, Wm. Mitchusson, Esquires.

At the suit Mary Williams against Thomas Edghill Junr the Deft in this Suit Prays an appeal and it is Granted him Tot he next court of Common Pleas Oyer and Terminer & C to be held at Ninety[six] the 16th of April Next whereupon he the said Thos Edghill Deft Together with Jas Finney his Security Entred into [**Page 68**] and Acknowledged their Bonds, To prosecute said Appeal.

[18 March 1786]

Edwerd Mitchuson Plt vs Jas & Susannah Allison Def. Trespass. This Suit is orderd to be continued Till June court Next, on oath being made by Deft that he could not Enforce the attendance of his Witness assentially necessary in this Tryall.

Robert McNees Plt vs John Martin Deft. In Debt. This day came the plt by J. Brown & J. Yancey his Attorneys and the Deft by William Shaw his attorney and Thereupon came also a Jury to wit, John McElroy, Joshua Arnold, Charles Swillivant, Saml Scott, Col. John Rodgers, James Saxon, James Watson, Robert Culbertson, James Adair, Stephen Potter, Andrew Rodgers & James Waldroup who being Elected, Tried & Sworn the Truth to Speak upon the Issue Joind upon their Oaths find for the Plt £7 s17 d1½ his Debt in the Declaration Mentioned, with one shilling Damages & Intrest for one year, beside his costs. Therefore it is considered by the court that the Plt Recover against the said Deft his Debt amounting to £7 17 1½ sterl'g and his Damages aforesaid in form aforesaid assesst and his Cost by him in this behalf Expended and the said Deft in Mercy &c.

Clerks fees   £ 14 8
Sheriffs Fees   6 8
Attorney's fees   1 1 9
                     £2 3 1.

Page 69: Mary Williams vs Thomas Edgehill Ju'r Deft. Execution haveing been Granted in this Case after Verdict, The Parties Came into Court and agreed that the s'd Execution should be withdrawn by Mutual Consent, and to Carry the said Suit up to the Circuit Court, at Ninety six, for another hearing and all advantages on all Parties with Regard to the s'd Execution are Relinquisht that Justice may be Done in the said Circuit Court. Thos Edghill Ju'r.

Ann Hendrix Plt vs Wm Briggs Deft. Attachment. This day came the Plt by Danl Brown her Attorney and the Attachment being Returnd Executed in Part and the Deft not appearing to Replevy &C it is Considered by the Court that the Plt Recover against the s'd Deft her Debt amounting to £5 s8 sterling and her cost by her in this behalf Expended, and the s'd Deft. in Mercy &c. Orderd that Property attacht be exposed to publick sale according to the act of Assembly in that Case made & provided and the moneys arising from such sale pay to the Plt towards Satisfaction of this Judgement and the overplus if any there be return to the Deft &c.

Clerks fees   £ 10
Sheriffs Fees
Attorney's fees   1 1 9

LAURENS COUNTY SC COURT MINUTES 1786-1789

[18 March 1786]
A Lease and Release for the Conveyance of 500 acres of Land from Jas Killgore to John McElroy proved by the oath of Saml Cob in open court & ordred to be Recorded.

Page 70: George Caldwell Plt vs David Allison Deft. Came the Plt by Danl Brown his Attorney and the Deft by J. Brown, J. Yancy & Charles Goodwin his Attorneys and Thereupon Came also a Jury to wit Joshua Arnold, Charles Swillivant, John Rodgers, Jas Watson, Robert Culbertson, James Adair, Stephen Potter, Andw Rodgers, James Waldroup, Saml Frank, Michal Waldroup, and John McElroy who being Elected Tried and Sworn well and Truly to Try the issue Joind upon their Oaths do say That the Plt hath Sustaind Damages by Accation of the Deft Detaining the Debt in the Declaration Mentioned to one shilling Sterling besides his Cost, Therefore it is considerd by the court that the Plt Recover against the s'd Deft his Debt in the Declaration Mentioned Amounting to £28 s11 d5 and his Damages aforesaid in form aforesaid assesst and his cost by him in this behalf Expended and the said Deft in Mercy &C. Stay of Execution Eight months.

Clerks fees   £ 19 8
Sheriffs Fees   6 8
Attorney's fees   1 1 9
                    £2 3 1.

Bryan McCarty Pl vs Ann Tindsley Deft. Debt. This suit by consent of the Parties is orderd to be Continued till June court next.

Edwerd Mitchusson Pl vs John Stubblefield Deft. In Debt S. P. This day came the Plt by James Yancey his Attorney and the Deft being Solemnly calld came not but made Default and says nothing in Barr or preclution of the Plts action by which he remains therein against him Undefended. Therefore it is considered by the court that the Plt Recover against the s'd Deft [**Page 71**] his Debt Amounting to £2 s6 d8 Sterl'g and his cost by him in this behalf Expended.

Clerks fees   £ 11
Sheriffs Fees   3 6
Attorney's fees   14
                    £1 8 6.

Michael Waldrop Plf vs William Austin Deft. In Debt S. P. Came the Plf by James Yancey his Attorney and the Deft being Solemnly calld came not but made Default and says nothing in Barr or preclution of the Plts action by which he remains therein against him Undefended. Therefore it is considered by the court that the Plt Recover against the s'd Deft his Debt Amounting to £1 s3 d4 Sterl'g & his cost by him in this behalf Expended.

Clerks fees   £ 11
Sheriffs Fees   3 6
Attorney's fees   14
                    £1 8 6.

LAURENS COUNTY SC COURT MINUTES 1786-1789

[18 March 1786]

John Box Plt vs Patrick Reyley Deft. Trover & Convertion. S. Process. Came the Plf by Danl Brown his Attorney and the Deft by J. Brown and J. Yancey his Attorneys and upon Consideration of the Evidence Produced and other Circumstances, it is considered by the court that the Plt Recover against the said Deft £5 sterling and his cost by him in this behalf Expended and the said Deft in Mercy &c.

Clerks fees	£ 14 6
Sheriffs Fees	6
Attorney's fees	14
	£1 14 6.

Page 72: Thos McClurkin P vs Alexd & Jane Grant and Robt Ross Defts. In Debt. Came the Plt by Danl Brown his Attorney and the Deft in his Proper person & the Defts sayeth they Cannot Gain say the Plts action for £125 s17 d6 old currency to be Depreciated, whereupon it is considered by the court that the Plt Recover against the s'd Defts his Debt aforesaid & his Cost by him in this behalf Expended and the s'd Deft in mercy &c.

Clerks fees	£ 11
Sheriffs Fees	3 6
Attorney's fees	14
	£1 8 6.

Thomas McClurkin Plt vs Alex & Jean Grant Executors of Geo: Moore Dec'd. In Debt. Came the Plt by Danl Brown his Attorney and the Deft tho Solemnly Calld came not Nor does he or they say anything in Barr or preclusion of the Plts action by which he Remains therein against him undefended. Therefore it is Considered by the Court that the Plt by proving his Debt should recover against the s'd Deft his Debt Amounting to £16 s16 d6 currency with the Intrest thereon and his cost by him in this behalf Expended and the s'd Defts in Mercy &c.

Clerks fees	£ 11
Sheriffs Fees	3 6
Attorney's fees	14
	£1 8 6.

Page 73: Reuben Pyles Plt vs Bartholomew Craddock & John Martin Defts. In Debt. Came the Plt by James Yancey his Attorney and Proveing his Debt by John Rodgers Esq'r it is considered by the Court that he Recover against the said Defendants his Debt amounting to £3 s2 d6 and his cost by him in this behalf Expended and the s'd Defts in Mercy &c.

Clerks fees	£ 13 6
Sheriffs Fees	8 6
Attorney's fees	14
	£1 16.

LAURENS COUNTY SC COURT MINUTES 1786-1789

[18 March 1786]

James Adair Plt vs Thos Hughes and Charles Saxon Defts. In Debt. Came the Plt by James Yancey his Attorney and the Defts in their Proper Person and Confessed Judgment for £1 s15 d10¼ sterl'g. Thereupon it is Considered by the Court that the Plt Recover against the s'd Defts his Debt aforesaid and his cost by him in this behalf Expended and the s'd Defts in Mercy &c.

Clerks fees	£ 11
Sheriffs Fees	3 6
Attorney's fees	14
	£1 8 6.

Tho's McClurkin Plt vs Alex'd & Jane Grant Executors of Geo: Moore Dec'd. In Debt. Came the Plt by Danl Brown his Attorney and the Deft being arested and not appearing Tho Solemnly Calld on Motion of the Plt by his attorney aforesaid it is ordred that Judgment be Entred for the Plt. against the s'd Deft for the Debt in the Declaration Mentioned to be Levied of the Goods and Chattles of the s'd George Moore Dec'd if so much thereof the said Def't hath in his hands to be Administred, unless the said Deft shall appear and plead to Issue at the next Court.

Page 74: Ezekiel Griffin Plt vs Andrew Cunnigham Deft. In Debt. The Suit is ordred to be Discontinued.

Clerks fees	£ 11
Sheriffs Fees	3 6
Attorney's fees	14
	£1 8 6.

Robert Taylor Plt. vs John Cargill Deft. Case. This day came the Deft. in his proper Person and the Plt. failing to appear and Prosecute his suit it is Considered by the court be non Suited & that the Deft Recover against the sid Plt five shillings Damages besides his costs by him about his Defence in this behalf Expended, according to the act of Assembly &c.

Clerks fees	£ 9
Sheriffs Fees	4 8.

Thos Jones Plt. vs Rich'd Hicks Deft. In Case. The Deft being aresest and not appearing Tho Solemnly Calld on Motion of the Plt by J. Yancy his Attorney it is ordred that Judgment that Judgment be Entred for the Plt for what Damages the Plt hath Sustaind by Accation of the Defts non performance of the assumption in the Declaration Specified to be Inquired of by a Jury unless the said Deft shall appear and Plead to Issue at the next court.

Nathan Kemp Plt vs Joseph Mayhon Deft. Debt. Came the Deft by Charles Goodwin his Attorney and the Plt. Tho Solemnly calld came not but made Default nor is his suit further Prosecuted. Therefore on Motion of the Deft it is Considered by the Court that he be non suited and that the Deft Recover against the said Plf five shillings Damages besides his cost by him about his Defence in this behalf Expended.

Clerks fees	£ 10
Sheriffs Fees	4 8
Attorney's fees	1 1 9
Total	£1 1 9.

Page 75: [18 March 1786]

Robert Faris Plt vs Wm Austin Deft. In Debt. The Deft being Arrested and not appearing tho Solemnly Calld on the Motion of the Plt by James Yancey his attorney it is ordred by the court that Judgment be Entred for the Plt against the s'd Deft for the Debt in the Declaration unless the Deft shall appear and plead to Issue at the next court.

John Williams Plt. vs John Donohoe Deft. In Debt. The Deft. being arrest and not appearing tho Solemnly called on the Motion of the Plt by Danl Brown his attorney it is ordred by the court that Judgment be Entred for the Plt against the s'd Deft for the Debt in the Declaration unless the Deft shall appear and plead to Issue at the next court.

William Millwee Plt vs John Craddock Deft. Attachment. Trespass. The Attachment being Returned Executed and the Deft not appearing to Replevy on Motion of the Plt. by J. Yancey & Wm Shaw his Attorneys it is ordred that Judgment be entred for the Plt. for what Damages he hath Sustaind by accation of the Trespass in the Declaration Mentioned to be assertained by an Inquiry thereof to be made by a Jury unless the Deft. shall appear and plead to Issue at the next Court.

John Blalock Plt vs Thos McDonald Deft. Attachment. The Attachment being Returned Executed and the Deft not appearing to Replevy tho Solemnly calld on Motion of the Plt. by Wm Shaw his Attorney it is ordred that Judgment be entred for the Plt. for what Damages he hath Sustaind by accation of the Trespass in the Declaration Mentioned to be assertained by an Inquiry thereof to be made by a Jury unless the Deft. shall appear and plead to Issue at the next Court.

Page 76: John Caldwell Plt vs Rich'd Lang Deft. Trespass. The Attachment being Returned Executed and the Deft not appearing to Replevy tho Solemnly calld on Motion of the Plt. by Daniel Brown his Attorney it is ordred that Judgment be entred for the Plt. for what Damages he hath Sustaind by accation of the Trespass in the Declaration Mentioned to be assertained by an Inquiry thereof to be made by a Jury unless the Deft. shall appear and plead to Issue at the next Court.

Ayres Gorely Plt vs Wm Price Deft. New Trial ordred at Next June court.

LAURENS COUNTY SC COURT MINUTES 1786-1789

[18 March 1786]

David Welch Plt vs John Barnet Deft. Ordred that a Dedimus Issue for the Examination of Saml Brown a Witness for the Deft in this Suit, Living in North Carolina, Rutherford County.

On Motion Made on Oath by Benj'n Killgore a Witness for Henry White at the Suit of Wm Thomason it is ordered That the said William Thomason pay him Ten shillings for four Days attendance at this court.

On Motion made by Sam'l Cob on oath a Witness in the sute Edward Mitchuson against James and Susannah Allison ordered That the Plt. pay him Fifteen shillings for six Days attendance at this court.

Pursuant to Law the Court appointed Jonth'n Downs and Silvanus Walker Esquires inspectors of the Clerks office this Year.

Court adjourned till Court in Course. Minets signed by James Montgomery, Charles Saxon, Joseph Downs, Wm. Mitchuson, John Rodgers, Esquires.

Page 77: At a Court held for the County of Laurens in the State of South Carolina at the Courthouse of the Said County the Second Monday in June being the 12th day 1786 and in the Tenth year of the Independence of the United States of America. Present the Worshipfull Jonth'n Downs, James Montgomery, Joseph Downs, Silvanus Walker, John Hunter, George Anderson, Wm. Mitchusson, Esquires.

Ordered by said Court that Marshall Franks be and is hereby appointed overseer of that Part of the high way Leading from Little River Near to the Courthouse of this County to Duncanks Creek, it being that Part of the high way of which Hugh McVay was Overseer last year, Ordred that he the said Marshall Franks case all the free male Inhabitants & Slaves Contigious to and Convenient to said Road to work thereon, and to Cause the Same to be kept in good Repair for on Year from this Date as the law Directs.

A Lease and Release for the Conveyance of Ten acres of Land from John Rodgers Esq'r and Margaret Rodgers his wife to Lewis Saxon acknowledged in open court, the wife being first Privily Examined apart from her husband as the Law directs and Ordered to be Recorded.

James Yancey Esq'r Produced in open [court] a Licence signed by the Hon. Henry Pendleton, Edanus Burk, John F. Grimkey, Esqr's, Judges of the Courts of Common Pleas within this State to Practice as an Attorney, in any of the Courts of Law or Equity within this State. Whereupon after the said Licence being Publickly Read in open Court, he the said James Yancey was ordred to be Enroled as an Attorney in this Court.

LAURENS COUNTY SC COURT MINUTES 1786-1789

Page 78: [12 June 1786]

A Lease and Release for the Conveyance of 150 acres of land from David Anderson to Charles Simmons Proved the last term by Lewis Devall and ordred to lie for further proof and now Proven in open court by William Mitchusson Esq'r and ordred to be Recorded.

Bryan McCarty vs Ann Tindsly. Debt. By Consent of the Parties this Suit is ordred to be Discontinued.

Ann Tindsly vs Bryan McCarty. Debt. By Consent of the Parties this Suit is ordred to be Discontinued.

Charles Swillivant vs John & Shadrach Martin. By Consent of the Parties this Suit is ordred to Dismist at the Defendants Costs.

Ayres Gorely vs Patrick Obryan. Slander. This Suit is ordred to be Dismist at the Defendants Costs.

Robert Harper vs John McElory. In Debt S. P. Ordred that this Suit be discontinued at Plts Costs.

James Swillivant vs Sarah Cargill. On motion of Mr. Goodwin & Consented to be the Opisite Counsil, Ordered that the Testimony of Dycey Martin a Witness for the Plaintiff be Taken on Oath before Esq'r Walker & Notice Given to the Defendant.

Ordered that an award Determined by John Ritchey, Marmaduke Pinson & Jonathan Downs Esq'r between Charity Parker and Andrew Rodgers Junr of the One Part and James Abercrumbie of the Other Part this day Present in Court be Entred upon Record.

Court Adjourned Till Tomorrow Morning 9 Oclock. Minets Signed by Jonth'n Downs president, James Montgomery, John Hunter, Joseph Downs, Wm. Mitchuson.

Page 79: Court met according to adjournment the 13th June 1786. Present Jonth'n Downs, James Montgomery, Joseph Downs, Charles Saxon, Wm Mitchuson, John Hunter, George Anderson.

John Hunter and George Anderson Esquires Produced in Open Court a Commission Signed by his Excellency William Moultrie Esq'r Governor &C. Baring Date the 23d day of March AD 1786 Commissioning them as Justices of the Peace in and for the county of Laurens, which said Commission being Publickly Read in open Court was ordred to be Recorded to wit.

State of South Carolina, By his Excellency William Moultrie, Esquire, Governor and Commander in Chief in and over the State aforesaid, To John

LAURENS COUNTY SC COURT MINUTES 1786-1789

Hunter and George Anderson, Esquires. In pursuance of an Act of the Legislature passed 24 March 1785, I commission the said John Hunter and George Anderson to be Justices of the Peace for the County of Laurens [**Page 80**], given at Charleston 23 March 1786. Peter Freneau, Dy Secy.

[13 June 1786]

A Lease and Release for the Conveyance of 150 acres of land from Thomas Edghill Junr to Thomas McDanald Proven in open Court by the oaths of Hugh Oneal and William Ozborn and ordered to be Recorded.

A Lease and Release for the Conveyance of 433 acres of land from Nathaniel Henderson to Thomas Tod Proven in open Court by the oaths of Stephen Williams and James Cleaton and ordered to be Recorded.

A Lease and Release for the Conveyance of 200 acres of land from Nathan hampton to Joseph Pinson proven according to the former act, and ordred to be Recorded.

A Lease and Release for the Conveyance of 200 acres of land from Joseph Pinson and Mary his wife to Stephen Wood Proven in open Court by the oaths of Jonth'n Downs & George Anderson, Esquires, and ordered to be Recorded.

A Lease and release for the Conveyance of 100 acres of land from William Martin to Alex'd Hambleton acknowledged in open court and ordered to be Recorded.

Page 81: On application of Charles Hutchings he is Admitted to keep Publick Tavern at his house where how now lives on the Plantation formerly the Property of John McCrary lying on Duncans Creek on the highway from Hammonds old Store on bush river to Joneses old mill on Enoree River for the space of One year from the Date hereof whereupon he the said Charles Hutchings together with Robt McCrary and James Dillard his securitys entred into and Acknowledged their bond according to Law.

State vs Nancy Babb. Bastardy. Ordred that the Defendant be Dismist on paying Cost of Prosecution.

John Caldwell vs Richard Long. Case on an attachment. The Sheriff to whom the said attachment was Directed now Returning the same Executed on 150 acres of Land the Property of the said Rich'd Lang, and he the said Defendant not appearing to Replevy the same thereupon Came a Jury to wit Wm Norris, Alex'd Hambleton, Saml Fleming, Isaac Rodgers, Ezekiel Griffen, Theophiless Gooden, Joseph Parsons, Holoway Power, Richard Roland, Thos Blakely, Robt McNees & John Brown who being Sworn well and Truly to Inquire of Damages upon their Oaths do say that the Plaintiff hath Sustained Damages by Accation of the Nonperformance of the Promises and assumptions in the Declaration Mentioned to £50 sterling therefore it is Considered by the Court that the Plt. Recover against the said Defendant his Damages aforesaid amounting to £50 in form aforesaid assessed and his Cost by him in this behalf Expended, and the said Deft in Mercy &c.

Page 82: [13 June 1786]

A Lease and Release for the Conveyance of 100 acres of Land from William Freemon and Mary his wife to James Little proven in open court by the oaths of John Hunter Esqr. and Richard Golden and Ordered to be Recorded.

State vs James Young. Indictment for Selling Liquor above the Rates Established by our said County of Laurens. No Person appearing to Prosecute, it is Ordred that the Deft by Dismist on Paying Cost of Suit.

State vs James Young. Indictment as overseer of the high Road. This day came the Parties by their Attorneys and thereupon came also a Jury to wit William Norris, Alexander Hambleton, Saml Fleming, Isaac Rodgers, Ezekiel Griffen, Theophiless Gooden, Joseph Parsons, Holoway Power, Rich'd Roland, Thos Blakely, Robert McNees & John Brown who being Sworn well and Truly to Try this Issue Joined upon their Oaths do say that the Deft is Not Guilty as is Complaind against him. Therefore it is Considered by the Court that the Deft be Dismist on paying the Cost of Prosecution.

A Lease and Release for the Conveyance of 100 acres of land from Robt Goodwin to David McDavid acknowledged in open Court & ordered to be recorded.

A Lease and Release for the Conveyance of 100 acres of land from Littleberry Harvey to Robt Goodwin acknowledged in open Court and Ordred to be Recorded.

Page 83: A Lease and Release for the Conveyance of 200 acres of land from John Craddock to Sarah Craddock Proved in open Court by the oaths of Tandy Walker & John Ozburn and Ordred to be Recorded.

A Lease and Release for the Conveyance of 120 acres of land from Alex'd Menary to Margaret Richey acknowledged in open Court and Ordred to be Recorded.

A Lease and Release for the Conveyance of 100 acres of land from John Craddock to Rich'd Hicks proved in open Court by Lumpy John Martin & Martin Martin Junr and Ordred to be Recorded.

State vs Alex'd Adair. Bastardy. Came Daniel Brown, County attorney, into Court and the Defendant in his Proper person and because he will not contend with the County, Submitted himself to the Jurisdiction and Mercy of the Court, and Sayeth that he is the father of a bastard Child Begotten on the

LAURENS COUNTY SC COURT MINUTES 1786-1789

body of Ann McCluer in manner and form as is alledged against him. Therefore it is Considered by the Court that he the said Alex'd Adair Pay unto the county a fine of £3 s11 & cost of Suit.

[13 June 1786]

State vs Ann McCluer. Bastardy. Came into Court the said Ann McCluer and Submitted her Self to Discression and Jurisdiction of the court and sayeth she is Guilty of haveing a bastard Child and that Alex'd Adair is the father of said Child, whereupon the Court after considering the matter find her for s'd offence £3 s11 & cost. Ordered that the said Ann McCluer & Alex'd Adair enter into bond Jointly severally in the sum of £50 [**Page 84**] with Sufficient Security to save harmless and Indemnified the said County from the Maintainance of the said Bastard Child for Ten years.

Alex'd Adair and Ann McCluer & Samuel Ewing came into Court and acknowledged themselves Indebted to the County in the sum of £50 sterling to be levied of their Goods and Chattels, lands and tenements. Yet upon Condition that they will Save harmless and Indemnified the said County from the Maintainance of the said Bastard Child on the body of the said Ann McCluer by the said Alex'd Adair. Acknowledged in open Court.

State vs Nancy Terry. Bastardy. Came into Court the said Nancy Terry and Submitted herself to the Jurisdiction and Mercy of the court and sayeth she is Guilty of haveing a bastard Child and that George Berry is the father of said Child, whereupon it is Considered by the Court that she pay unto the said County a fine of £3 s11 & cost of Suit. Ordered that she enter into bond with sufficient security in the in the sum of £50 for the Maintainance of the said Bastard Child.

State vs George Berry. Bastardy. Came into Court the said George Berry and Submitted himself to the Jurisdiction of the court and sayeth he is Guilty of being the father of a bastard Child begotten on the body of Nancy Terry, whereupon it is Considered by the Court that he pay unto the said County a fine of £3 s11 & cost of Suit and enter into bond with sufficient security to save harmless and Indemnified the said County from the maintainance of the said Bastard Child.

Page 85: George Berry, Nancy Terry, Stephen Potter, and William Terry, came into Court and acknowledged themselves indebted to the County in the sum of £50 sterling to be levied Jointly and severally of their Goods and Chattels, lands and tenements, yet upon condition that they save harmless and Indemnified the said County from the Maintainance of a Certain Bastard Child begotten on the body of s'd Nancy Terry for the Term of Ten years. Acknowledged in open Court.

LAURENS COUNTY SC COURT MINUTES 1786-1789

[13 June 1786]

A Lease and release for the conveyance of 300 acres of Land from James Steen to John Lindsey Proved according to the former act and ordred to be Recorded.

A Deed of Conveyance from Benjamin Brown to Abraham Gray for the Conveyance of 160 acres of land, Proven in open court by John Lindsey and Henry Hambleton and ordred to be Recorded.

State vs Elizebeth Raburn. Bastardy. Came into Court the said Elizebeth Raburn and Submitted herself to the Mercy and Jurisdiction of the court and sayeth she is Guilty of haveing a bastard Child and that Elijah Watson is the father of the same. Therefore, it is Considered by the Court that she pay a fine of £3 s11 sterling & cost of Suit. Ordered that she enter into bond with for the Maintainance of the said Bastard Child.

State vs Elijah Watson. Bastardy. Came into Court the said Deft and Because he will not content with the County sayeth he is Guilty of being the father of a bastard Child begotten on the body of Elizebeth Raburn, and submitted himself to the Mercy and Jurisdiction of the Court, whereupon it is Considered by the Court that he the said Elijah Watson pay unto the said County a fine of £3 s11 & cost of Suit. Ordred that he the said Elijah Watson and enter into bond with sufficient security to save harmless and Indemnified the said County from the maintainance of the said Bastard Child.

Page 86: Bond of Elijah Watson, Elezebeth Raburn, William Watson, and Thomas McGrigger, 15 June 1786, to save harmless and Indemnified the County from the Maintainance of a certain Bastard Child. Elijah Watson, Elezebeth Raburn, William Watson, Thos McGrigger. Test, Lewis Saxon, C. C.

A Deed from Benjamin Brown to John Lindsey for the Conveyance of 40 acres of Land Proven in Court by Abraham Gray and Henry Hambleton and Ordred to be Recorded.

I agree to Pay my fine of £3 s11 at next court, or execution to Issue against me Immediately. George Berry.

We Confess a Judgment for £7 s1 sterling for fines due from us Elijah Watson, Elizebeth Raburn, to the county for Bastardy. William Watson, Elijah Watson. Ordred that Execution be stayed till next Court.

Page 87: Court adjourned till Tomorrow morning 9 Oclock. Minets signed by Jonth'n Downs, Joseph Downs, James Montgomery, John Hunter, George Anderson, Esquires.

LAURENS COUNTY SC COURT MINUTES 1786-1789

Court met according to adjournment 14th June 1786. Present Jonathan Downs, Joseph Downs, James Montgomery, John Rodgers, Silv's Walker, Esquires.

A Lease and Release for the Conveyance of 200 acres of Land from Benjamin Rainey to Nicholas White Proved in Open Court by the oaths of Daniel Wright and Saml. P. Jones and Ordred to be Recorded.

A Lease and Release for the Conveyance of 135 acres of Land from Nathaniel Norwood to Thomas Gafford Proven according to the former Act and Ordered to be Recorded.

A Lease and Release for the Conveyance of 107 acres of land from Charles Allin and Susannah Allin his wife to Robt McNees Acknowledged by the said Charles Allin in open Court and the said Susannah Allin not being able to Travel to our County Court, it is Ordred that a Commission Issue to Two or more Justices to go unto her house and take her Examination and make Return of the same to our next Court.

Ordred that the Defaulters on the Grand Jurors that were Summoned to Attend this Court be Cited to appear at the next Court to Shew Cause if any they have, why the fines allowed by Law should not be Levied on them.

Page 88: A Lease and Release for the Conveyance of 110 acres of land from Mary Hillon and John Hillon to James Adair Proven in Open Court by the Oaths of George Ross and John Cammel & Ordred to be recorded.

A Lease and Release for the Conveyance of 140 acres of land from Mary Hill and John Hillon to John Cammel Proven in Open Court by the Oaths of George Ross and James Adair & Ordred to be recorded.

State vs Clement Davis. On an indictment for Assault and Battery. This day Came the Parties by their Attorneys and Thereupon Came also a Jury to wit William Norris, Alex'd Hambleton, Samuel Fleming, Isaac Rodgers, Ezekiel Griffen, Theophiless Goodwin, Joseph Parsons, Holoway Power, William Taylor Junr, Thos Blackley, Robert McNees & John Brown who being Sworn well and Truly to Try the Issue Joind upon their Oaths do say that the Defendant is Guilty of the Charges in the Indictment mentioned or alledged against him, Whereupon the Court will Take time to Consider of the Judgment to be Passed against him. Ordered that the Defendant go Give bail for to abide by and Perform the said Judgment of the Court.

Know all men by these Presents that we Clement Davis and Col. Rob't McCrary are held and firmly bound unto the Justices of our said Court in the sum of £50 which payment well and Truly to be made we bind out selves and our Heirs, Executors & Administrators Jointly, severally, and firmly by these Presents, 14 June 1786, **[Page 89]** that Clement Davis do not Depart from this Court untill he hath Performed the Judgment and Order of the same.

LAURENS COUNTY SC COURT MINUTES 1786-1789

[14 June 1786]

Ordred that the Order of last Court for the laying out a Road from McDowalls Store on Bush River the Nearest and Best way to Graves ford on Salludy, be Void & Set aside and that the Overseers appointed to work on said road desist from the same.

On application of John Rodgers Esq'r he is Admitted to keep a Publick Tavern at the Courthouse of this County, being the Place where he the said John Rogers now lives, for and during the full space and term of One year from this Date whereupon he the said John Rodgers Esq'r Together with Robt McNees and Nehemiah Franks his securitys entred into and Acknowledged their bond according to Law.

John Entrekin vs Charles Swillivant. Debt. Summary Process. By Consent of the Parties this Suit is ordred to be Dismist at the Plts Costs.

Page 90: Charles Swillivant vs John Mading. In Debt. This Suit is Ordred to be continued till next Court at the Defts Costs.

Court adjourned till Tomorrow morning 9 Oclock. Minets signed by Jonathan Downs, James Montgomery, Silv's Walker, Joseph Downs, and George Anderson, Esq'rs.

Court met according to adjournment 15th June 1786. Present Jonth'n Downs, James Montgomery, John Hunter, Silv's Walker, George Anderson, Esquires.

An Indenture of Apprenticeship Between Jean White of the One Part and Jean Taylor of the Other Part was Acknowledged before a Justice of the peace and Ordered to be Recorded.

James Waldroup vs Samuel Henderson. Case. S. P. By Consent of the Parties by their Attorneys the[y] Mutually Submitted all matters In difference between them to the Determination of James Yancey & Jacob Brown Esq'rs and their award to be made the Judgment of the Court and the same was Ordered accordingly who now Return the same in these words that the Deft. Pay unto the said Plft. Twenty shillings & cost of Suit. In Confirmation whereof it is Considered by the Court that the Plft. Recover against the said Deft the said Sum of Twenty Shillings & His cost by him in this behalf Expended &c.

Page 91: A Bill of Sale for the Conveyance of a Certain Negro woman Named Hannah from Hain & Burke & James Tinker to Lewis Saxon Proved in open court and ordered to be Recorded.

Patrick Reyley vs William Thomason. Slander. By Consent of the Parties they Mutually Submitted the Determination of this Suit to Wm Wood, Chas. Swillivant, Saml Boling, James Abercrumbie, John Goodwin & James Stinson whose award to be made the Judgment of the Court and the same is Ordered accordingly.

[15 June 1786]

Patrick Reyley vs William Thomason. Case. By Consent of the Parties who this Suit to the Determination of Wm Wood, Chas. Swillivant, Saml Boling, James Abercrumbie, Jno Goodwin & James Stinson whose award is to be made the Judgment of the Court & the same was Ordered accordingly.

Ordred that Elizebeth Obryan Committed to Joal[?] for Bastardy Declare on oath who the father of said Bastard Child is, or on her Refusal to Swear as aforesaid to Give Sufficient Security for her appearance at the next Court to be held at Ninety Six on the 26th day of November next.

Page 92: Josiah East, Daniel Davis, John Hunter & James Saxon, bound to the Justices of said County Court of Laurens in the sum of £50, 15 June 1785, that the said Josiah East and Daniel Davis to appear at next court on the second Monday in Sept next and abide by the Judgment and Order of the same.

Ordered that John Martin desist from Acting as Constable in this County of Laurens and is hereby Suspended therefrom.

On motion of Josiah East, Henry Myers, Saml Niel, & Daniel Davis on oath as Witnesses for the State against Clement Davis, it is ordered that Clement Davis pay unto each of them above mentioned the sum of Twelve Shillings & Six pence Each for five Days attendance at this Court.

Page 93: On motion on oath of Saml Cob, James Downen and Wm Bratcher, witnesses for Patrick Reyley against William Thomason, it is ordered that Wm. Thomason pay them the Several sums hereinafter mentioned to wit
Samuel Cob 7 days attendance @ 2/6   17/6
James Downen 9 days @ 2/6   £ 1 2 6
William Bratcher 9 days @ 2/6   £ 1 2 6
Ordered that William Thomason pay the said several sums for the services above mentioned.

Thomas Jones vs Richard Hicks. Case. By consent of the Parties by their Attys all matters in Diference between them to the Determination of Silvanus Walker Esqr and Andw Rogers Junr & Mark Moor, and their award to be made the Judgment of the Court & the same was ordred accordingly.

Court adjourned till Tomorrow morning 9 Oclock. Minets Signed by Jonth'n Downs, Silv's Walker, George Anderson, William Mitchuson, Esquires.

Court met according to adjournment 16th June 1786. Present Jonth'n Downs, James Montgomery, George Anderson, William Mitchuson, Esquires.

[16 June 1786]

State vs Clement Davis. Indictment. The Court Proceed to Pass Judgment on the Defendant in Consequence of his being found Guilty by a Verdict on an Indictment for Assault and Battery, which is that he pay a fine of £20 sterling and the cost of Prosecution.

Page 94: William Shaw Esqr. haveing committed a Breach of the Peace by Assault and Battery on the Person of Mr. Alexander McDowall, the said William Shaw came into Court and Submitted himself to the Mercy and Discretion of the same, whereupon it is ordered that the said Wm Shaw pay a fine of Twenty Shillings which was Immediately Paid in open court.

Bond of Clement Davis and Gilbert Menary to the County Court of Laurens, in the sum of £40 sterling, 16 June 1786, on condition that said Clement Davis pay to the Sheriff of said county £20 on or before the second Monday in Sept next.

George Berry is appointed Overseer of that part of the high Road leading from Duncans Creek to Enoree River it being a Part of the New Road leading from the Courthouse of this County to Enoree River, ordered that he cause the several free male Inhabitants & slaves Contiguous [**Page 95**] to and Convenient to said Road to work thereon and to cause the same to be kept in good repair for one year from this date as the law directs.

Ordered that Joseph Adair be appointed Overseer of that part of the high Road leading from Duncans Creek to Hendrixes old Place on the South fork of Duncans Creek from thence to the County line, and that he cause the same to be kept in good repair for one year from this date as directed by law.

Thos Ewing is appointed Overseer of that part of the high way leaving from Jones's old mill on Enoree River to James Youngs on Bush River & that he cause the several free male Inhabitants & slaves Contiguous to and Convenient to said Road to work thereon & cause the same to be kept in good repair for one year from this date as the law directs.

Ayres Gorely vs William Price. In Case. Sum Process. This day came the Plt by J. Yancy his Attorney and the Deft. in his Proper Person and the Plt makeing oath that £4 s16 d8 the Ballance of his account as it stands stated whereon his action is founded is Justly due to him, therefore it is Considered by the Court that the Plt. Recover against the said Defendant the said sum of £3 s16 d8 & his cost by him in this behalf expended.

Page 96: Robt Kellogh vs Andw Rodgers Junr. In Trover. By consent of the Parties this Suit is ordred to be Dismist at the Plaintiffs Cost.

Reubin Pyles vs James Millwee. Debt. Sum'r Process. The Plaintiff Proveing his note against the said Deft. for £3, it was considered by the court that the

LAURENS COUNTY SC COURT MINUTES 1786-1789

Plaintiff Recover against the said Defendant by his Debt Amounting to £3 & his Costs by him in this behalf expended.

[16 June 1786]

Reubin Pyles vs Andw Rodgers Senr. Ordered to be Continued till next Court.

William Anderson vs Claburn Sims. Case S. P. Ordered to be Continued till next Court.

Robert McNees vs Jean Hardy. Case S. P. This suit is ordered to be Continued till next Court.

James Adair vs Jonth'n Gilbert. Debt S.P. By Consent of the Parties this suit is ordered to be Continued till next Court.

State vs Elizebeth Obryan. Bastardy. Ordered that the Deft. be Admitted on Paying of all Cost and Charges on this Suit, and Giving Sufficient Security to the Sheriff for his Return at the next Court to be held for this County to go unto the Place where the said Bastard Child was born, and Produce from that County Certificates of her haveing made Satisfaction for the said offence.

Page 97: John Tune vs George Martin. In Trover. The Defendant being arest and not appearing tho Solemnly Called, on Motion of the Plaintiff by Jacob Brown his Attorney it is Ordered that Judgment be Entered for the Plt for what damages he hath Sustain by accation of the Trover and Convertion in the Declaration Specified to be Inquired of a Jury unless the said Defendant shall appear at the next court and Plead to Issue.

Michael Waldrop vs And'w Cunningham. Attachment. By Consent of the Parties this Suit is ordred to be Dismist at the Plaintiffs Costs.

Hugh Woods vs Nehemiah Franks. Assault & Battery. This day Came the Defendant by William Shaw and J. Yancey his Attorneys and the Plaintiff tho Solemnly Called came not but made Default neither is his suit further Prosecuted, therefore on motion of the Deft by his Attorneys aforesaid, it is Considered by the Court that the Deft. Recover against the said Plt five shillings Damages besides his cost by him about his Defence in this behalf expended according to the form of the Act of Assembly in that Case made & Provided.

James Montgomery vs Thomas Persons. Attachment. This day came the Plaintiff by J. Yancey his Atty and the attachment being Returned Executed, and the Deft not Replevying by appearance & putting in Special Bail tho Solemnly called, on motion of the Plaintiff by his atty aforesaid it is ordered that Judgment be entered for the Plt for what damages he hath Sustained by Accation of the Trover and Convertion in the Declaration mentioned [**Page**

98] to be Inquired of by a Jury unless the said Defendant shall appear at the next court and Plead to Issue.

[16 June 1786]

James Adair vs Thos Persons. Attachment. Trover. This day came the Plaintiff by J. Yancey his Atty and the attachment being Returned Executed, and the Deft not Replevied by appearance or put in Special Bail tho Solemnly called, on motion of the Plaintiff by his atty aforesaid it is ordered that Judgment be entered for the Plt for what damages he hath Sustain by Accation of the Trover & Convertion in the Declaration mentioned to be Inquired of by a Jury unless the said Defendant shall appear and Plead to Issue at the next court.

Charles Saxon vs Thomas Persons. Attachment. Trespass. This day came the Plaintiff by J. Yancey his Atty and the attachment being Returned Executed, and the Deft not Replevied by appearance or put in Special Bail tho Solemnly called, on motion of the Plaintiff by his atty aforesaid it is ordered that Judgment be entered for the Plt for what damages he hath Sustain by Accation of the Trover & Convertion in the Declaration mentioned to be Inquired of by a Jury unless the said Defendant shall appear and Plead to Issue at the next court.

Page 99: James Saxon vs Joshua Nun. Attachment. Trover. This day came the Plaintiff by J. Yancey his Atty and the attachment being Returned Executed, and the Deft not Replevied by appearance or put in Bail tho Solemnly called, on motion of the Plaintiff by his atty aforesaid it is ordered that Judgment be entered for the Plt for what damages he hath Sustain by Accation of the Trespass in the Declaration mentioned to be Inquired of by a Jury unless the said Defendant shall appear and Plead to Issue at the next court.

Robert McCrary vs James Jones. Attachment in Debt. This day came the Plaintiff by J. Yancey his Atty and the attachment being Returned Executed, and the Deft not appearing to Replevy tho Solemnly called, on motion of the Plaintiff by his atty aforesaid it is ordered that Judgment be entered for the Plt against the said Deft. for his Debt the Declaration mentioned to be Inquired of by a Jury unless the said Defendant shall appear and Plead to Issue at the next court.

Jacob Duckett vs Notley Mastes. Attachment. Debt. This day came the Plaintiff by W. Shaw his Attorney and the attachment being Returned Executed, and the Deft not appearing to Replevy tho Solemnly called, on motion of the Plaintiff by his atty aforesaid it is ordered that Judgment be entered for the Plt against the said Deft. for his Debt the Declaration mentioned to be Inquired of by a Jury unless the said Defendant shall appear and Plead to Issue at the next court.

LAURENS COUNTY SC COURT MINUTES 1786-1789

Page 100: [16 June 1786]

George Reed vs John Megee. Attachment. Case. This day came the Plaintiff by Wm. Shaw his Attorney and the attachment being Returned Executed, and the Deft not appearing to Replevy tho Solemnly called, on motion of the Plaintiff by his atty aforesaid it is ordered that Judgment be entered for the Plaintiff for what Damage the Plt hath Sustained by accation of the non performance of the Promises and assumptions in the Declaration mentioned to be Inquired of by a Jury unless the said Deft shall appear and Plead to Issue at the next court.

James Downen is appointed Overseer of that part of the high way Leading from John Fords old Bounds to Thomasons mill on Reaburns Creek, it being that part of the high road of which Saml Boling was overseer the Last year & that he cause the same to be kept in Repair for one year as the law Directs.

Edward Mitchuson is appointed Overseer of that part of the high way Leading from the Antiant boundry Line to Dirbins Creek, being that part of which Joseph Burchfield was overseer the Last year; Ordered that he cause the same to be kept in Repair for one year as the law Directs.

Ordered that all the States business in this County for the future be Transaction on the Thursday in Every Term or Session.

Page 101: Joseph Downs Esquire is appointed Treasurer for the County of Laurens. Ordered that he Enter into bond with Sufficient Security in the sum of £500 sterling money for the faithful discharge of his duty.

Ordered that the Sheriff or any other Officer in the said County who shall collect or Receive any Publick money due by County Taxes or fines pay the same unto the said County Treasurer.

Ordered that Two Constables do attend this Court Every Term or Session, the said Constables to be appointed or assign'd to this Post by the Court Every Term, and on their Producing a Certificate from the Court of their Attendance, the County Treasurer shall pay them for this attendance at the Court as aforesaid the sum of 4/8 p'r day.

James Floyd vs James McNees. Debt. This Suit by Consent of the Parties is Ordered to be Dismist at Plf Cost.

Ordered that a Summons issue against Ebenezer Moss to appear at our next court to be held for this County on the second Monday in Sept. next to declare as a Garnishee on oath what affects, debts, moneys, or Book accounts he hath in his hands the Property of Robert Harison, in an attachment brought by Joseph Parsons.

LAURENS COUNTY SC COURT MINUTES 1786-1789

Page 102: [16 June 1786]

Ordered that the Sheriff or County Treasurer Pay unto Lewis Saxon on his Producing a copy of this Order the sum of £12 s10 for his Extra or Publick Service done by him in his office and Take his Receipt for the same.

Court adjourned Till Court in Course &c. Minets signed by James Montgomery, George Anderson, Wm. Mutchuson, John Rodgers, Esquires.

At a Court held for the County of Laurens in the State of So Carolina at the courthouse of the said County the 11th day of Sept 1786. Present Jonathan Downs, Silvanus Walker, Charles Saxon, Esqrs.

Peter Carnes Esq'r is Admitted to Practice as an Attorney in this Court On condition that he produce to the Court Legal Credentials of his haveing been Regularly admitted to Practice as an Attorney within this State, which said Credentials to be produced to the next court to be held for this county the 2d Monday in December next.

Thomas P. Carnes Esq'r produced in open Court a License signed by the Hon. John Rutledge and Richard Hutson, Esqrs., Judges of the Court of Court of Chancery and the Hon. Edanus Burke & Thomas Haward, Esq'rs, Judges of the Court of Common Pleas of his the said Thos P. Carnes being Regularly admitted to Practice as an attorney in any of the courts of Law or Equity within this State Whereupon it is Ordered that he be Entered and Enrol'd as such in this Court.

A Deed of Conveyance of 250 acres of Land from Wm. Huggins and Mary his wife to Wm. Salmon Proven in Court by the oaths of Richard Watts and John Perry and ordered to be recorded.

[Pages 103-126 are missing.]

LAURENS COUNTY SC COURT MINUTES 1786-1789

[13 December 1786]

Page 127: A Deed of Conveyance from Thos Dendy & Mary his wife to David Burn for 130 acres of land Proven in Court by Silvanus Walker & Thos Lewis & Ordered to be Recorded.

A Lease and Release for the Conveyance of 200 acres of land from John Lewis and Presilla his wife to Joshua Teague proven according to the former act & Ordered to be Recorded.

A Lease and Release for the Conveyance of 350 acres of land from George Norwood to Joshua Teague proven according to the former act & ordered to be recorded.

A Lease and Release for the Conveyance of 300 acres of land from George Weir and Mary his wife to William Cason proven according to the former act & ordered to be recorded.

A Lease and Release for the Conveyance of 100 acres of land from Joseph Pearson to James McClintick proven in open Court by John McClintick & Wm Fowler and Ordered to be Recorded.

A Lease and Release for the Conveyance of 300 acres of land from John McCrary and Jean his wife to Charles Hutchings Proven by Jas Montgomery & Robt McCrary and Ordered to be Recorded.

A Lease and Release for the Conveyance of 150 acres of land from John McCrary and Jean his wife to Charles Hutchings Proven by Jas Montgomery & Robt McCrary and Ordered to be Recorded.

James Montgomery Esqr. Reported to the Court that the above named Jean McCrary freely & Willingly signed and acknowledged before him the 2 Setts of Conveyances from John McCrary & herself to Charles Hutchings.

Page 128: Ezekiel Smith vs Richard Polard. By Consent of the Parties this Suit is Ordered to be Continue till Next Court.

James Crooks is appointed Overseer of that Part of the High way Leading from the Beaverdam Creek the Charleston Road to Aaron Linches, it being that Part of the high way of which John McClintick was overseer. Ordered that he cause the same to [be] kept in Repair for one year from the Date hereof.

Ordered that Silvanus Walker and John Hunter Esquires appointed Commissioners to Confer with Robt Gilliam and William Caldwell, Esquires, about the execution of a bridge over Little River on the Road Leading from the Island ford on Salluda River to Odels for on Enoree River & Let the same in Conjunction with the Commissioners agreeable to the Order of Newberry

County and that the Clerk forward an Order to the Commissioners Reporting the same.

[13 December 1786]

William Young Plff vs James McNees and Hugh Young Deft. By Consent of the Parties this Suit is Ordered to be Continued till Next Court.

Edward Mitchusson Plff. vs James & Susannah Allison Defts. Admr. of John York decd. In Trover and Convertion. This day came the Parties by their attys and thereupon Came also a Jury to wit Bazel Prator, Wm Huddleston, Martin Doyall, Joseph Glen, James Dorough, James Downen, John Gray, George Bush, Josiah Prator, Clem't Deal, James Grier, and John Watson who being Elected Tried & Sworn the truth to Speak upon the Issue Joind upon their Oaths do say that the Dec'd John York was Guilty of the trover & Convertion in the Declaration Mentioned & they do assess the Plff Damages by acation thereof to £11 s 11 besides his Cost. Therefore it is Considered by the Court that the Plff **[Page 129]** Recover against the s'd Defts. his damages aforesaid in form aforesaid assesst Together with his Cost by him in this behalf Expended, To be levied of the s'd Testators Goods & Chattels in the hands of the s'd Defts unadministered, if so much thereof he hath, if not, to be levied on the future assets when they shall come to the hands of the s'd Admr to be administred and the said Deft in Mercy &c.

On Motion of Joshua Fowler a Witness for Edward Mitchusson against James Allison admr. of John york decd, it is ordered that the s'd Jas Allison pay unto him the s'd Joshua Fowler the sum of 50 shillings for 20 days attendance at 2/6 p'r day & that the same be taxed in the bill of Cost.

On Motion of Samuel Cob on oath, a witness for Edwerd Mitchusson against James and Susannah Allison admr of John York decd it is ordered that the sum of £2 7/6 be Taxed in the Bill of Cost for the said Saml Cob for 19 days attendance a 2/6 P'r day.

Mary Williams Plff vs Samuel Scott Deft. By Consent of the Parties this Suit is Ordered to be Continued the next Court.

Joseph Smith Pff. vs Joseph Paterson Deft. Ordered that this Suit be tried the first Cause Tomorrow morning.

On Motion of Richard Hix on oath, a Witness for Sarah Cargill vs James Sullivant, it is Ordered that James Sullivant pay him the sum of 22 shillings and 6 pence for 9 days attendance a 2/6 p'r day. Ordered the same be taxed in the bill of cost.

On Motion of Richard Hix on oath a witness for Elizebeth Tindsley vs Robert McNees, Ordered that Robert McNees pay him 20 shillings for 8 days Attendance @ 2/6 P'r day.

LAURENS COUNTY SC COURT MINUTES 1786-1789

[13 December 1786]

Hugh McVay Plff vs Lewis Banton Deft. By Consent of the Parties this Suit is Ordered to be Continued till Friday next.

Page 130: Court adjourned till Tomorrow Morning Nine OClock. Minets signed by John Hunter James Montgomery, Silv's Walker, Esq'rs.

Court met according to adjournment the 14th Dec'r 1786. Present James Montgomery, Wm Mitchusson, Silvanus Walker, John Rodgers, Esquires.

Thomas Jones Plff vs Richard Hix. Deft. In Case. The Parties haveing Mutually submitted all Matters in Difference between them to the Determination of Silvanus Walker Esqr and And'w Rodgers Junr and agreed that their award thereupon should be made the Judgment of the Court, and the said Silv's Walker and And'w Rodgers, this day Returned their award into Court, upon the premises, in Confirmation whereof it is Considered by the Court that the Plff recover against the s'd Deft. the sum of £16 and each party paying their own Cost in said Suit Expended.

State Plff vs David Allison Deft. Indictment. Assault & Battery. John Blackwell & Chas England witnesses in behalf of the state upon the Bill of Indictment sworn & sent.

The State Plff vs John Blackwell & Charles England Defts. Indictment. Assault & Battery. David Allison witness in behalf of the state on s'd Bill of Indictment order to be sworn & sent to the Grand Jury.

Robert McCrary foreman, Saml Whorton, Tully Choice, John Stephens, John Boyd, Robert Ross, Thos Cunningham, Jas Finney, William Bucks[?], James Abbercrumbie, Thos Cason, James Cook, and John Ritchey were sworn Grand Jurors of Inquest for the body of this County, and after haveing received their Charge Retired from the barr to Consult & their Verdict and after [**Page 131**] sum time Returned into Court and Presented as follows We of the Grand Jury for the County of Laurens Present as a Greavance John Martin Constable for the Escape of James Stinson. We further Present Jonathan Downs for Encourageing a Royett between Robert Franks and Dickson Mayhon.

The State Pff vs John Coker Deft. Indictment. Assault & Battery. Returned by the Grand Jury into a True Bill.

The State Plff vs John Blackwell & Charles England Defts. Indictment. Assault & Battery. Returned into Court by the Grand Jury a True Bill against England. John Blackwell clear.

State Plff vs David Allison Deft. Indictment. Assault & Battery. Returned into Court by the Grand Jury a True bill.

LAURENS COUNTY SC COURT MINUTES 1786-1789

[14 December 1786]

State Plff vs John Ritchey Deft. Indictment. Assault & Battery. Returned into Court Not a True bill.

Ordered that Process Issue against the Several Persons this Day Presented by the Grand Jury to appear here at the next court to answer to the Presentments against them Respectively.

On application of Jonathan Johnston to obtain Licence to Retail Spiritous Liquores at his Store in this County in any less Quantity than Three Gallons, Ordered to be Granted at next March Court & that he continued sell & retail Spiritous Liquors until that time by Virtue of his former Licence.

Page 132: Charles Hutchins Plf vs James Dillard Deft. In Slander. By Consent of the Parties this Suit is Ordered to be Dismist Each Party Paying their own cost.

The State vs David Allison. Indictment. Assault & Battery. The Deft comes into Court & Confesses the Charges in the Indictment Alleged against him and puts himself upon the Mercy of the Court, whereupon it is Considered by the Court that the Deft Pay a fine of five shillings & Cost of Prosecution.

The State vs Charles England. Indictment. Assault & Battery. The Deft Came into Court & Confessed that he was Guilty of the Charges in the Indictment alledged against him, and put himself upon the Mercy of the Court, whereupon it is Considered by the Court that he pay a five of 5/ & Cost of Prosecution.

Joel Burgess vs Thomas Evans. Assault and Battery. By consent of the parties this suit is ordered to be dismist at Defts Cost.

Joseph Smith Plff vs Joseph Patterson Deft. In Trover. This day came the Parties by their attys & thereupon came also a Jury to wit Bazel Prator, Wm Huddleston, Martin Doyall, Joseph Glen, Ja's Dorough, James Downen, John Gray, George Bush, Josiah Prator, Clem't Deal, James Grier, and John Watson who being Elected Tried & Sworn the truth to Speak upon the Issue Joind upon their Oaths do say that the Deft is not Guilty of the Trover & Convertion in the Declaration Mentioned. Therefore it is Considered by the Court that Deft go hence without day & recover against the s'd Plff his Cost about his Defence in this behalf Expended.

Page 133: On Motion made on oath by Thomas Mcgregory a witness for Joseph Patterson vs Joseph South, Ordered that the Sum of 30 shillings for his attendance at 2/6 P'r day 12 days be Taxed in the Bill of Cost.

On Motion made on oath by Reubin Dollar a witness for Joseph Patterson vs Joseph South, Ordered that the Sum of 30 shillings be Taxed in the Bill of

LAURENS COUNTY SC COURT MINUTES 1786-1789

Cost, also mileage for coming & returning from Court fifteen miles three times for 12 days attendance at 2/6 P'r day amt. 45/.

[14 December 1786]

On Motion made on oath by John Watson a witness for Joseph Patterson vs Joseph South, Ordered that the Sum of 25 shillings be Taxed in the Bill of Cost for him for 10 days attendance at 2/6 P'r day & mileage for going & coming out of Spartanburgh County 13 Miles three times.

On Motion made on oath by John Histelo a witness for Joseph Patterson against Joseph South, Ordered that Joseph Patterson pay him 30 shillings for 12 days attendance at 2/6 P'r day.

On Motion made on oath by William Watson a witness for Joseph Patterson against Joseph South, Ordered that Joseph Patterson pay him the sum of 25 shillings for 10 days attendance at 2/6 P'r day.

On Motion of Mr. Yancey atty for John Newman, Ordered that a Mortgage from Robt H. Hughes to John Newman for 170 acres of land and a mill on Enoree River, be filed in the office of be recorded, & that the Clerk Issue Subpoenas for John Briggs, John Robertson, & Richd Burgess to appear here at the next court to prove the same.

Court adjourned till tomorrow morning 9 Oclock. James Montgomery, Silv's Walker, Wm Mitchusson, Esqrs.

Page 134: Court met according to adjournment the 15th Decr 1786. Present Silv's Walker, Jas Montgomery, Wm Mitchusson, John Rodgers, George Anderson, Esquires.

Richard Collins Plt. vs Reubin Stone Deft. Debt. This day came the Deft by his Atty and the Plft. thos solemnly calld came not but made Default, nor is his Suit further Prosecuted therefore on motion of the Deft. by his atty it is Considered that the Plf. be Nonsuited and that the Deft. Recover against the s'd Plff 5/ damages according to an act of Assembly in that Case made and Provided and his cost by him about his Defence in this behalf Expended &c.

On Motion made on oath by Francis Allison a Witness Reubin Stone vs Rich'd Collins, ordered that Reubin Stone pay him the sum of 47 and six pence for 18 days attendance at 2/6 p'r day & that the same be taxed in the bill of Cost.

David Welch Plft. vs John Barnet Deft. In Debt. By consent of the Parties by their attys they have mutually submitted the Determination of this Suit to Nathan Barksdale, James Adair and Charles Simmons and agreed that their award thereupon should be made the Judgement of the Court, which s'd aware was Ordered to be Returned into Court Immediately.

[15 December 1786]

The said Arbitrators the same day Returned their award into Court in these words to wit that the Deft pay unto the Plt Two shillings & six pence P'r Bushell for what Corn is Due in the note, with six months intrest, to be paid on demand if Paid in Property the Property to be Rated at Cash Price and the Plf pay Cost of s'd suit, whereupon it is Considered by the Court that the Plf Recover against the s'd Deft the sum of £6 s18 d6 the amount of the corn due on the note at 2/ P'r Bushell, and the said Plff pay Cost of suit.

Page 135: On Motion of Michael Wallace a Witness for David Welch vs John Barnett, Ordered that David Welch pay him the sum of 20 shillings for 8 days attendance @ 2/6 p'r day.

Charles Sullivant Plf vs Abel Boling Deft. In Trover & Convertion. This day came the Parties by their attorneys and thereupon came also a Jury to wit Bazel Prator, Wm Huddleston, Joseph Glen, James Dorough, James Downen, John Gray, George Bush, Josiah Prator, Clem't Deal, James Grier, John Watson and Martin Doyall who being Elected Tried & Sworn the truth to Speak upon the Issue Joind returned a Verdict into Court in these words to wit, we of the Jury for want of Evidence find for the Def't. The Plf by D. Brown his atty moved the Court that a Judgment be not Entered for the Deft but a new trial granted as the Trial was bought on by surprise, the Verdict was Ordered to be set aside and a New Trial Granted accordingly on payment of the cost of suit.

Hugh McVay Plt vs Lewis Banton Deft. In Case. On Motion of the Deft by his Atty to Rule the Plf to Give security for the Cost of said suit if he should be cost, which s'd motion was over ruled, and ordered to go immediately to Trial. Whereupon Came the Parties by their attorneys and thereupon Came also a Jury to wit, Bazel Prator, Wm Huddleston, Martin Doyall, Joseph Glen, James Dorough, James Downen, John Gray, George Bush, Josiah Prator, Clem't Deal, James Grier, and John Watson who being Elected Tried & Sworn the truth to Speak upon the Issue Joind upon their oaths do Say, that the Deft. is Guilty of the promises and assumptions in the Declaration mentioned & they do assess the Plff damages by accation thereof of £5 s8 d9 besides his Cost, therefor it is Considered by the Court that the Plf Recover against the s'd Deft his Damages aforesaid in form aforesaid assesst and his Cost by him in this Behalf Expanded & the sd Deft in Mercy &c.

Page 136: On Motion of Winney Fuller a Witness for Hugh McVay against Lewis Banton, Ordered that the sum of £3 s1 d6 be Taxed in the bill of Cost for her the said Winney Fuller for 25 days attendance @ 2/ p'r day.

On Motion of Robert Ross a Witness for Hugh McVay against Lewis Banton, Ordered that the Plff pay him 30 shillings for 12 days attendance @ 2/ p'r day. & that the same be Taxed in the Bill of Cost.

LAURENS COUNTY SC COURT MINUTES 1786-1789

[15 December 1786]

On motion of Abraham Neighbours a Witness for Lewis Banton against Hugh McVay, Ordered that Hugh McVay pay him £ 3 s15 for his attendance 30 days @ 2/ p'r day.

On Motion of Joshua Arnald a Witness for Hugh McVay against Lewis Banton, Ordered that Hugh McVay pay him £3 s15 for his attendance 30 days @ 2/ p'r day.

On Motion of Stephen Potter a Witness for Hugh McVay against Lewis Banton, Ordered that Hugh McVay pay him £3 s7 for his attendance 25 days @ 2/ p'r day.

William Anderson Plf vs Claburn Sims Deft. Summary Process. By Consent of the Parties this suit is Ordered to be Dismist at Plfts. Cost.

William Anderson Plf. vs Charity Parker Deft. In Trover. By Consent of the Parties this Suit is Ordered to be Dismist Each party paying their own Cost.

Samuel Cob Plf vs James & Susanna Allison admr. of John York decd. Deft. Trover. Plea Entered an Abatement as to susanna Allison, She not being one of the admr's of s'd York's Estate which Plea was Sworn to and allowed, Whereupon it is Considered that the said Susannah Allison Recover vs the said Saml Cob his Cost by her in this behalf Expended &c.

Page 137: Charles Sullivant Plf vs John Mading Deft. In Case. This day came the Plf D. Brown his attorney & the Deft by C. Goodwin his atty & thereupon came also a Jury to wit Bazel Prator, Wm Huddleston, Martin Doyall, Joseph Glen, James Dorough, James Downen, John Gray, George Bush, Josiah Prator, Clem't Deal, James Grier, & John Watson who being Elected Tried & Sworn the truth to Speak upon the Issue Joind on their own find a Verdict for the Plff for £9 s13 & his Cost. Therefore, it is Considered by the Court that the Plf Recover against the s'd Deft his Debt amounting to £9 s13 and his Cost by him in this Behalf Expended and the said Deft in Mercy &C.

James Cunningham Plf vs James Stinson Deft. On attachment. The attachment being Returned Executed on Two horse Creatures the Property of the Deft. and the Deft. not appearing to Replevy the same, The Plff. Came into Court and Proved an acct. against the s'd Deft. to the amount of £10 & thereupon it is Considered by the Court that the Plft Recover against the s'd Deft the sum £10 & his Cost by him in this behalf Expended. Ordered that the Sheriff expose to publick sale the s'd two Horses the Property of the Deft attcht in behalf of the Plff Providing thereon as if Taken by a writ of Fieri facias and the moneys arising from such sale to pay unto the Pltt toward the Satisfaction of this Judgment & the Overplus if any there be return to the Deft.

[15 December 1786]

William Thomason Plff vs William Martin Deft. Attachment. Returned not Executed & thereupon it is Ordered to be Struck off the Docket & The same was done accordingly.

Page 138: Ordered that Nathaniel Austin be & is hereby appointed Constable to attend this Court Every Term & to be Allowed the sum of 2/9 for his Attendance at Every Term.

Court adjourned till Tomorrow Morning 9 Oclock. James Montgomery, Silv's Walker, George Anderson, Esquires.

Court met according to adjournment the 16th Decr 1786. Present Silvanus Walker, James Montgomery, George Anderson, Esquires.

On motion of George Brooks a Witness for John Barnet against David Welch, Ordered that the sum of £2 s1 d8 be Taxed in the Bill of Cost against the said David Welch, for the said George Brooks for 14 days attendance at 2/6 P'r day and Milage going and comeing out of Spartanburgh County 30 miles twice at /2 Pr Mile.

John Smith Plff. vs George Winters Deft. On Attachment. The Attachment being Returned Executed and the Deft not appearing to Replevy the same, the Plf came into Court and Proved his Acct against the Deft. Amounting to £10, it is thereupon considered by the Court that the Plff Recover against the said Deft. the sum of £10 and his cost by him in this behalf Expended and the s'd Deft in Mercy &c.

Ordered that the Goods and Chattels the Property of the Deft. attacht in Behalf of the Plf be Exposed to Publick Sale, and the moneys ariseing from such sale, pay unto the Plff towards satisfaction of the Judgment and the Overplus if any there be Return to the Deft.

Page 139: Isaac Mitchel Plft vs Jonathan Childs Deft. In Slander for words. The Deft being arested and not appearing tho Solemnly calld on Motion of the Plff by C. Goodwin his atty, it is ordered that Judgment be Entered for the Plff against the said Deft for what Damages the Plff hath Sustained by accation of the said Defts Speaking the words in the Declaration mentioned to be Inquired of by a Jury, unless the said Deft. shall appear and Plead to Issue at the next Court.

Richard Hancock Plff vs John Phindly Deft. In Debt. The Deft being arested and not appearing tho Solemnly calld on Motion of the Plff by his atty Peter Carnes, it is ordered that Judgment be Entered for the Plff against the said Deft for his Deft in the Declaration mentioned unless the said Deft. shall appear and Plead to Issue at the next Court.

LAURENS COUNTY SC COURT MINUTES 1786-1789

[16 December 1786]

Joseph Goodman Plff vs Jean Tolds Deft. In Slander. The Sheriff Haveing Returned that the Deft is not Found within his County, on the motion of the Plft by D. Brown his atty, and alias Capias is awarded him against the s'd Deft. Returnable here the Next Court.

Edward Arnald Plft vs Richard Collins Deft. In Trover & Convertion. This day Came the Plft by C. Goodwin his atty and the Deft. by W. Shaw his Atty and thereupon came also a Jury to wit Bazel Prator, William Huddleston, Martin Doyall, Joseph Glen, James Downen, John Gray, George Bush, Josiah Prator, Clem't Deal, James Grier, James Dorough, & John Watson who being Elected Tried & Sworn the truth to Speak upon the Issue Joind on their oaths do say that the Deft is Guilty of the Trover and Convertion in the Declaration mentioned [**Page 140**] and they do assess the Plf. Damages by accation thereof to £10 besides his Cost. Therefore, it is Considered by the Court that the Plf Recover against the s'd Deft his damages aforesaid in form aforesaid assesst, and his Cost by him in this Behalf Expended and the said Deft in Mercy &C.

Patrick Reyley Plf vs William Thomason Deft. In Slander. Ordered that this Suit be Discontinued at Plffs Cost.

Reuben Pyles Plft. vs Andrew Rodgers Senr. Deft. Summary Process. In Case. This day came the Plff into Court and Proved an Acct. against the said Deft for £1 s7 d11 and thereupon it was Considered by the Court that the Plff Recover against the said Deft. the sum of £1 s7 d11 and his cost by him in this behalf Expended and the said Deft in Mercy &C.

Patrick Reyley Plf vs William Thomason Deft. In Case. Ordered that this Suit be Discontinued at Plffs Cost.

John Williams Plff vs John Donohoe Deft. In Debt. This day came the Plft by D. Brown his atty and the Deft. Tho Solemnly [called] Came not, and Thereupon came also a Jury to wit, Bazel Prator, William Huddleston, James Dorough, James Downen, Martin Doyall, Joseph Glen, John Gray, George Bush, Josiah Prator, Clem't Deal, James Grier, and John Watson who being Elected Tried & Sworn the truth to Speak upon their oaths do say that the Deft doth owe the Debt in the Declaration mention, amounting to £10, therefore it is Considered by the Court that the Pltf. Recover against the said Deft. his Debt as aforesaid amounting to £10 & his Cost by him in this behalf Expended and the said Deft in Mercy &C.

Page 141: John Willson Plff vs Notley Mastes Deft. On an Attachment. ordered to be Discontinued and Struck off the Dockett.

Samuel Dilrumple Plft vs Samuel Bydston Deft. In Covenant. The Deft. being arested and not appearing thos Solemnly Calld on Motion of the Pltf by W. Shaw his Atty it is ordered that Judgment be Entered for the Plft against the s'd Deft for what Damages that Plft hath Sustain by accation of the Breech of the Covenant in the Declaration mentioned unless the said Deft. shall appear at the next Court & Plead Issue.

[16 December 1786]

Isaac Williams Plft vs Mary Griffen Deft. In Debt. By Consent of the Plft by James Yancey his Atty it is ordered that this suit be Discontinued at Plfts. Cost.

on Motion made on oath by Hendrix Arnald a Witness for Edwerd Arnald vs Richard Collins, Ordered that Richard Collins pay him 22 shillings and 6 pence for 9 days Attendance at 2/6 p'r day & that the same be Taxed in the bill of Cost.

Court adjourned Till Court in Course. Minets signed by Silvanus Walker, James Montgomery, George Anderson, Esquires.

At a Court held for the County of Laurens in the State of So Carolina at the Courthouse of said County, the 12th day of March 1787. Present Silvanus Walker, Charles Saxon, Joseph Downs, George Anderson, Esquires.

On application of Edmond Craddock he is Admitted to keep a Publick Tavern at the place where he now lives, formerly the property of John McCrary, for the Term of One whole year from thence next Ensuing, whereupon the s'd Edmond Craddock Together with James and Saml Saxon his securities entered into and acknowledged their bonds according to Law.

Page 142: A Lease and Release for the Conveyance of 400 acres of Land from Solomon Niblet to Joshua Saxon proved in open Court by Joseph Downs Esqr. and Robert Cooper and Ordered to be Recorded.

A Deed from Wm Prator & Mary his wife to John Powell for the Conveyance of 100 acres of land Acknowledged in open Court & ordered to be Recorded.

A Lease and Release for the Conveyance of 100 acres from James Waldroup to John Farrow proven in open Court by Thomas Farrow & Vinson Brown and Ordered to be Recorded.

A Lease and Release for the Conveyance of 250 acres from Thos McClurkin to Andrew Endsley, Proven in open Court by Reubin Pyles & John Glenn and Ordered to be Recorded.

A Lease and Release for the Conveyance of 150 acres from Robert Plunkett to Abijah Oneal, proven in open Court by Elisha Ford & Hugh Oneal and Ordered to be Recorded.

LAURENS COUNTY SC COURT MINUTES 1786-1789

[12 March 1787]

A Lease and Release for the Conveyance of 200 acres from Samuel Pearson & Messer Babb to Elisha Ford, proven in open Court by Hugh Oneal and Saml Kelley and Ordered to be Recorded.

A Lease and Release for the Conveyance of 500 acres from Wm Anderson to Saml Kelley Junr, proven in open Court by Saml Kelley Senr & Jas Docherty & Ordered to be Recorded.

A Lease and Release for the Conveyance of 150 acres from James Abercrumbie to Richard Childers, proven by John Childers and Ordered to be Recorded.

A Lease and Release for the Conveyance of 78 acres of land from Charles Saxon to Robert Young acknowledged in open Court & ordered to be Recorded.

Ordered that an Order Entered Last September Court for a Deed to be Recorded from George Anderson & Molley his wife to John Pamplin for the Conveyance of 150 acres of land, be & is hereby set aside, & is Void to all intents & purpusses, Ordered that a Deed for the Conveyance of the same 150 ares of land from the s'd George Anderson & Molley his wife to Meriah Goodman **[Page 143]** be Entered upon Record, being proven in open court by Saml Wharton & Charles Sullivant.

A Lease and Release for the Conveyance of 150 acres from Col. Robt McCrary to John Prude, proven according to the former Act, and Ordered to be Recorded.

A Mortgage for 270 acres of land with a Griss mill, from Robt H. Hughes to John Newman, proven in open Court by Richard Burgess & John Brigs, & ordered to be recorded.

A Lease and Release for the Conveyance of 100 acres from James Roseman to Lewis Graves proven in open Court by David Anderson & David McCaa & Ordered to be Recorded.

William Harris is appointed overseer of that Part of the Highway Leading from Michael Waldroups to James Youngs. Ordered that the said Wm Harris Cause the several free male Inhabitants and Slaves Contiguous to and Convenient to said road to work thereon and to Cause the same to be kept in Repair for One year from this date as the Law Directs.

On Application of John D. Kern he is Admitted to sell & Retail all kinds of Spirituous [Liquors] at his store in said County in as small a Quantity as one quart for the Term of One year from this Date he complying with the Revenue act of s'd state.

LAURENS COUNTY SC COURT MINUTES 1786-1789

[12 March 1787]

A Lease and Release for the Conveyance of 220 acres of land from John Redman to Jesse Goodwin proven in open Court by James Barton & Ordered to Ly for further proof and now proven by Saml Cob & Ordered to be Recorded.

A Lease and Release for the Conveyance of 100 acres from of land John Redman to James Barton, Proven in open Court by Jesse Goodwin & Ordered to Ly for further proof and now proven by Saml Cob & Ordered to be Recorded.

John Caldwell vs Rich'd Lang. Attachment. Judgment for Plft. for £50 & Cost. Ordered that the Sheriff Expose to Publick Sale the goods and Chattels lands & tenements of the Deft. attacht by the Sheriff, or so much as will be Sufficient to Satisfy **[Page 144]** the s'd Plft for his Judgment aforesaid.

William Shaw vs Charles Sullivant. Summary Process. Debt. Came as well the Plft as the Deft in their Proper persons and the Deft Confessed Judgment to the Amount of £2 s3 d6 whereupon it is Considered by the Court that the Plft. Recover vs the s'd Deft the said Sum of £2 s3 d6 & his Cost by him in this behalf Expended.

A Deed for the Conveyance of 30 acres of land from Robert Young to James Cook Acknowledged in open Court & ordered to be Recorded.

Thomas Wadsworth & Turpin vs John Ozburn. Sum Process. Debt. Continued by Consent till next Court.

John Martin vs Robert Franks. Trespass Assault & Battery. Dismist by Consent of the Parties at the Defts Cost.

The State vs Robert Franks. Indictment Assault & Battery. The Deft Came into Court and Sayeth that he will not Contend with the State, as he is Guilty of the Charges in the Indictment Aledged against him and Submitted himself to the Mercy of the Court. Thereupon it was considered by the Court that he the Deft. pay a fine of one shilling & Cost of Prosecution.

Court adjourned till Tomorrow Morning 9 Oclock. James Montgomery, Joseph Downs, Charles Saxon, Esquires.

Page 145: Court met according to adjournment the 13 March 1787. Present Silvanus Walker, James Montgomery, George Anderson, Esquires.

Charles Goodwin vs James Sullivant. Sumr Process. Case. By Consent this Suit is Ordered to be Dismist at Defts Cost.

LAURENS COUNTY SC COURT MINUTES 1786-1789

[13 March 1787]

A Lease and Release for the Conveyance of 320 acres of land from John Denny to William Ray acknowledged in open Court and Ordered to be Recorded.

A Lease and Release for the Conveyance of 63 acres of land from John Caldwell to Gilbert Turner proven in open Court by Hugh Oneal and Haisten Doyall and Ordered to be Recorded.

A Lease and Release for the Conveyance of 150 acres of land from Thomas Edgehill Junr to Tho's McDanald proven in open Court by Hugh Oneal and Edm'd Drake & Ordered to be Recorded.

A Lease and Release for the Conveyance of 100 acres of land from John Weir to Haisten Doyal, proven in open Court by Wm Boyd & Saml McClurkin & Ordered to be Recorded.

A Lease and Release for the Conveyance of 200 acres of land from Ferrell Reyley to Wm Cason Senr proven in open Court by William Cason Junr & Peter Hitt and Ordered to be Recorded.

A Lease and Release for the Conveyance of 2 tracts of land, one for 250 acres and the other for 89 acres of land, from Thos Clark to Saml Eakin, proven according to the former Act & Ordered to be Recorded.

A Lease and Release for the Conveyance of 180 acres of land from Sam'l Eakin and Jean his wife to Peter Hitt, proven in open Court by Thos Wm Fakes and Wm Cason & Ordered to be Recorded.

A Lease and Release for the Conveyance of 440 acres of land from Saml Dillard & Agness his wife to James Dillard acknowledged in open Court & Ordered to be Recorded.

Page 146: James Criswell vs William Shaw. Sum Process. Case. This day came the Parties by their attys after both Parties being heard by the Attys it was Considered by the Court that the Deft Recover against the said Plft. his Cost by him in this behalf Expended.

Wadsworth & Turpin vs Michael Waldroup. Sum Process. Debt. Judgment for the Plft for £9 s18 d10 with the Intrest thereon & his Cost by him in this behalf Expended.

A Lease for the Conveyance of 200 acres of land from John Young & Mary his wife to George Anderson proven in No Carolina by Archibald Young & Now proven in open Court by James Young & Ordered to be Recorded.

LAURENS COUNTY SC COURT MINUTES 1786-1789

[13 March 1787]

A Lease and Release for the Conveyance of 52 acres of land from Susannah Deen to John Edwards acknowledged in open Court and Ordered to be Recorded.

John Hall vs James Russell. Sum Process. Case. Came the Parties by their Attys and after hearing the Matter Debated by the council on both sides, it was Considered by the Court that the Plft Take nothing by his bill, but for his false Clamour be in Mercy & that the Deft. go home without Day and Recover against the s'd Plft his cost by him in this behalf Expended.

A Lease and Release for the Conveyance of 250 acres of land from John Entrekin & Elizebeth his wife to Susannah Deen proven according to the former Act & Ordered to be Recorded.

Page 147: On application of John Simpson he is admitted to sell and Retail all kinds of Spirituous at his Store in this County in any less quantity than three Gallons for and During the full space of one year from this date, he complying with the Revenue Act.

A Power of Atty from Ann Browster to James Irwin Presented in open Court by the said James Irwin and ordered to be Recorded.

A Power of Atty from Agness Irwin to James Irwin acknowledged in Pennsilvania by the said Agness Irwin, and now presented in open Court by James Irwin and ordered to be Recorded.

A Lease & Release for the Conveyance of 200 acres of land from Thomas Haisten to Alex'd Irwin proven according to the former Act and Ordered to be Recorded.

William Thomason vs William Martin. Attachment. Enoch Bramblet being Summoned as a Garnishee came into Court and being Duly sworn according to Law, sayeth that he hath in his Possession of the Property of the Deft, Twelve & a half Barrels of Corn, three cheers, two baggs, and no more, and the Constable Returning the attachment, that there was no other goods & Chattells of the Deft to be found within this County, the Plf proveing his Demand against the Deft to the amount of £14, thereupon it is Considered by the Court that the Plf. Recover against the s'd Deft the s'd sum of £14 *& his cost by him in this behalf Expended.

Ordered that the Sheriff or Constable Expose to publick sale the Goods and Chattells the Property of the Deft. Attach't in behalf of the Plf. and the moneys arising from such sale pay unto the Pft towards Satisfaction of this Judgmt.

LAURENS COUNTY SC COURT MINUTES 1786-1789

[13 March 1787]

Thos W. Fakes foreman, Andrew Rodgers Senr, Geo Young, Kitt Smith, Saml Boling, Richard Griffen, Nehemiah Franks, Marshel Franks, Charles Simmons, Robt Lard, Joseph Grier, James Adair, James Burchfield were sworn Grand Jurours of Inquest for the body of this County & after haveing rec'd [**Page 148**] their Charge, Retired from the Bar to Consult of their Verdict and after sum time Returned into Court and Presented as follows to wit.

We Present as a Grievence that there is no Overseer from Mill Creek to Little River & That an Overseer be appointed for that Purpose.

We Present as a Grievence that the Commissioners from Heads ford on Enoree to the County Line, at the Cross Roads below Joseph Ramages, are not Tolerated to Build a Bridge most Sutable to Trade for the Benefit of Travellers, where both Roads might Conveniently Cross at One Bridge.

The State vs Clem't Davis. Indictment. Assault & Battery. Returned into Court a True bill by the Grand Jury.

The State vs Mansfield Walker, John Blackwell. Indictment. Sabbath braking. Returned into Court by the Grand Jury not a True Bill. Thos W. Fakes foreman, George Young, Kitt Smith, Rich'd Griffen, Marshell Franks, Robt Lard, Nehemiah Franks, Charles Simmons, And'w Rodgers, Ja's Burchfield, James Adair.

A Lease and Release for the Conveyance of 100 acres of land from Thomas Jones Senr to William Stone proven in Open Court by Thos W. Fakes and Ordered to Ly for further Proof.

Page 149: John Rogers vs Thos Rodgers. Trover. The Parties mutually submitted all matters in Deference Between them to the Determination of Rob't Gilliam, Anthony Griffen, Daniel Mcgin, and Hugh Oneal, which said arbitrators now returned their award into Court viz that the Deft pay unto the Plft on or before the first of August next Ensuing the Just and full sum of £4 s7 and each Party pay their own Cost, whereupon it is Considered by the court that the Plft recover against the s'd Deft the sum of £4 s7 & each Party their own Cost.

Duncan Obryan vs William Thomason. Sum Process. Case. The Parties mutually submitted all matters in Deference Between them to the Determination of David Dunlap & James Sullivant whose award was to be made a Judgment of court, which s'd arbitrators now returned their award in to Court as follows to wit that the Deft pay unto the Plft the sum of nineteen shillings and four pence, whereupon it is Considered by the court that the Plft recover against the s'd Deft the sum of nineteen shillings and four pence and his Cost by him in this behalf Expended.

[13 March 1787]

Richard Hancock vs John Phindley. Writ Debt By Consent of the Parties this suit is Ordered to be Dismist at the Plfts cost Except the Clerks fees.

John Brown vs Lewis Duvall. Trover. By Consent of the Parties this Suit is Ordered to be Continued till next Court.

A Lease and Release for the Conveyance of 150 acres of land from Clem't Davis to Thos East proven by Alex'd Morison & John Chapman and Ordered to be Recorded.

Page 150: David Allison vs Thomas Palmour. Sum Process. Debt. Came the Parties by their Attorneys and the Deft Petitioned for a Jury at his own Cost, and thereupon Came also a Jury to wit, Thos Dendy, Wm. Dendy, Saml Eakins, James Underwood, Wm. Green, Robt Spence, Wm. Tweedy, Michael Waldroup, Saml Powell, Martin Martin, John Owin and Patrick Obryan who being Elected Tried & Sworn the truth to Speak upon the Issue Joind, upon their Oaths find for the Plft £8 s8 d10 & his cost by him in the this behalf Expended.

The State vs Clement Davis. Assault & Battery. The Deft Came into Court and Confessed that he was guilty & Submitted himself to the Mercy of the Court, whereupon it was considered that the Deft. Pay a fine of five shillings & Cost of Prosecution.

Court adjourned till tomorrow Morning 9 OClock. Minets signed by Silv's Walker, Jas Montgomery, George Anderson.

Court met according to adjournment the 14th March 1787. Present Silv's Walker, George Anderson, James Montgomery, Joseph Downs, Esq'rs.

Thomas Dendy vs John Martin. Trover. By Consent of the Parties this Suit is Ordered to be Dismist at Defts Cost.

Page 151: A Deed of Gift from Michael Waldrop to Jas & Shadrach Waldroup, proved in Open Court by Isaac Couch & Ordered to Ly for further proof.

Saml Cob vs James & Susannah Allison. Trespass. By Consent of the Plft. this Suit is Ordered to be Dismist at his cost.

Charles Sullivan vs Abel Boling. Continued By Consent till Next Court.

George Anderson vs William Price. By Consent this is ordered to be Dismist at Plfts. Cost.

LAURENS COUNTY SC COURT MINUTES 1786-1789

[14 March 1787]

James Adair vs Henry Johnston & David Simpson. By Consent this Suit is ordered to be Dismist at Plfts. Cost.

Ezekiel Smith vs Richard Pollard. By Consent of the Parties this Suit is Ordered to be Continued till Next Court.

Colo. George Reede vs John Mcgee. Attachment. The Attachment being Returned Executed on a Tract of land supposed to Contain 300 acres Lying & Being in this County and the Deft. Failing to Appear and Plead to the Plfts action agreable to the former order to this Court, Came the Plfts into Court by Wm. Shaw his Atty whereupon Came also a Jury to wit Thos Dendy, Wm. Dendy, Ja's Underwood, Wm. Green, Robt Spence, Wm. Tweedy, Michael Waldroup, Saml Powell, Martin Martin, John Owin, Patrick Obryan, and Wm Young who being Elected Tried & Sworn well and truly to Inquire what Damages the Plft hath Sustained by accation of the Defts not performing the promises & Assumptions in the Declaration mentioned, upon their oath do say that the Plft hath sustained Damages by accation thereof to £36 s11 d8 3/4 with cost. [Page 152] Whereupon it is Considered by the Court that the Pflt Recover against the s'd Deft the sum of £36 s11 d8 3/4 & his Cost by him in this behalf Expended.

Ordered that the Sheriff Expose to Publick Sale the said Tract of 300 acres of land, and the moneys ariseing from such sale pay unto the Plft towards Satisfaction of this Judgment & the Overplus if any there be return to the Deft.

William Hanna vs Benjamin Rainey. By Consent of the Parties this Suit is Ordered to be continued till Next Court.

William Jackson vs John Motley. Discontinued.

On Application of James Pollock he is Admitted to Sell and Retail all kinds of Spirituous Liquors at his house where he now lives in this County for and During the full space and Term of one whole year from thence next Ensuing in any Less Quantity than three Gallons, he complying with the Revenue act of this State.

A Lease and Release for the Conveyance of 49 acres of land from Susannah Deen to Josiah East acknowledged in open Court & ordered to be Recorded.

On Application of Jonathan Johnston he is Admitted to Sell and Retail all kinds of Spirituous Liquors at his Store in this County in any Less Quantity than three Gallons for and During the full space & Term of one whole year from thence next Ensuing, he complying with the Revenue act of this State.

LAURENS COUNTY SC COURT MINUTES 1786-1789

[14 March 1787]

A Lease and Release for the Conveyance of 100 acres of land from David Weir & Jean his wife to Haisten Doyall, proven in Open Court by Wm. Boyd and Saml McClurkin & Ordered to be Recorded.

Robert Cooper vs Abraham Boyd. Trover. By Consent, this Suit is Ordered to be Dismist at the Plfts Cost.

Page 153: Thomas Mars vs John Ritchey. False Imprisonment. This day came the Parties into Court by their Attys and thereupon came also a Jury to wit, Thos Dendy, Wm. Dendy, James Underwood, Wm. Green, Robt Spence, Wm. Tweedy, David Burn, Saml Powell, Martin Martin, John Owin, Patrick Obryan, & Wm Young who being Elected Tried & Sworn the truth to Speak upon the Issue Joined, upon their Oaths do say, that the Deft is Guilty of the Trespass assault and false Imprisonment in the Decl'n Mentioned, and they do assess the Plft. Damages by accation thereof to £2 s1 besides his costs, thereupon it was considered by the Court that the Plft. Recover against the said Deft. his Damages aforesaid in form aforesaid assest and his cost by him in this behalf Expended and the said Deft. in Mercy &c.

On Motion made on oath by John Saxon a witness for Thos Mars against John Ritchey, Ordered that John Ritchey pay him the sum of £2 s10 for 20 days attendance at 2/6 P'r day, and that the same be Taxed in the bill of Cost.

On Motion made on oath by Sam'l McClurkin a witness for Thos Mars against John Ritchey, Ordered that John Ritchey pay him the sum of £2 s2 for 17 days attendance at 2/6 P'r day, and that the same be Taxed in the bill of Cost.

Mary Williams vs Samuel Scott. Debt. Ordered to be the first Cause Tried in the Morning.

Court Adjourned till Tomorrow Morning Eight OClock. Minets Signed by Silv's Walker, Joseph Downs, George Anderson, James Montgomery, Esquires.

Court met according to adjournment the 15th March 1787. Present James Montgomery, Joseph Downs, George Anderson, Esquires.

Page 154: On Application of Duke Williams he is Admitted to keep a Publick Tavern at the place where he Joseph Goodman formerly kept a Public Tavern in this County, for and During the full Space and Term of One whole year from thence next Ensuing, whereupon he the s'd Duke Williams Together with John Williams and James Criswell his securities came into court and acknowledged their bonds according to Law.

A Lease and Release for the Conveyance of 130 acres of land from Saml Henderson & Mary Ann his wife to Luke Waldroup, proven in Open Court by Wm. Ozburn and Richard Henderson & Ordered to be Recorded.

LAURENS COUNTY SC COURT MINUTES 1786-1789

[15 March 1787]

Mary Williams vs Saml Scott. Debt. By Consent of the Parties this Suit is Ordered to be Dismist at Defts Cost.

Nathan Kemp vs Joseph Mayhon. By Consent of the Parties this Suit is Ordered to be Continued till Next Court.

Robert Hunter Vs Robert Franks. Case. This day came the Parties by their Attys & thereupon Came also a Jury to wit, Thos Dendy, Wm. Dendy, James Underwood, Wm. Green, Robert Spence, Wm. Tweedy, Micha'l Waldrop, Saml Powell, Martin Martin, John Owin, Patrick Obryan, and Wm Young who being Elected Tried & Sworn well and truly the truth to Speak upon the Issued Joind upon their Oaths do say that the Deft. is Guilty of the Premises and Assumptions in the Declaration Mentioned & and they do assess the Plft Damages by accation thereof to £3 s9 & costs of Suit, whereupon it was Considered by the Court that the Plft Recover against the s'd Deft his Damages aforesaid in form aforesaid assest and his cost by him in this behalf Expended and the said Deft in Mercy &c.

Page 155: Anthony Golden is Appointed Overseer of that Part of the highway Leading from Mill Creek to Little River, at Mr. Williams's, and that he cause all the hands within Two Miles of the said Road both of Laurens and Newberry Countys to work thereon and to Cause the same to be kept in Good Repair for one year as the Law directs.

William Davis is Appointed Overseer of that Part of the County Road Leading from Bush River to Indian Creek and all the free Male Inhabitants and slaves within Two Miles of the s'd Road to work thereon and to Cause the same to be kept in Repair for one year as the Law directs.

Reubin Pyles & James McNees vs Col. Robert McCrary. Sum Process. Case. This day came the Parties by their Attys whereupon it was Considered by the Court, after several Witnesses being sworn and Examined Tuching the Premises & the Council heard on both sides, that the Plf Recover against the said Deft against the said Deft £4 s4 d6 and his Cost by him in this behalf Expended.

Ludwick Lard vs Andrew Rodgers Junr. By Consent of the Parties this Suit is Ordered to be Continued till Next Court.

Court Adjourned till Tomorrow Morning Eight OClock. Minets Signed by James Montgomery, Joseph Downs, Silv's Walker, George Anderson, Esquires.

Court met According to adjournment the 16th March 1787. Present James Montgomery, Joseph Downs, Silv's Walker, George Anderson, Esquires.

[16 March 1787]

Wm Tweedy is Appointed Overseer of that Part of the highway Leading from Little River to Michael Waldrops, and that he cause all the Several free male Inhabitants & slaves within Three Miles of the said Road to work thereon and to Cause the same to be kept in Good Repair for one year as the Law directs.

Page 156: A Bill of Sale from Thomas Ship to Mark Moore Bareing Date the 16th instant which said Bill of Sale was Acknowledged in Open Court by the said Thos Ship and ordered to be Recorded.

On Motion made on oath by Wm Glidewell a Witness for Rob't Hunter vs Robert Franks, Ordered that Robt Franks pay him the sum of £2 s5 for 18 days attendance @ 2/6 p'r day & that the same be Taxed in the bill of Cost.

A Lease and Release for the Conveyance of 250 acres of land from John and Saml Boyd to Vinson Glass Senr acknowledged in open Court by the [said] John & Saml Boyd & ordered to be Recorded.

Nehemiah Franks vs Thomas McClurkin. Case. This day came into Court the Parties by their Attorneys and thereupon Came also a Jury to wit Thomas Dendy, Wm. Dendy, James Underwood, Wm. Green, Robt Spence, Wm. Tweedy, Michael Waldroup, Saml Powell, Martin Martin, John Owin, Patrick Obryan, & Wm Young who being Elected Tried & Sworn the truth to Speak upon the Issue Joined find a Verdict for the Plt for £8 s4 & d3 with Cost of Suit, Whereupon it was Considered by the Court that the Plft Recover against the s'd Deft the sum of £8 s4 & d3 and his Cost by him in this behalf Expended and the said Deft in Mercy &c.

On Petition of Susannah Web or Tiber filed in this Office for a Guardian to Prosecute her suit for her freedom, Ordered that John Ridgeway be appointed her Guardian for the above purpose.

Pyles & McNees vs James Floyd. Sum Process. Case. By Consent of the Parties this Suit is Ordered to be Continued till next Court.

Thomas Entrekin vs John Gammel. Assault & Battery. Discontinued at Plfts Cost.

James Montgomery vs David Allison. Attachment. The Attachment being Returned Executed and the Deft not appearing to Replevy the same, the Plf came into Court and Proved his demand against the s'd Deft. to the Amount of £6 s9 d4, whereupon it was Considered by the Court that the Plff Recover against the s'd Deft. the sum of £6 s9 d4 and his cost by him in this behalf Expended.

Page 157: Ordered that the Sheriff or Constable Expose to Publick sale the Goods & Chattells by him attacht the property of the Deft. in behalf of the

LAURENS COUNTY SC COURT MINUTES 1786-1789

Plft. and the moneys arising from such sale pay unto the Plts Towards Satisfaction of the Judgment and the Overplus if any there be Return to the Deft and it not Sufficient Execution to Issue for the balance.

[16 March 1787]

James Sullivant vs Thomas Portswood. Attachment. Returned by the Sheriff that he had Summoned Charles Sullivant as a Garnishee, which said Charles Sullivant came into Court and made oath according to Law and saith that he owed the said Thomas Portswood the sum of £10 Virginia Money with Intrest from the 10th April 1786 & no more.

Ordered that Clement Davis be Committed to prison for a Contempt offered in Open Court by the s'd Clem't Davis.

John Wallace vs Mary Williams Exec'r of James Williams decd. Case. This day came the Parties by their Attys and thereupon came also a Jury to wit, Thomas Dendy, Wm. Dendy, Ja's Underwood, Robt Spence, Wm. Tweedy, Michael Waldroup, Saml Powell, Martin Martin, John Owin, Patrick Obryan, & Wm Young who being Elected Tried & Sworn the truth to Speak upon the Issue upon their [oaths] do say that Dec'd James Williams in his life time did undertake in manner & form as the Plft against him **[Page 158]** has Declared and they do Assess the Plt Damages by accation of the nonperformance of the promises & Assumptions in the Declaration mentioned to £30 s18 d9½ with Intrest from 1782, Whereupon it was Considered by the Court that the Plft Recover against the s'd Deft his Damages aforesaid in form aforesaid assesst & his cost by him in this behalf Expended to be Levied of the Goods & Chattells of the s'd dec'd in the hands of the said Deft to be Administered.

On Motion made on oath by Bartlet Saturwhite a Witness for John Wallace vs Mary Williams, Ordered that Mary Williams pay him the sum of s25 for 5 days attendance @ 2/6 p'r day & Milage going and coming 25 Miles 3 Times out of Newberry County & that the same be Taxed in the bill of Cost.

Thomas McClurkin vs Alex'd & Jean Grant, Exrs. of George Moor decd. In Debt. This day came the Plft by D. Brown his Atty and the Defts being Solemnly Call'd Came not but made Default, and thereupon Came a Jury to wit Thomas Dendy, Wm. Dendy, Ja's Underwood, Wm. Green, Rob't Spence, Mich'l Waldrop, Saml Powell, Martin Martin, John Owin, Patrick Obryan, and Wm Young who being Elected Tried & Sworn well and truly the truth to Inquire of Damages in this Suit, upon their Oaths do find for the Plft the sum of £9 s19 d8½ & costs, thereupon it was Considered by the Court that the Plft recover of the said Defts. Exr's of George Moore decd the said sum of £9 19 8½ & his Cost by him in this behalf Expended.

Mary Williams vs Robt Toombs. By Consent of the Parties this Suit is Ordered to be Continued till Next Court.

LAURENS COUNTY SC COURT MINUTES 1786-1789

Page 159: [16 March 1787]

James Montgomery vs Thos Pearson. Attachment. Trespass. This day came the Plft by his Attys and the Attachment being Returned Execution on 300 acres of land the Property of the Deft and the said Deft not appearing to Replevy the same or Plead to the Plfts Declaration agreeable to a former Order of this Court, Therefore upon a Jury to wit Tho's Dendy, Wm. Dendy, Ja's Underwood, Wm. Green, Rob't Spence, Wm Tweedy, Mich'l Waldrop, Saml Powell, Martin Martin, John Owin, Patrick Obryan, and Wm Young who being Sworn well and truly to Inquiry what Damages the Plft hath Sustain'd by accation of the Trespass in the Declaration mentioned, upon their oaths do say that the Plft hath Sustained Damages by accation thereof to £20 besides his cost, thereupon it was Considered by the Court that the Plft Recover against the s'd Deft his damages aforesaid in form aforesaid assest and his cost by him in this behalf Expended.

James Adair vs Thomas Pearson. This day came the Plft by his Attys and the Attachment being Returned Execution on 300 acres of land the Property of the Deft and the said Deft not appearing to Replevy the same or Plead to the Plfts Declaration agreeable to a former Order of this Court, Therefore upon a Jury to wit Tho's Dendy, Wm. Dendy, Ja's Underwood, Wm. Green, Rob't Spence, Wm Tweedy, Mich'l Waldrop, Saml Powell, Martin Martin, John Owin, Patrick Obryan, and Wm Young who being Sworn well and truly to Inquiry what Damages the Plft hath Sustain'd by accation of the Trespass in the Declaration mentioned, upon their oaths do say that the Plft hath Sustained Damages by accation thereof to £20 besides his cost, thereupon it was Considered by the Court that the Plft Recover against the s'd Deft his damages aforesaid in form aforesaid assest and his cost by him in this behalf Expended and the s'd Deft in Mercy &c.

Page 160: Joseph Adair vs Thomas Pearson. This day came the Plft by his Attys and the Attachment being Returned Execution on 300 acres of land the Property of the Deft and the said Deft not appearing to Replevy the same or Plead to the Plfts Declaration agreeable to a former Order of this Court, Therefore upon a Jury to wit Tho's Dendy, Wm. Dendy, Ja's Underwood, Wm. Green, Rob't Spence, Wm Tweedy, Mich'l Waldrop, Saml Powell, Martin Martin, John Owin, Patrick Obryan, and Wm Young who being Sworn well and truly to Inquiry what Damages the Plft hath Sustain'd by accation of the Trespass in the Declaration mentioned, upon their oaths do say that the Plft hath Sustained Damages by accation thereof to £20 besides his cost, thereupon it was Considered by the Court that the Plft Recover against the s'd Deft his damages aforesaid in form aforesaid assest and his cost by him in this behalf Expended.

Ordered that the Clerk pay unto Nathaniel Austin £1 1 9 out of the Publick Moneys in his hands for attending upon the Pettit Jury this Court.

Ordered that all Publick Business be continued over till next Court.

LAURENS COUNTY SC COURT MINUTES 1786-1789

[16 March 1787]

Jean Kellet vs Wm Martin. Attachment. Returned Executed by Summoning King Chandler as a Garnishee and the s'd King Chandler failing to Appear, James Russell came into court and made oath that the said King Chandler acknowledged to him that he owed the Deft the sum of thirty shillings Virginia money whereupon it was Considered by the Court that the Plft Recover against the said Deft the s'd sum of thirty shillings Virginia money.

Page 161: Court Adjourned till Tomorrow Morning Eight OClock. Minets Signed by Joseph Downs, Silv's Walker, George Anderson, Esquires.

Court met According to adjournment the 17th March 1787. Present James Montgomery, Joseph Downs, John Rodgers, Wm Mitchusson, Esquires.

Ordered that the Clerk pay unto John Martin constable Two Guineas out of the public money in his hands for his attending the Court.

Court adjourned till Court in Course. James Montgomery, Joseph Downs, Wm. Mitchusson, Esq'rs.

At a Court held for the County of Laurens at the Courthouse of said County in the State of South Carolina, the Eleventh day of June 1787. Present Jonathan Downs, Joseph Downs, George Anderson, Charles Saxon, Anguish Campbell, John Rodgers, Wm Mitchusson, Daniel Wright, Esquires.

A Lease and Release for the Conveyance of 170 acres of Land from Daniel Abbercrumbie to Elias Brock Proven in Open Court by the Oaths of Haisting Doyall & John Pearson & Ordered to be Recorded.

A Deed from Silvanus Walker, James Burnsides & Sarah Walker to Francis Lester for the Conveyance of 110 acres of Land proved in Open Court by the oaths of Saml Saxon and John Williams and Ordered to be recorded.

Page 162: A Deed from George Anderson to James Burnsides for the Conveyance of 110 acres of land Acknowledged in open Court and Ordered to be Recorded.

A Deed from Robert Dunlap and Elizebeth his wife to Absolem Bobo acknowledged in open court & ordered to be Recorded.

A Lease and Release for the Conveyance of 200 acres of land from John Lucust and Sarah his wife to Zachariah Bailey, the said Sarah Lucust came into Court and acknowledged the same, Ordered to Ly for further proof.

A Lease and release for the Conveyance of 150 acres of land from John Harvey to Thos Blackley, proven in open court by Wm. Harris and Phillip Harvey & ordered to be recorded.

LAURENS COUNTY SC COURT MINUTES 1786-1789

[11 June 1787]

Abraham Neighbours is Appointed Overseer of that part of the highway Leading from Little River to Duncans Creek in the Room of Marshall Franks, Ordered that he Cause the several free male Inhabitants & Slaves contiguous to & convenient to said Road, to work thereon & to cause the same to be kept in Repair for one year as the Law Directs.

John Sims is Appointed Overseer of that part of the highway Leading from James Sullivants to Carters old fields in the Room of Aaron Starnes, Ordered that he Cause the several free male Inhabitants & Slaves contiguous to & convenient to said Road, to work thereon & to cause the same to be kept in Repair for one year as the Law Directs.

A Lease and Release for the Conveyance of 50 acres of land from Patrick Reyley to Rob't Sims, proven in open Court by Drury Boyce and Wm. Faris and Ordered to be Recorded.

A Lease & Release for the conveyance of 100 acres of land from Joseph Kellet to Robert Sims proven according to the former act and Ordered to be Recorded.

A Lease and Release for the Conveyance of 200 acres of Land from Wm Baugh to Thomas Palmore, proven in Open Court by Saml Whorton & Ordered to Ly for further Proof.

On Application of Lewis Saxon, Clerk of the Court, he is Admitted to build an office on the Publick land laid out for the use of the County, Round the Courthouse of the same.

Page 163: Court Adjourned till Tomorrow Morning Ten OClock. Minets Signed by Jonathan Downs, George Anderson, Anguish Campbell, Joseph Downs, Daniel Wright, Esquires.

Court met according to adjournment the 12th June 1787. Present Jonathan Downs, Joseph Downs, John Hunter, Wm. Mitchusson, James Montgomery, Charles Saxon, Esquires.

A Lease and Release for the Conveyance of 374 acres of land from John Polock to Robert Scott proven in open Court by John Hunter Esq'r and Sam'l Ewing & ordered to be Recorded.

A Mortgage from John Oneal to Charles Willson for 100 acres of land Acknowledged in Open Court and Ordered to be Recorded.

A Lease and Release for the Conveyance of 100 acres of land from Isaac Williams to Mary Griffen, Proven heretofore by John Hunter Esqr., and now proven in open court by Josiah East & Ordered to be Recorded.

LAURENS COUNTY SC COURT MINUTES 1786-1789

[12 June 1787]

A Deed from Charles Saxon to James Hulsey for the Conveyance of 150 acres of land Acknowledged in Open Court and Ordered to be Recorded.

A Deed from Haisting Doyal & Rebecca his wife to John Tod, Proven in open Court by Rob't Tod & Wm. Hubbs and Ordered to be Recorded.

A Lease and Release for the Conveyance of 150 acres of Land from David Huggins & Susannah his wife to Th's Cason, proven in open Court by Richard Pollard and John Cook and Ordered to be Recorded.

Clement Deal is appointed Overseer of that part of the highway Leading from Mill Creek to the Island ford on Salluda River, Ordered that he Cause the several free male Inhabitants & slaves Contiguous to & Convenient to s'd Road to work thereon, and to Cause the same to be kept in Repair for one year as the Law Directs.

Page 164: Sarah Lucust vs Martin Martin. By Consent the Suit is Ordered to be Dismist at Plfts Cost not Attys fee to be Taxed in the bill of Cost.

Ezekiel Smith vs Richard Pollard. Discontinued at Plfts. Cost.

A Deed of Gift from Daniel McClain to Mary Hutson acknowledged in open Court & Ordered to be Recorded.

On Application made in open Court by James Dillard a Commission is awarded him to Examine & Take the Acknowledgement of John Sanders & his wife to a Conveyance from the s'd John Sanders & his wife to the s'd James Dillard for ____ acres of land, to be taken before Two Justices of the Peace in Culpepper County in the State of Virginia, and Make Return of the s'd Examination Together with the Commission to this Court within one Year from this Date.

A Deed from Nehemiah Franks to Charles Smith for the Conveyance of 100 acres of land, acknowledged in open Court and ordered to be Recorded.

On Application of Martha Moore widow of Joshua Moore Deceased, Ordered that Letters of Administration of all & singular the Goods & Chattels, Rights and Credits of the said Joshua Moore Deceased, be Granted to her the s'd Martha Moore, She haveing Taken the Oaths Prescribed by Law, Whereupon she with Andrew Rodgers & John Ritchey her Securities Entered into & acknowledged their Bonds in the Penalty of £500 with Condition According to Law.

Ordered that a Warrant of Appraisement Issue to four Good & Lawfull freeholders to appraise the Estate of the Personal Estate of the s'd Joshua

Moore, being first Sworn before a Justice of the Peace of this County and make Return thereof within the Time Prescribed by Law.

[12 June 1787]

The last will and Testament of Joseph Kellett Deceased was Presented in open Court by Jane Kellett & Wm. Kellet the Executors therein named, and proven by Martin Mehaffy and Curnelius McMahon Witnesses thereunto & ordered to be Recorded.

Page 165: On Motion of the said Executors who made Oath according to Law, Ordered that Letters Testamentary be Granted them in due form.

A Lease and Release for the Conveyance of 250 acres of Land from Lewis Duvall & Terisy his wife to John Simpson, Proven in Open Court by John Hunter & Michael Waldrop & ordered to be recorded.

Ordered that a Precept Issue against John Shirly at the Request of Edward Box to shew cause if any he hath why he keeps Hester Williams out of the Possession of a Tract of land her Property on which he the said John Shirly now lives, She the s'd Hester Williams being Incapable of Transacting her own business & that the Sheriff made Return of the s'd Precept to next Court.

A Lease and Release for the Conveyance of 250 acres of land from John Kellet and Susannah his wife to William Kellett acknowledged in open court she being first privily Examined apart from her husband and Ordered to be Recorded.

The Court Proceeded to the Choice of a Sheriff, when David Anderson was by a Majority of the Justices Chosed Sheriff for the County of Laurens & the same was Ordered to be Recorded and a Certified Copy thereof Given to him.

Court adjournd for half an hour. Court met according to Adjournment. Present Jonathan Downs, John Hunter, Daniel Wright, Silv's Walker.

James Adair, son of James Adair, is appointed Overseer of that Part of the highway Leading from Hughes's mill on Enoree to James Young's on Bush River in the room of Tho's Ewing. Ordered that he Cause the free male Inhabitants and Slaves contiguous to & convenient to said Road, to work thereon & to cause the same to be kept in Repair for one year as the Law directs.

A Lease and Release for the Conveyance of 200 acres of land from Francis Bryan to Wm Arnold proven in open Court by Silv's Walker & Rich'd Watts & ordered to be Recorded.

LAURENS COUNTY SC COURT MINUTES 1786-1789

Page 166: [12 June 1787]

A Lease and Release for the Conveyance of 50 acres of land from James Dillard to Silas Garrat acknowledged in Open Court and ordered to be Recorded.

David Burn vs Clement Davis. By Consent by his atty this Suit is Ordered to be Continued at Defts Cost till Next Court.

A Lease and Release for the conveyance of 75 acres of land from Silas Garrat to John Garrat acknowledged in open court and Ordered to be Recorded.

Susannah Web vs Nathan Kemp. By Consent, this suit is Ordered to be Continued till next court.

Thomas Lowery vs Thos Gorman. Discontinued at Plfts Cost.

Pyles & McNees vs John Boyd. Continued by Consent till next Court.

John Westmoreland being arrested and Taken into Custody, no person appearing to prosecute him he was Ordered to be Discharged, and was Discharged accordingly by Proclamation made at the door of the Courthouse.

Robert Hannah foreman, Andrew Rodgers, Thos Ewing, Wm Harris, Lewis Banton, Zachariah Bailey, Joseph Burchfield, John Abbercrumbie, joseph Parsons, Roger Brown, John Goodwin, Theophiless Goodwin & Wm Burton was Sworn Grand Jurours of Inquest for the body of this County haveing Received their Charge Retired from the Bar, and after some time Returned into Court and Presented as follows to wit.

We Present that Part of the highway Leading from Michael Waldrops to the Cross near Thomas Dendys being our of Repair.

We Present Benjn Carter, John Carter, Mr. Molden who lives at Joseph Carters old place, for Turning Cason's Road from above Cain Creek below Joseph Carters old place and making the same Impassible.

We Present that the Road from Mill Creek to Little River being our of Repair on the Ninety Six Road.

Page 167: State vs Edmond Craddock. Indictment for keeping Disorderly house or Tavern. Returned into Court by the Grand Jury a True Bill.

State vs John D. Kern. Indictment for Retailing Liquor without Licence. Returned into Court by the Grand Jury a True Bill.

The Presentments were signed by the whole of the Grand Jury.

Court adjourned till Tomorrow morning Ten OClock. Minutes signed by Jonathan Downs, James Montgomery, John Hunter, Daniel Wright, Joseph Downs.

Court met according to adjournment the 13th June 1787. Present Jonathan Downs, Joseph Downs, John Hunter, James Montgomery, Esquires.

Pyles & McNees vs James Floyd. S. P. Case. Continued by Consent till Next Court.

John Wallace vs John Martin. S. P. Case. This day Came the parties by their Attorneys after several witnesses being sworn & Examined Touching the Premises, and the council for both Parties heard, it was Considered that the Plft Recover against the said Deft. the sum of £6 & his cost by him in this behalf Expended.

On Motion made on oath by Elisha Brooks a Witness for John Wallace against John Martin, Ordered that John Martin pay him the sum of 5/ for Two days attendance & the sum of 8/4 for Coming & Going 25 miles out of Newberry County a /2 P'r mile & that the same be Taxed in the Bill of Cost.

also the sum of 5/ To John Satterwhite Snr a Witness for Two Days Attendance as a Witness for John Wallace against John Martin, also the sum of 8/4 for Coming & Going 25 miles out of Newberry County a /2 P'r mile & that the same be Taxed in the Bill of Cost.

Page 168: Ordered that the sum of £3 be paid out of the Publick Moneys Collected in this County to Ann Hendrix after all Publick Demands now against the County shall be Discharged, she being of the Poor of this County or Parish.

Ordered that Letters of Administration of all & singular the Goods & chattels Rights & Credits of John Lucust late of this County Dec'd be Granted to Sarah Lucust his widow, She being Duly sworn according to law Whereupon she together with Andrew Rodgers Junr and Thomas Hughes her Securitys Entered into & acknowledged their Bonds in the sum of £500 with condition according to law.

Ordered that a Warrant of Appraisement Issue to James Burnsides, Wm. Bailey, Robert young & Saml Powell, who being first sworn before a Justice of Peace to appraise the Estate of the s'd John Lucust Dec'd & make Return of the s'd Appraisement to Next Court.

A Lease and Release for the Conveyance of 100 acres of land from James Waldrop to John Waldrop, proven in open Court by James Waldrop & Michael Waldrop and ordered to be Recorded.

LAURENS COUNTY SC COURT MINUTES 1786-1789

[13 June 1787]

To the Intent that all appeals hereafter Granted by any Justice in this County to any Person Considering himself Agrieved by the Judgment of such Justice, May be Regularly Granted and Obtained, It is Ordered that the Justice Granting such Appeal Take a bond of the Person praying the same at the Time such appeal shall be granted with Good security for the prosecuting the Appeal with affects & to pay all cost of Damages awarded to the Appeallee if the Judgment of the s'd Justice should be affirmed. All appeals granted or brought up without such bond being Given and produced in Court, shall be null & void.

A Lease and Release for the Conveyance of 100 acres of land from George Adams to Richard Turner proven in open Court by Richard Watts & ordered to Ly for further Proof.

John Adair vs Seth P. Pool. Si. P. This day came the Parties by their attys & after several witnesses being sworn & examined tuching the premises of the Council heard on both sides it is Considered by the Court that the Plft Adair [Page 169] Recover against the said Pool Deft. the sum of £2 s6 & his cost by him in this behalf Expended.

Henry Meredith vs John Journey. Attachment. Ordered that Deft appear either by himself or by his Atty & Plead to the Plfts. Declaration on or before the Second Monday in June next, otherwise Judgment by Default will be Given against him.

State vs John Ripley. Arested for Incouraging a Royet. Ordered that he be bound to his Good Behaviour for Twelve months, that he Enter himself in Recognizance in the sum of £50 & two Good Securitys in the sum of £25 each.

State vs Ambrose Ripley & John Murrey. Being Taken into Custody for being Concerned in & Incouraging a Roiet. Ordered that they be Committed to the Common Joal of this county & there to Remain Ten days & then to Give Security for their Good Behaviour for one years, themselves in the sum of £25 each & two Good Securities each in the sum of £12 each, to stand committed until Cost of Prosecution is paid, and the above Requisition is Complyed with.

Saml Saxon vs Joshua Nunn. Attachment. The Deft not appearing to Plead to the Plts Declaration agreeable to a former Order of this Court, tho Solemnly calld it is Considered by the Court that Judgment be Entered up for the Plft against the said Deft for what Damage the Plft hath justly sustained to be Ascertained by an Inquiry thereof to be made by a Jury, unless the Deft. shall appear and Plead to Issue at the Next Court.

The last Monday in July next is appointed by the Court to Settle the publick affairs of this County. Ordered that all Public Officers belonging to the

LAURENS COUNTY SC COURT MINUTES 1786-1789

County Court of Laurens that have Collected or Received any Publick Money for the Use of the County, do appear on the Day aforesaid at the Courthouse of this County in order to Render the Public money or an Acc't thereof.

Page 170: John Ripley, Saml Saxon, and Thomas Wm. Fakes bound to the Justices of the County Court of Laurens for £100, 13 June 1787, that John Ripley shall be of the Good People of this State for one year.

Court adjourned until Court in Course. Minutes signed by Jonathan Downs, James Montgomery, Joseph Downs, John Hunter, Esq'rs.

At a Court held for the County of Laurens in the State of So Carolina at the Courthouse of said County, on Monday the 10th day of September 1787. Present Jonathan Downs, James Montgomery, Joseph Downs, George Anderson, Charles Saxon, Daniel Wright, Esquires.

David Anderson Esquire Produced a Commission Signed by his Excellency Thomas Pinckney, Esqr., Gov. of SC, dated **[Page 171]** 10 Aug 1787 appointed him Sheriff for the County of Laurens, and he entered into bond with George Anderson & John Rodgers, Esqrs., his Securitys, in the sum of £1500. Commission to Continued in force for Two years.

Page 172: Bond of David Anderson, dated 10 Sept 1787, witnessed by Lewis Saxon, C. C.

Page 173: A Lease and Release for the Conveyance of 150 acres of land from John Williams to John Owins proven according to the former Act & Ordered to be Recorded.

A Deed from Samuel Weathers & Martha his wife to Mary & Margaret Durrum for the Conveyance of 100 acres of land proven in open court by the oaths of David Mcglathery & John Carter & Ordered to be recorded.

A Lease & Release for the Conveyance of 100 acres of land from Joseph Babb & Mary his wife to John Furguson proven in Open Court by Hugh Abernathy & Ordered to lie for further proof.

A Lease & Release for the Conveyance of 183 acres of land from William Helloms & Constant his wife to John Helloms Proven in Open Court by John Coker & Saml Williams Junr & Ordered to be Recorded.

A Lease and Release for the Conveyance of 200 acres of land from David Spence to Robert Spence proven in Open Court by John Rodgers Esqr. & Wm. Taylor Junr & Ordered to be Recorded.

A Lease and Release for the Conveyance of 270 acres of land from John Newman to Robert H. Hughes proven in Open Court by Edmond Craddock & John Pinson & Ordered to be Recorded.

LAURENS COUNTY SC COURT MINUTES 1786-1789

[10 September 1787]

Patience Tenney vs John Cason. Assault & Battery. By Consent of the Parties this Suit is Ordered to be Dismist at Defts. Cost.

A Lease and Release for the Conveyance of 200 acres of land from John Ripley to Nathan Kemp Acknowledged in open Court by the said John Ripley & Ordered to be Recorded.

Articles of Agreement entered into between Wm. Simpson, Benj. Carter & Duncan Obryan of the one part and James Furguson and Mary Furguson of the other part, proven in open Court by Wm. Millwee and Ordered to be Recorded.

A Deed from Francis Logan to Wm. Anderson for the Conveyance of 150 acres of land, proven in Open Court by George Anderson Esq'r & Tested by Esq'r Flack in the State of No Carolina & Ordered to be Recorded.

Page 174: A Deed from Bartlet Brown to John Lindsey for the Conveyance of 150 acres of land, proven according to the former Act and Ordered to be Recorded.

A Deed from Benjamin Brown to Andrew Cunningham for the Conveyance of 100 acres of land proven in open Court by Abraham Gray & John Lindsey & Ordered to be Recorded.

A Deed from Andrew Cunningham to Abraham Gray for the Conveyance of 100 acres of land, proven in Open Court by John Lindsey, and Ordered to Lye for further proof.

Court Adjourned till Tomorrow morning 10 Oclock. Minutes signed by Jonathan Downs, James Montgomery, Charles Saxon, Daniel Wright, Esquires.

Court met according to Adjournment the 11th Sept 1787. Present Jonathan Downs, James Montgomery, John Rodgers, Charles Saxon, George Anderson, Daniel Wright, John Hunter, Esquires.

James Downen is appointed Overseer of that part of the high way leading from Thomasons Mill on Reaburns Creek to the Ridge above Curnelius McMahons in the Room of Saml Bolings. Ordered that he cause the Several free male Inhabitants & Slaves Contiguous to & Convenient to said road to work thereon & to cause the same to be Kept in Good Repair for one year as the Law Directs.

A Lease and Release for the Conveyance of 100 acres of land from William Caldwell & Elizabeth his wife to Jas Templeton acknowledged in open court by the s'd William Caldwell & Ordered to be Recorded.

LAURENS COUNTY SC COURT MINUTES 1786-1789

Page 175: [11 September 1787]

Ordered that Thos Cahoon, Edward Gideon & Stephen Wood attend this Court as Constables.

A Deed from John Bailey to Saml Powel for the Conveyance of 200 acres of land proven in Open Court by Silvanus Walker & James Bailey & Ordered to be Recorded.

Ordered that the Road leading from Haisting Doyall's old field to Hugh ONeal's Mill on Little River be Altered and Turned the Nearest and best way from Doyal's old field aforesaid to Neal's Mill, and that Daniel Megin continue to act as Overseer of the Road & Direct the Clearing & opening the same.

The State vs John Clardy. The s'd John Clardy being bound to appear to this Court, on a Charge of Felony, and there being no Grand Jury, the Court ordered him to be further Recognized to appear at Next Court & that he be Continued in Custody of the Sheriff untill he Give Security as aforesaid.

Joseph Reed vs John Shirley. Debt. By Consent of the Parties this Suit is Ordered to be Dismist Each party paying their own cost.

Thos Evans vs Jones Winn. Attachment. By Consent this Suit is Ordered to be Dismist at Defendants cost.

Henry Ridgeway vs Saml Ridgeway. Assault & Battery. By Consent this Suit is Ordered to be Discontinued.

John Brown vs Lewis Duvall. By Consent this Suit is Ordered to be Continued till next Court.

Wadsworth & Turpin vs John Ozburn. S. Process. Case. Ordered to be Dismist at Defts Cost.

Clement Davis vs Reubin Pyles. By Consent of the Plt. this suit is Ordered to be Dismist at his cost.

Reubin Pyles vs Clement Davis. By Consent of the Plt. this suit is Ordered to be Dismist at his cost.

Page 176: David Ross vs James Stinson. Attachment. Ordered to be Discontinued at Plfts. Cost.

John Ritchey vs Noltey Mastes. Attachment. Ordered to be Discontinued at Plfts. Cost.

LAURENS COUNTY SC COURT MINUTES 1786-1789

[10 September 1787]

David Bevin vs Clement Davis. Sum Process. Case. The Deft moved to the Court that the Trial of this Suit be Submitted to a Jury, Ordered to be Granted at his own Cost.

Robert Goodloe Harper produced in open Court Credentials signed by the Hon. John Rutledge and Richard Hudson, Esquires, Judges of the Honorable the Court of Chancery, and the Hon'ble Henry Pendleton, Esquires, one of the Judges of the Court of Common Pleas in this State, Admitting him the said Robt. G. Harper to practice as an attorney & Solicitor in any of the Courts of Law or Equity in this State. Whereupon it was Ordered that the s'd Robt G. Harper be Admitted to practice as such in this Court.

Absolem Filbay vs Joseph Martindale. S. Process. This day came the Parties by their Atto's and after Hearing Evidence that was Admm'd & the Council of Either side, it was Considered by the Court that the Plft. Recover against the s'd Deft the Sum of £4 s2 d4 & his cost by him in this behalf Expended. Ordered that the Plft Deliver to the Deft the Note and Order Received of him.

On Motion made on Oath by John Robison a Witness for Joseph Martindale vs Filbay, Ordered that Martindale pay him the sum of 2/6 for One days Attendance.

Elizebeth Gary vs Jacob Gibson & Mary Gibson. S. Process Case. Ordered to be Continued till Friday next at which time this Suit is Ordered to be Tried.

Page 177: William Boling is appointed Overseer of that Part of the Highway leading from Duncans Creek to Hendrix's old place on the south fork of Duncans Creek in the place of James Craig. Ordered that he cause the several free male Inhabitents and Slaves contiguous to & convenient to s'd Road to work thereon & to cause the same to be kept in Good Repair for One year as the Law Directs.

A Lease and Release for the Conveyance of 250 acres of land from David Cuningham to William Bald proven by John Sadler & Benjn Hatter & ordered to be Recorded.

A Deed from John Sanders to James Dillard for the conveyance of 100 acres of land, Signed and acknowledged before James Pendleton, James Jett and John Stroud, Justices of the peace in the state of Virginia, who was authorized to take the s'd Acknowledged by a Commission from this Court for that purpose, which s'd Commission was this day Returned into court annexed to the s'd Deed, Together with a Certificate of the Acknowledgement of the s'd John Sanders signed by the Justices aforesaid, which s'd Commission Certificate & Deed being Presented in open Court by Jas Dillard was thereupon Ordered to be Recorded.

LAURENS COUNTY SC COURT MINUTES 1786-1789

[11 September 1787]

A Deed from James Dillard to Saml Dillard for the Conveyance of 261 acres of land acknowledged in open court by the said James Dillard & Ordered to be Recorded.

Stephen Wood Constable fined five shillings for Neglect of Duty.

John Ford vs John Brown. By Consent of the Parties this Suit is Ordered to be Dismist at Defts Cost.

Charles Sullivant vs Abel Boling. By Consent of the Parties this Suit is Ordered to be Dismist at Plfts Cost.

A Deed of Gift from Micajah Hendrix to Margaret Hendrix proven according to the former act & Ordered to be Recorded.

Page 178: A Lease and Release for the Conveyance of 107 acres of land from Robert McNees and Mary his wife to Joshua Saxon Acknowledged in open Court, she being first privately Examined apart from her husband as the law Directs & Ordered to be Recorded.

A Lease and Release for the Conveyance of 150 acres of land from Robt McCrary to Charles Jones acknowledged in open Court & ordered to be Recorded.

A Deed from John Gray to Charles Jones for the Conveyance of 65 acres of land acknowledged in Open Court & ordered to be Recorded.

The State vs John Vance. The s'd John Vance being bound in Recognizance to appear at this Court to answer a Charge of felony, Made his appearance & was discharged with proclamation on payment of Cost for which Saml Saxon enters himself Security.

A Lease & Release for the Conveyance of 300 acres of land from William Millwee Sheriff to James Montgomery Esq'r acknowledged in open Court & ordered to be recorded.

A Lease & Release for the Conveyance of 100 acres of land from Robt Taylor to John McCelvey acknowledged in open Court & Ordered to be Recorded.

A Deed from Robt Taylor to Robt Ross for the Conveyance of 43 acres of land, Acknowledged in open Court & Ordered to be Recorded.

David Burn vs Clement Davis. S. Process. Case. This day came the Parties by their Atto's & thereupon came also a Jury to wit Aron Starns, Wm. McFarson, John Hall, Jonathan Pucket, Saml Weathers, James Dorough, Waterman Boatman, Wm. Taylor, Michael Wallace, John Carter, Robt Finney &

LAURENS COUNTY SC COURT MINUTES 1786-1789

Nathaniel Nickols [Page 179] who being Elected Tried & Sworn the Truth to Speak upon the Issue Joind upon their Oaths do say that the Deft is Guilty of the Promises and assumptions by the Plft alledged and they do assess the Plft. Damages by Accation thereof to £2 d13 d4 & the note to be Given up, whereupon it was Considered by the Court that the Plft. Recover against the said Deft. the sum of £2 d13 d4 and his Cost by him in this behalf Expended. And the s'd Deft in Mercy &c.

[11 September 1787]

On Motion made on oath by Josiah East a Witness for Clem't Davis vs David Burn, Ordered that Clem't Davis pay him the sum of 10/ for four days attendance at 2/6 p'r day.

Also to David Burn Jun'r a Witness for David Burn vs Clem't Davis, Ordered that Clement Davis pay him the sum of 12/6 for 5 days attendance at 2/6 p'r day.

Also to John Edwards a Witness in said suit, Ordered that the Deft. Davis pay him the sum of 10/ for four days attendance at 2/6 p'r day & that the same be Taxed in the Bill of Cost vs the Deft.

Samuel Wharton was this day appointed Deputy Sheriff for the County of Laurens, by David Anderson, Sheriff of s'd County & with the approbation of the Court. The said Samuel Wharton came into Court & took the oath of allegiance to the state, together with the oath of office according to Law.

A Bond from John Grier to Ruth Adair Conditioned to make a sufficient right & Title to 150 acres of land proven in open Court by James Montgomery & James Grier & ordered to be Recorded.

Christian Langston being Recognized to appear at this Court to answer a charge of Bastardy. Bazel Hollen one of her Securities for her appearance aforesaid agrees & undertakes to Surrender her at the next court to be held for this County.

Court adjourned till Tomorrow morning 10 OClock. Minutes signed by Jonathan Downs, James Montgomery, George Anderson, Esquires.

A Deed from And'w Rodgers & Letty his wife to James Clardy for the Conveyance of 240 acres of land Proved [in] court by George Anderson & John Rodgers & Ordered to be Recorded.

Page 180: Court met according to adjournment the 12th Sept 1787. Present Jonth'n Downs, John Hunter, Danl Wright, Charles Saxon, John Rodgers, Esquires.

[12 September 1787]

A Release from Vardry McBee & Benjamin Killgore to John Martin acknowledged in Open Court & Ordered to be Recorded.

A Lease and Release for the Conveyance of 152 acres of land from Robt Goodwin Senr to Danl Wright Proven in Open Court by Josiah Fowler & Wm. Gilbert & ordered to be Recorded.

James Waddleton vs John Russell. Case on Attachment. By Consent of the Parties this Suit is Ordered to be Dismist at Plfts. Cost.

Bazaleel Ackley vs Martin Williams. Slander. By Consent of the Plft. this Suit is Ordered to be Discontinued.

A Deed from William Willson to Lewis Saxon for the Conveyance of 100 acres of land proven in open Court by David McCaa & John Hughes & Ordered to be Recorded.

Mr. Yancy Motioned the Court that they would Receive the Bridge built over little river on the road leading from the Island ford on Salluda to Enoree River, he producing a Certificate from Newberry Court of their haveing Receivd & Excepted the s'd Bridge on their Part. Ordered that this Court do Receive the s'd Bridge on their Part and that the Clerk give an Order on the County Treasurer to pay one Half of the contract money with the Undertaker out of the moneys in the hands of the Treasurer belonging to the County.

Page 181: A Lease and Release for the Conveyance of 80 acres of land from John Kellett & Hanna his wife to Martin Mehaffey acknowledged in open Court, the wife being first privily Examined apart from her s'd Husband as the law directs & ordered to be Recorded.

A Deed from Joshua Arnald to Marshall Franks for the conveyance of 130 acres of land Acknowledged in Open Court & Ordered to be Recorded.

A Deed from Nehemiah Franks to Marshell Franks for the conveyance of 20 acres of land acknowledged in Open Court & Ordered to be Recorded.

John Garner & Mary Chumney Ex'rs of Wm Chumney decd Petitioned this Court praying this Court that Joseph Chumney Infant Son of the s'd William Chumney dec'd should be bound an apprentice to Joshua Saxon, whereupon Consideration of the s'd petition it is Ordered, that the s'd Joseph Chumney be bound as an apprentice to the said Joshua Saxon for the space & Term of seven years &c.

Thomas Mars vs Saml Scott. False Imprisonment. This day came the parties by their attys and thereupon came also a Jury to wit Aron Starns, Wm. McFerson, John Hall, Jonathan Pucket, Saml Weathers, Wm Bailey,

LAURENS COUNTY SC COURT MINUTES 1786-1789

Waterman Boatman, Wm. Taylor, Michael Wallace, John Carter, Robt Finney & Nathaniel Nickols who being Elected Tried & Sworn the Truth to Speak upon the Issue Joind upon their Oaths do say that the Plft is not Guilty of the false Imprisonment in the Declaration mentioned. Whereupon it is Considered by the Court that the Plft Take nothing by his bill but for his false Clamour be in Mercy And that the Deft go notice without day & recover against the said Plft his Cost by him in this Behalf Expended &c.

[12 September 1787]

On Motion made on oath by John Ritchey a Witness for Saml Scott vs the s'd Thos Mars, Ordered that the s'd Thos Mars pay him the sum of 5/ for 2 days attendance at 2/6 P'r day.

Page 182: On Motion made on oath by Alex'd Snell a Witness for Thos Mars vs Saml Scott, Ordered that the s'd Thos Mars pay him the sum of 5/ for 2 days attendance at 2/6 P'r day & the same be Taxed in the bill of Cost.

William Young vs James McNees & Hugh Young. In Debt. By Consent this Suit is Ordered to be Continued till Next Court at Defts Cost.

George Anderson vs Curnelius Dendy. Trover. This Suit is Particularly Ordered to be Tried on Fryday next.

A Lease and Release from Elizebeth Lethes & Margaret Lethes to Richard Hatter for the Conveyance of 50 ares of land proven by Wm Bald, and Ordered to Lie for further proof.

Saml Saxon vs Joshua Nun. Attachment. The Attachment being Returned Executed on 100 acres of land the Property of the Deft, after being Regularly Gazetted, & the Deft tho solemnly called came not & thereupon came a Jury to wit Aron Starns, Wm. McFerson, John Hall, Jonathan Pucket, Saml Weathers, Wm Bailey, James Dorough, Waterman Boatman, Wm. Taylor, Michael Wallace, John Carter, Robt Finney & Nath'l Nickols who being Elected Tried & Sworn the Truth to Speak upon the Issue Joind upon their Oaths do say that the Plft hath Sustained Damages by accation of the Trover & Conversion in the Declaration mentioned to £50 besides his Cost. Thereupon it was considered by the Court that the Plt recover against the s'd Deft the sum of £50 & his cost by him in this behalf expended.

Page 183: Ordered that the Sheriff Expose to Public Sale the said tract of 100 acres of land the property of the s'd Deft Joshua Nun and the moneys arising from such sale pay unto the Pltf towards Satisfaction of the Judgment &c.

Benjamin Griffeth vs James Allison. Continued by Consent till Next Court.

A Deed from John Boling & Josiah Prater for the Conveyance of 94 acres of land acknowledged in Open Court & Ordered to be Recorded.

LAURENS COUNTY SC COURT MINUTES 1786-1789

[12 September 1787]

William Gilbert vs Mastin Williams. Continued by Consent till Next Court.

Isaac Mitchell vs Jonathan Childs. Slander. By Consent of the Parties this Suit is Ordered to [be] Dismist at Defts Cost.

Court Adjourned Till Tomorrow Morning Ten OClock. Minets signed by James Montgomery, Charles Saxon, Danl Wright, Esq'rs.

Court met according to Adjournment the 13 Sept 1787. Present Jonathan Downs, James Montgomery, John Hunter, Danl Wright.

A Lease & Release for the Conveyance of 100 acres of land from Rebecca Brown now Bishop to Roger Brown acknowledged in open Court & Ordered to be recorded.

Thos Mars vs John Moore. False Imprisonment. Discontinued at Plts Cost.

Page 184: Thomas Mars vs John Gocher. False Imprisonment. Discontinued at Plts Cost.

Thos Mars Plaintiff vs David Alexander Junr. False Imprisonment. Discontinued at Plts Cost.

On application of Sarah Ward, widow of Jeremiah Ward Dec'd, Ordered that Letters of Administration of all & Singular the Goods & Chattels Rights & Credits of the s'd Dec'd be Granted & Committed to her the s'd Sarah Ward, She being Duly sworn in Open Court as the law Directs. Whereupon she the said Sarah Ward Together with Duncan Obryan & Thos W. Fakes her Securities Entered into and acknowledged their bonds in the penalty of £500 with Condition according to Law.

Ordered that a Warrant of Appraisement Issue to four freeholders Directing them to appraise the Estate of the s'd Dec'd and that Anguish Campbell be desired to Qualify s'd appraisers.

State vs John D. Kern. Indictment. Retailing Liquors without Licence. This day came the parties by their attys and thereupon came also a Jury to wit Aron Starns, Wm. McFerson, John Hall, Saml Weathers, James Dorough, Waterman Boatman, Wm. Taylor, Mich'l Wallace, John Carter, Nath'l Nickols & Wm Bailey who being Elected Tried & Sworn the Truth to Speak upon the Issue Joind upon their Oaths do say that the Deft is not Guilty of the Charges in the Indictment mentioned. Whereupon it was considered by the Court that the Deft be acquited on payment of the Cost of Prosecution.

LAURENS COUNTY SC COURT MINUTES 1786-1789

Page 185: [13 September 1787]

A Lease & Release for the Conveyance of 100 acres of land from Robert Sims to Micajah Sims acknowledged in open Court & Ordered to be Recorded.

A Deed of Conveyance of 270 acres of land from William Dendy & Clary his wife to Thos Dendy proven in Open Court by Silvanus Walker Esq'r & Silvanus Walker Junr & Ordered to be Recorded.

William Jackson vs Danl Megin. Trover. Dismist by Consent Each party Paying their Own Cost.

John Honeycut vs Joseph Mayhon. Sumry Process. Continued by Consent till next Court.

William Bailey vs John Cargill. Attachment. Ordered that the land be Advertised according to law.

James McLaughlin vs Benjn Killgore. Case. Continued by Consent till next Court.

Edwerd Bryan vs John Ritchey. Trover. Discontinued at Plfts. Cost.

Court Adjourned till to Morrow Morning ten OClock. Jonth'n Downs, John Hunter, Joseph Downs, Esq'rs.

Court met according to Adjournment the 14th Sept 1787. Present Jonth'n Downs, Ja's Montgomery, Silvanus Walker, Joseph Downs.

Page 186: George Barns vs William Price. Assault & Battery. This day came the Plft by J. Yancy his atty and the Deft. being against Solemnly called but came not, thereupon came also a Jury to wit Aron Starns, Wm. McFerson, John Hall, Saml Weathers, James Dorough, Waterman Boatman, William Taylor, Michael Wallace, John Carter, Nath'l Nickols, James Bailey & Wm. Bailey who being Elected Tried & Sworn the Truth to Inquire of Damages in this Suit upon their Oaths do say that the Plft hath Sustained Damages by accation assault & Battery in the Declaration Mentioned to £20 whereupon it was considered by the Court that the Plft Recover against the s'd Deft the s'd sum of £10 & his cost by him in this behalf Expended & the s'd Deft in Mercy &c.

On Motion made by Robt Saxon a Witness for the Pltf ordered that the sum of 12/6 be Taxed in the bill of Cost vs the Deft for him the s'd Robt Saxon for 5 Days Attendance at 2/6 P'r day.

Elizabeth Gary vs Jacob Gibson & Mary Gibson. Sumr Process. By Agreement this Suit is Ordered to be Dismist at Defts Cost.

LAURENS COUNTY SC COURT MINUTES 1786-1789

[13 September 1787]

John Ridgeaway vs Nathan Kemp. Sumr. Process. Dismist at Mutual Cost by Consent.

Page 187: The State Plft vs Edmond Craddock. Indictment for keeping a Disordily house. This day came the Parties by their Attys & thereupon came also a Jury to wit Aron Starns, Wm. McFerson, John Hall, Saml Weathers, Ja's Dorough, Waterman Boatman, Wm. Taylor, Michael Wallace, John Carter, Nath'l Nickels, Wm Bailey & James Bailey who being Elected Tried & Sworn the Truth to Speak upon the Issue Joind upon their Oaths do say that the Deft is not Guilty of the Charges in the Indictment alledged. Whereupon it was considered by the Court that the s'd Deft be Acquited from the Same, on payment of Costs.

Clement Deal vs Thos Edghill. Attachment. Ordered that the Return of Hugh Oneal Summoned as a Garnishee in this Suit be Rec'd & filed.

Ordered that a Rule to shew Cause at the next Court be Issued against Ambrose Hudgins Senr Another Garnishee in the s'd Attachment, Why he should not pay the Condemnation Money in Case he does not make a Return.

Court Adjourned till Court in Course. James Montgomery, Charles Saxon, John Hunter, Joseph Downs, Esq'rs.

Page 188: At a court held for the County of Laurens at the Courthouse on the 10th Decem'r 1787. Present Jonathan Downs, John Hunter, Charles Saxon, Joseph Downs, John Rodgers, Esquires.

A Deed from John Manly Junr to Wm Willson for the Conveyance of 100 acres of land Proven in open Court by the oaths of Rob't Tod & Charles Megaffey & Ordered to be Recorded.

A Lease & Release for the Conveyance of 50 acres of land from Rob't Allison to Beverly Barton Acknowledged in open Court and Ordered to be Recorded.

A Lease and Release for the Conveyance of 150 acres of land from John Cox & Elizebeth Cox his wife to Charles Henderson proven in open Court by Thos Henderson & Wm. Dodd and Ordered to be recorded.

A Lease and Release for the Conveyance of 10 acres of land from Lewis Saxon & Salley his wife to John Rodgers proven in open Court by John Garner & David McCaa and ordered to be recorded.

A Lease and Release for the Conveyance of 100 acres of land from Jonathan Downs to David Ridgeway acknowledged in open Court & ordered to be recorded.

LAURENS COUNTY SC COURT MINUTES 1786-1789

[10 December 1787]

A Lease and Release for the conveyance of 100 acres of land from William Pitts to Rob't Young Proven in open Court by John Watson & Jacob Neil & ordered to be Recorded.

A Lease and Release for the conveyance of 100 acres of land from George Anderson to Rob't Young Acknowledged in open Court and ordered to be Recorded.

Page 189: On Motion made in Open Court by Silvanus Walker Esq'r that a Deed of Gift from John Falkner to him the s'd Silvanus Walker should be Recorded. Also Nathaniel Hall Motioned to the Court that a Deed of Gift from s'd John Falkner to the s'd Nathaniel Hall should be Recorded. Ordered that Neither of the s'd Deeds of Gift be at this time or at any time hereafter admitted to Record in this Court on Suspicion of fraud.

Pyles & McNees vs James Floyd. S. Process. Case. By Consent of the parties this Suit is ordered to be Discontinued at Mutual Cost.

Lenoir Westmoreland vs Lewis Wells. Slander. By Consent of the parties this Suit is Ordered to be Discontinued at Plfts. cost.

Thomas Hambleton & Temperance Hambleton vs Benjamin Varford Defendant. Trover. Dismist off the Docket.

Court Adjournd Till Tomorrow Morning Nine OClock. Minets signed by John Hunter, Joseph Downs, John Rodgers, Esquires.

Court met according to Adjournment the 11th Decem'r 1787. Present James Montgomery, John Rodgers, Charles Saxon, Dan'l Wright.

A Lease and Release for the Conveyance of 200 acres of land from John Widowman & Barbery Widowman his wife to William Head Proven in Open Court by the Oaths of John head & David Childers and Ordered to be Recorded.

Page 190: A Lease and Release for the Conveyance of 300 acres of land from Charles Hutchings & Elizebeth Hutchings his wife to John Elmore Proven in Open Court by the oaths of Samuel Saxon & Robert H. Hughes and Ordered to be Recorded.

Ordered that a Commission Issue to Esquire Montgomery to Examine and take the acknowledgement of Elizabeth Hutchings to the above mentioned Deeds of Conveyance and make Return of the s'd Commission & Acknowledgement to Next Court.

LAURENS COUNTY SC COURT MINUTES 1786-1789

[11 December 1787]

A Deed for the Conveyance of 150 acres of land from Jacob Bowman to John Bowman Proven in Open Court by George Anderson Esq'r & Saml Wharton & Ordered to be Recorded.

Pyles & McNees vs John Boyd. Sum. Process. Case. Continued by Consent till Next Court.

A Deed from Frederick Little to Wm. Hubbs for the Conveyance of 100 acres of land proven in open Court by Robt Todd & Chas Megaffie & ordered to be recorded.

A Lease and Release for the Conveyance of 164 acres of land from Charles Hutchings & Elizebeth his wife to Robt H. Hughes proven in Open Court by John Trotter & John Gorely & ordered to be Recorded.

John Honeycut vs Joseph Mayhon. Sum. Process. Case. Ordered to be Discontinued at Plfts. Cost.

A Deed from Joshua Arnald to Nehemiah Franks for the Conveyance of 228 acres of land Acknowledged in Open Court and Ordered to be Recorded.

A Deed from Joshua Arnald to Samuel Franks for the Conveyance of 132 acres of land Acknowledged in Open Court and Ordered to be Recorded.

A Lease and Release for the Conveyance of 100 acres of land from Wm. Huddleston & Jane his wife to Matthew Hunter proven by George Leveston & Ja's Huddleston & Ordered to be Recorded.

Page 191: Wm Brown vs Joseph Glen. Appeal. This day came the parties by their attorneys, the Court after hearing the Council on Both sides confirmed the Judgment of the Justice by whom the s'd appeal was certified. And it is considered that the s'd Glenn Recover against the s'd William Brown the sum of £2 s2 d10 together with his cost in this behalf Expended.

A Lease and Release for the Conveyance of 250 acres of land from Thomas Boyce to John Adams, acknowledged in open Court & ordered to be recorded.

Court adjourned Till Tomorrow Morning Nine OClock. Minets signed by James Montgomery, Danl Wright, George Anderson, Esquires.

Court met according to Adjournment the 12th Decem'r 1787. Present James Montgomery, Charles Saxon, John Rodgers, George Anderson, Esquires.

LAURENS COUNTY SC COURT MINUTES 1786-1789

[12 December 1787]

An Award of Edward Musgrove, Samuel Ewing, Robt Hanna & John Hunter as Arbitrators in a Difference between Charles Hutchings and John D. Kern which award was agreed to & signed [by] the s'd Parties, proven in Open Court by Edw'd Musgrove & ordered to Ly for further Proof.

James Russell vs Patrick Rieley. Debt. By Consent of the Parties this Suit is Ordered to be Continued Till Next court.

Page 192: Absent Charles Saxon, Esquire.

Charles Saxon vs Thomas Pearson. Attachment. The Attachment being returned Executed on a Tract of 300 acres of land the Property of the Deft, and the Deft not appearing to Replevy the same or plead to the Plft's Declaration according to a former order of this Court, tho Again solemnly called, Thereupon came a Jury to wit John Walker, Robt Scott, Adam Bell, Charles Hutchings, Robt Long, Luke Waldrop, Benjn Adair, Robt McNees, Wm. Price, Wm Young, Joseph Young & Bazel Hollon who being Elected well & truly to Inquire of Damages in this Suit, upon their Oaths do say that the Plft hath Sustained Damages by accation of the Trespass in the Declaration mentioned to £20 besides his Cost. Thereupon it was considered by the Court that the Plt recover against the s'd Deft the sum of £20 & his cost by him in this behalf expended.

Benjamin Griffith Plaintiff vs James Allison Adm'r of John York Decd. In Trover. By Consent of the Plft, this suit is ordered to be Dismist at his Cost.

George Anderson vs Curnelius Dendy. In Trover. This day came the Parties by their Attys & thereupon came also a Jury to wit Jno Walker, Robert Scott, Adam Bell, Charles Hutchings, Robt Long, Luke Waldrop, Benjn Adair, Robt McNees, Wm. Price, Wm Young, Joseph Young & Bazel Hollon who being Elected Tried & Sworn the truth to speak upon the Issue Joind, upon their Oaths do say that the Deft is not Guilty of the Trover & Convertion in the Declaration mentioned, Whereupon it was considered by the Court that the Deft take nothing by his bill but for his false Clamour be in Mercy & that the Deft go home without day of Recover against the s'd Plft, his cost by him in this behalf expended &c.

Page 193: A Lease and Release for the Conveyance of 50 acres of land from Wm Young to Alexander Harper, proven by Benj'n Rainey & Wm Jackson and Ordered to be recorded.

John Brown vs Lewis Duvall. In Trover. The Parties came into Court & Agreed that this Suit should be Dismist at Mutual Cost. Whereupon it was ordered accordingly.

LAURENS COUNTY SC COURT MINUTES 1786-1789

[12 December 1787]

State vs Nathaniel Austin. Indictment. Misdemeanor. The Grand Jury Returnd a True Bill.

State vs James Sullivant. Indictment for an Assault on David Anderson, Esq'r. The Grand Jury Returned not a True Bill.

State vs Joseph Smith. Indictment for keeping a Tavern. The Grand Jury Returnd a True Bill.

James McNees vs Goyn Gibson. ordered that a Commission Issue to three Justices of the Peace in North Carolina, Linkon County, to Examine William Hutcheson on the Part of the Deft and to Cross examine the s'd Witness & to Return the s'd examination sealed up with the commission there to be read in Evidence, the Deft Giveing the Plt ten days notice of the time & Place of such Examination & the s'd Justices do swear the s'd evidence if he is not intrested in the event of the Suit.

John Blalock vs Thomas McDanald. Attachment. Whereas the Plff in this Action did on the 13th day of Decem'r 1787 file his Declaration in the Clerks office of this court, against the Deft. who is absent from & without the Limits of this State & hath neither wife nor Atty known within the s'd State upon whom a Copy of the Declaration with a Rule to plead thereto within a year & a Day might be served, it is therefore ordered that in pursuance of an [**Page 194**] Act of Assembly in that Case made & Provided that the said Deft, do appear & Plead to the s'd Declaration on or before the Second Monday in December in the year 1788. Otherwise final & absolute Judgment will be Given and awarded against him.

Edward Musgrove foreman, Nathan Barksdale, William Anderson, Joseph Parsons, John McClintock, John Lindsey, James McNees, Robt Young, Thos Ward, Shadrach Martin, Saml Saxon and John King were sworn as Grand Jurors of Inquest for the body of this County, Received their Charge & Retired from the Barr, and some time Returned into Court & Presented as follows to wit. We the Grand Jury for the County of Laurens, Present Elizabeth Briggs adm'r of the Estate of John Briggs Dec'd for Concealing a Set of Leases Contrary to her oath and administration, as appears with a View to Defraud the Heir of his Right.

We Inform the Court that the Road leading from John McClintock's to Michael Waldrop's is Very much out of Order.

We Inform the Court that the Road Leading from Jas Sullivant's to Hugh ONeal's is Very Much out or Repair.

We also inform the Court that the road from Reaburns Creek to the Widow Wards is out of Repair.

LAURENS COUNTY SC COURT MINUTES 1786-1789

[12 December 1787]

We present Martin Williams & Richard Collins for fighting & Profane Swearing Several Oaths.

Page 195: A Deed for the Conveyance of 400 acres of land from Alex'd McDowall to John Millwee Acknowledged in Open Court & ordered to be Recorded.

Benjamin Griffith vs Jas Allison. Ordered that the Plft pay unto Rolley Bowin a Witness for the Plt vs the s'd Deft the sum of 40/ for 16 days attendance at 2/6 P'r day.

Also to Holloway Power the sum 42/6 for 17 days attendance at 2/6 P'r day as a Witness in s'd Suit.

Saml Boyd Ex'r of Jas Boyd Decd vs Sarah Cargill admx of Curnelius Cargill Decd. By Consent this suit is Ordered to be Dismist at Plfts cost.

Reubin Pyles vs James McNees. Case. By Consent of the Parties this suit is ordered to be Continued till Next Court.

James McNees vs Reubin Pyles. Detinue. By Consent of the Parties this suit is ordered to be Continued till Next Court.

James McNees vs Reubin Pyles. Slander. By Consent of the Parties this suit is ordered to be Continued till Next Court.

Mary Williams vs Robt Toombs. Case. By Consent of the Parties this suit is ordered to be Continued till Next Court.

Jean Tolds vs Joseph Goodman. By Consent of the Parties this suit is ordered to be Continued till Next Court.

Daniel Dyson vs Clough Harris. Case. By Consent of the Parties this suit is ordered to be Dismist Each party paying their own Cost.

Page 196: Court Adjournd till Tomorrow Morning 9 OClock. Minets signed by Jonathan Downs, George Anderson, John Rodgers, Esquires.

Court met according to Adjournment the 13th Decem'r 1787. Present Jonathan Downs, Daniel Wright, John Rodgers, Esquires.

Whereas William Craig this day applied for Letters of Administration of all and Singular the Goods & Chattels rights & credits of Charles Edwerds Dec'd. Ordered that a Citation Issue, Citing and Admonishing the kindred and Creditors of the s'd Charles Edwerds decd to appear at the next Court to be held for this County on the Second Monday in March next to shew cause if

LAURENS COUNTY SC COURT MINUTES 1786-1789

any they [can] why Letters of Administration as aforesaid should not be granted.

[13 December 1787]

Charles Neil vs Jeremiah Webb. Attachment. The attachment being Returned executed & the Deft not appearing to Reply the same, therefore it was considered that a Judgment [be] entered for the Plft for the Debt in the Declaration mentioned unless the Deft shall appear & Plead to Issue at the next Court.

Page 197: A Deed from John Hearvey to Wm Rodgers for the Conveyance of 100 acres of land, Proven in open Court by Andw Rodgers Senr & John Garner & Ordered to be Recorded.

William Young vs James McNees & Hugh Young. In Debt. This day came the Parties by their Attys and thereupon came also a Jury to wit John Walker, Robert Scott, Adam Bell, Charles Hutchings, Robert Long, Luke Waldrop, Benjamin Adair, Wm. Price, Bazel Hollon, Zachariah Bailey, Saml Lemon & Joseph McDanald who being Elected tried & Sworn the Truth to Speak upon the Issue Joind, upon their Oaths find for the Plts £15 and Cost of Suit. The Deft Mooved for a New Trial which was Ordered to be brought on Tomorrow mourning.

Ordered that Thos Wadsworth & Richard Griffen & Samuel Henderson, be & is hereby appointed Commissioners to View a New Road Cut from Hugh ONeal's Mill to Mudlick Creek as aforesaid and that they the said Commissioners Report to next Court, which os the two Roads is the Nearest & Best & Convenients for the Publick.

A Lease and Release for the Conveyance of 100 acres of land from Adam Gorden to Samuel Dunlap acknowledged in open Court by the s'd Adam Gorden and Ordered to be Recorded.

Jones & Smith vs Wm Thomason. Case. By Consent of the Parties this Suit is Ordered to be Discontinued, Each party paying their own Cost.

A Lease and Release for the Conveyance of 100 acres of land from Robert Sulton to Danl Wright proven in open Court by Luther Smith & Michael Wallace & Ordered to be Recorded.

Page 198: A Lease and Release for the Conveyance of 100 acres of land from Wm. Price & Margaret his wife to John Saxon proven in Open Court by John Hunter & James Saxon and ordered to be Recorded.

A Lease and Release for the Conveyance of 100 acres of land from John Saxon to Robt Black acknowledged in open Court & Ordered to be Recorded.

LAURENS COUNTY SC COURT MINUTES 1786-1789

[13 December 1787]

Daniel Jackson vs James Sullivant & Harrison Sullivant. In Debt. This day came into Court the Parties & the Deft James Sullivant Sayeth that he cannot Gain say the Plts action for £10 s5 whereupon it was Considered by the Court that the Pltf recover against the s'd Defts the s'd sum of £10 s5 & his Cost by him in this behalf expended. And the Ptff agrees to Stay Execution till March Next.

Court Adjournd till Tomorrow morning 9 Oclock. Minets signed by Jonathan Downs, John Rodgers, Daniel Wright, Esquires.

Court met according to Adjournment the 15th Decem'r 1787. Present Jonathan Downs, John Hunter, Daniel Wright, John Rodgers, Esquires.

William Young vs James McNees & Hugh Young. The Defts Mooved for a New Trial, the Court after hearing both parties by their Attorneys, Ordered that a New Trial be Granted & Tried next Court.

Page 199: James Pucket vs Joseph Adair. Slander. By Consent of the Parties, this Suit is Ordered to be Continued till Next Court.

Wadsworth & Turpin vs Richard Carral. Case. This day came the parties by their attys & thereupon came also a Jury to wit John Walker, Robert Scott, Adam Bell, Charles Hutchings, Robt Long, Luke Waldrop, Benjn Adair, Wm. Price, Bazel Hollon, Robt McNees, Wm Young, Joseph Young who being Elected Tried & Sworn the truth to Speak upon the Issue Joind, upon their Oaths do say that the Plft hath Sustained Damages by accation of the nonperformance of the promises & Assumptions in the Declaration mentioned & they do assess the Plft Damages by accation thereof to £10 s4 d10 with Cost of Suit, Whereupon it was Considered by the Court that the Plts Recover against the s'd Deft the sum of £10 s4 d10 together with his Cost by him in this behalf expended &c. And the s'd Deft in Mercy &c.

Ordered that William Mitchusson and Daniel Wright, Esquires, Bind out James Scrugs, Pamela Scrugs & Sarah Scrugs in the following manner & form, the said James Scrugs until he is of the age of 21 years, the [said] Pamela and Sarah Scrugs until they attain to the age of 18 years, Respectively.

A Deed from Randolph Carsey & Charity his wife to Richard Robison for the Conveyance of 158 acres of land Proven by Wm. Donohoe & ordered to ly for further proof.

A Lease and Release for the Conveyance of 150 acres of Land from Richard Robinson to Wm Donohoe proven by Joel Burgess & Catharina Harris & Ordered to be Recorded.

LAURENS COUNTY SC COURT MINUTES 1786-1789

Page 200: [15 December 1787]

Charles Goodwin vs Charles Hunt. Sum. Process. Debt. This day came the parties by their attorneys, and the Court after Hearing both parties by their attys aforesaid Gave Judgm't for the Plft That he Recover against the s'd Deft the sum of £3 s5 d3 Together with his cost by him in this behalf expended & they agreed to Stay execution Three months.

John Rutledge made application to the Court of Letters of Administration of all & singular the Goods & Chattells rights & Credits of Reason Rutledge Decd. Ordered that a Citation Issue, Citing and Admonishing the kindred and Creditors of the s'd Reason Rutledge dec'd to appear at the next Court to be held for this County on the Second Monday in March next to shew cause if any they have why Letters of Administration as aforesaid should not be granted.

The State vs Abraham Neighbours. Indictment for keeping a Public Tavern without Licence. The Prosecutor Refuseing to prosecute any further. Ordered to be Dismist at Defts. Cost.

James Dillard vs Clement Davis. Slander. By Consent of the parties, it is ordered that a Commission issue to Esquire Hunter & Montgomery To examine and Take the Deposition of Ellenor Lewis a Witness in this Suit in behalf of the Deft. & that they return the said Commission & Deposition to Next Court, there to be read in Evidence in this Suit. The Deft. is ordered to Give to the Plft. Ten Days Notice of the time & Place of Such Examination that s'd Witness is to be Sworn on her Voire Dire whether she is Intrested in the event of the Suit.

Page 201: On application of Edward & Wm Mitchusson for Licence to keep a Public Tavern at the house of the s'd Edward Mitchusson, Ordered to be Granted for the Term of one year they complying with the Revenue act & enter into bond with Sufficient Security with the Clerk for the Support of the s'd Licence according to Law.

On application of John Garner he is Admitted to keep a Public Tavern at the where he now lives for the Term of one year, he complying with the Revenue act & enter into bond with Sufficient Security with the Clerk for the Support of the s'd Licence according to Law.

Ordered that no Licence Issue from the Clerks Office or be of force until the Duty is paid into the Clerks of County Treasurers Hands.

State vs Nathl Austin. Indictment for a Misdemeanor. The Deft. Pleads not Guilty by his atto. Wm. Shaw Traversed the Indictment, Ordered to be Tried next Court and that the Deft. be bound with Two Sufficient Securities in the sum of £50 the s'd Deft in the sum of £25 and the securities in the sum of £12 10 each for his the s'd Defts appearance at the next Court to be held for this

County. And that the Deft be continued in Custody of the Sheriff until such Security [be] given as aforesaid.

[15 December 1787]

The State vs John Coker. Indictment. Assault & Battery. Ordered to be Dismist and that the Deft. pay the Cost of Prosecution.

State vs Martin Williams. Indictment. Assault & Battery. The Deft. Confessed himself Guilty. Fined by the Court five shillings with Cost.

Page 202: State vs Richard Collens. Indictment. Assault & Battery. The Deft. Confessed himself Guilty. fined by the Court five shillings Together with Cost of Suit.

State vs Robt Sims. Indictment. Profane Swearing. Ordered to be Dismist on payment of the Cost.

State vs Gilbert Menary & John Cargill. Indictment. Profane Swearing. fined by the Court five shillings Each Together with Cost of Suit.

State vs James Farbarn. Indictment. Bastardy. Ordered to be Dismist on payment of Cost.

State vs Christian Langston. Indictment. Bastardy. Ordered to be Dismist on payment of Cost.

State vs Jacob Penington. Ordered that the s'd Jacob Penington on Complaint being made in open Court by Benj'n Rainey, That the s'd Penington be bound Tot he peace& Good Behaviour for one Year, with one Good Security in the sum of £30 viz the s'd Penington in the sum of £20 and his security in the sum of £10.

State vs Nathl Austin, Robt Goodwin & Robt Goodwin. In Debt. On Recognizance. Ordered to be Dismist & that the Defts Pay Cost of Suit.

State vs John Koewin. Indictment. Selling Liquors without Licence. Ordered to be Dismist at Defts Cost the prosecutor Refuseing to prosecute any further.

Page 203: Nicholass Brown is appointed Overseer of the Highway in place of George Berry, Ordered that he cause the several Free male Inhabitents & Slaves Contiguous to & Convenient to the s'd Road to work thereon & cause the same to be kept in Good repair for one year as the Law Directs.

Nathan Camp vs Joseph Mayhon. By Consent of the Parties Ordered that a Commission Issue to three Justices of the Peace in Rutherford County in the State of North Carolina viz Elias Alexander, George Moore & ____ Irwin to Examine James Brock, on the part and behalf of the Pltf & to Cross examine

& swear the s'd Brock on his Voire Dire whether he is Intrested in the event of the Suit & to Return the said examination Together with the Commission to next Court there to be read in evidence, The Plft giveing the Deft. Ten days Notice of the time & Place of such examination.

[15 December 1787]

Mary McDanald vs Edw'd Mitchusson. In Trover. By Consent of the parties this Suit is Ordered to be dismist at Defts Cost.

Wm Bailey vs John Cargill. Attachment. The attachment being Returned executed & the Deft not Replevying. Ordered that the Perishable property of the Defts. attacht be exposed to Publick Sale & the moneys arising from such sale to be Continued in the hands of the Sheriff untill Next Court.

Lewis Duvall vs Sarah Cargill. In Debt. By Consent of the Plft. this suit is Ordered to be Dismist at Pfts. Cost.

Mary Durham vs Elizebeth Tindsley. In Trover. This day came the Parties by their Attys & there **[Page 204]** upon came also a Jury to wit John Walker, Robt Scott, Adam Bell, Charles Hutchings, Robt Long, Luke Waldrop, Benjn Adair, Robt McNees, Wm. Price, Wm Young, Joseph Young & Bazel Hollen who being Elected Tried & Sworn the Truth to Speak upon the Issue Joind upon their oath do say that the Deft. is not Guilty of the Trover & Convertion in the Declaration mentioned, Whereupon it was Considered by the Court that the Plft take Nothing by his bill, but for her false Clamour be in Mercy & that the Deft. Go home without day & Recover against the s'd Pltf Her cost by her in this behalf expended and the s'd Pltf in Mercy &c.

On Motion made on oath by John Donohoe a Witness for the Deft against the Pltf Mary Durham, Ordered that the Plft pay him the sum of 25 shillings for 10 days attendance at 2/6 P'r day.

A Deed of Gift from Wm. Price to Mary Price, Ruth Price, Sarah Price and Jane Price, Acknowledged in open Court by the s'd Wm Price & Ordered to be Recorded.

A Deed of Gift from Wm Price to Isaac Price for 100 acres of land Acknowledged in open Court by the s'd Wm Price & Ordered to be Recorded.

Court Adjournd till Tomorrow mourning Ten OClock. Minets signed by Joseph Downs, Silvanus Walker, Danl Wright, Esquires.

Court met according to adjournment the 16th Decem'r 1787. Present Jonth'n Downs, Danl Wright, George Anderson, Joseph Downs, John Rodgers, Wm Mitchusson, Esquires.

LAURENS COUNTY SC COURT MINUTES 1786-1789

Page 205: [16 December 1787]

On application of James Ferguson for Letters of Administration of all & Singular the goods & Chattells, Rights and Credits of John Ferguson decd, as being next of kinn. Ordered that a Citation issue, Citing & Admonishing all & singular the kindred & Credits of the s'd Dec'd to appear at the next Court to shew Cause if any they have Why Letters of Administration as aforesaid should not Granted.

Whereas there was yesterday an Ordered Entered to Allow John Garner to keep a Publick Tavern at his house where he now lives, which order as it appears was entered threw mistake in the application, Ordered that the s'd order be & is hereby Reversed.

On Application of John Rodgers Esq'r he is admitted to keep a publick tavern at or near the Courthouse of this County for the term of one year from this Date, he Complying with the Revenue act. Ordered that the s'd John Rodgers enter into bond with Two Good & Sufficient Securities with the Clerk, Condition to support the s'd Licence according to Law.

Ordered that the following Estrays be sold at Public Sale by the Sheriff after being advertised ten days to wit.

A Bay Mare Taken up by George Elliott & Told before John Rodgers Esq'r.

A Dark Bay horse Taken up by Wm Glidewell & Told before James Montgomery.

A Black Horse Taken up by James Young & Told before George Anderson, Esq'r.

A Roand Mare Taken up by Hugh McWilliams & Told before James Montgomery Esq'r.

Page 206: Also 4 Barrows Taken up by Hugh Middleton &U Told before Jonathan Downs Esquire

for Cash or paper medium Giving Two Months Credit, Takeing Notes of the purchasers with sufficient security, payable to the County Treasurer.

Ordered that the following Estrays be sold by the Sheriff at Publick sale this day for Cash or paper medium giving Two Months Credit, Taking notes with Good Security from the Purchasers to wit.

A Black horse Taken up by Charles Pucket & Told before James Montgomery, Esquire.

LAURENS COUNTY SC COURT MINUTES 1786-1789

[16 December 1787]

A Bright bay mare taken up by Joseph Adair Jun'r & told before James Montgomery, Esqr.

A Black Mare taken up by Zachariah Sims & Told before George Anderson, Esqr.

A Sorrel Mare Taken up by John Watson & Told before Anguish Campbell, Esq'r.

Any Moneys that comes into the Sheriffs hands by Virtue of the Sale of the above Estrays, he is Ordered to pay into the hands of the County Treasurer as soon as is Convenient.

Court Adjourned for half an hour. Court met according to Adjournment. Court Adjourned till Court in Course. Minets signed by Jonathan Downs, George Anderson, Danl Wright, Esquires.

Page 207: At a Court held for the County of Laurens at the courthouse the Tenth day of March 1788. Present Joseph Downs, Charles Saxon, James Montgomery, John Rodgers, Esquires.

The following Persons were drawn to serve as Pettit Jurours at the next Court to be held for the County the second Monday in June next, to wit.

1. Matthew Hunter
2. Midleton Prater
3. Wm Niel
4. Joshua Nobles
5. Saml Niel
6. Chas Braudy
7. Hutchings Burton
8. Joel Burgess
9. Jacob Wright
10. John Sims
11. Charles Nickalls
12. Robt Franks
13. David Allison
14. John Filpot
15. Saml Hall
16. John Hughes
17. Wm Dunlap
18. Roger Murphey
19. Patrick Obryan
20. Abel Boling
21. Jonathan Pucket
22. Wm Sims
23. Michl Gafford
24. Abraham Neighbours
25. Thomas Dendy
26. James Pucket
27. John Box
28. Wm Donohoe
29. James Wells
30. John Willard

The following Persons were drawn to serve as Grand Jurours at the next Court

1. Marshall Franks
2. John Carter
3. Andrew Rodgers
4. David Bailey
5. Absolem Bobo
6. James Saxon
7. Benjamin Jones
8. Zachariah Bailey
9. John Abercrumbie
10. William Tweedy
11. James Young
12. Charles Allen
13. James Abercrumbie
14. Abner Babb
15. Charles Simmons
16. Daniel Ozburn
17. Thomas Boyce
18. Thomas Ship
19. Edmond Learwood
20. William Dendy

LAURENS COUNTY SC COURT MINUTES 1786-1789

[10 March 1788]

William Tate Esq'r Produced a Credential Signed by the Hon. Edanus Burke, John F. Grimkey, and Thomas Haward Junr, Esquires, Judges of the Court of Common Pleas in this State, Bareing Date the 20th day of February 1787, Admiting him the said William Tate to practice as a Solicitor and Attorney at Law or Equity in this State, Whereupon it was Ordered that he the s'd Wm Tate be Enroled as Such in this Court.

Page 208: A Lease and Release for the Conveyance of 100 acres of land from John Williams to Samuel Goodman, Acknowledged in Open Court and Ordered to be Recorded.

A Deed of Gift from Daniel McClain to Archebald Owins, proven in open Court by Wm. Obennian and John Hutson and Ordered to be Recorded.

A Deed from Joel Burgess & Elener his wife to Thos Ship for the Conveyance of 95 acres of land, Acknowledged in Open Court and Ordered to be Recorded.

A Deed of Gift from Wm Clinton to Robt Clinton, Mary Clinton & Pamela Clinton proven in open court by Thomas Gorman & John Cammel & Ordered to be Recorded.

John Donohoe vs Wm Boyce. Assault & Battery. By Consent of the parties this Suit is Ordered to be Dismist at Defendants Cost.

The Last Will and Testament of Hugh ONeal dec'd was presented in open court by Mercer Babb & Elisha Ford, Two of the Executors therein name, and proven by the oath of Patrick McDowell one of the Witnesses thereunto and ordered to be Recorded. On the Motion of the s'd Executors who made oath according to Law, Ordered that Letters Testamentary Issue Accordingly.

Ordered that a Warrant of Appraisement Issue to Wm Cason, Saml Henderson, James Henderson & Daniel Megin free holders who being first sworn before a Justice of the peace of s'd County, or any three of them, do repair to all such places within this County, as they shall be Directed unto by the s'd Executors &c.

On application of Wm Whealer for Letters of Administration of all and Singular the Goods and Chattels of Matthew Love, decd. Ordered that a Citation Issue, Citing and Admonishing the kindred and Creditors of the s'd dec'd to appear at the next Court to be held for this County on the Second Monday in June next to shew cause if any they have why Letters of Administration as aforesaid should not be granted as aforesaid.

Page 209: Daniel Davis vs Wm Barksdale. In Slander. By Consent of the Parties this Suit is Ordered to be Dismist at Defendants Cost.

LAURENS COUNTY SC COURT MINUTES 1786-1789

[10 March 1788]

A Lease and Release for the Conveyance of 50 acres of land from Joshua Cates to Millinton Couch, proven by John Templeton and Ordered to Ly for further proof.

A Lease and Release for the Conveyance of 50 acres of land from Joshua Cates to Joseph Cates proven in Open Court by James Montgomery and ordered to Ly for further proof.

A Deed of Gift from Mary Edwerds to James Edwerds, John Edwerds, and Mary Edwerds, proven in Open Court by John Nealy and Ordered to Ly for further proof.

A Deed from John Bull to Henry Davis for the Conveyance of 200 acres of land proven in Open Court by George Whitmore and Ordered to Ly for further proof.

Rob't Ross is appointed Overseer of that part of the highway leading from Theophiless Goodwins to Little River in the place of Abraham Neighbours, Ordered that he cause the Several free Male Inhabitents and Slaves Contiguous to and Convenient to s'd road to work thereon & to cause the same to be kept in Good repair for one year as the Law Directs.

John Fields is appointed Overseer of that part of the highway leading from Thomas Carter's old place to James Sullivants in the place of John Sims. Ordered that he cause the Several free Male Inhabitents and Slaves Contiguous to and Convenient to s'd road to work thereon & to cause the same to be kept in Good repair for one year as the Law Directs.

Lewis Banton is appointed Overseer of that part of the highway leading from Thomas Carter's old place to Swanceys ferry on Salluda. Ordered that he cause the Several free Male Inhabitents and Slaves Contiguous to and Convenient to s'd road to work thereon & to cause the same to be kept in Good repair for one year as the Law Directs.

A Lease and Release for the Conveyance of 100 acres of land from George Whitmore to Reuben Flanagan acknowledged in Open Court & ordered to be Recorded.

Page 210: Court adjourned Till Tomorrow Morning Nine OClock. Minets Signed by Joseph Downs, James Montgomery, John Rodgers, Esquires.

Court met according to Adjournment the 11th March 1788. Present James Montgomery, George Anderson, John Rodgers, Esq'rs.

A Deed from Enoch Bramblet to Thomas Higgins for the Conveyance of 100 acres of land Acknowledged in Open Court and Ordered to be Recorded.

LAURENS COUNTY SC COURT MINUTES 1786-1789

[11 March 1788]

A Deed from Joseph Atteway to Elisha Atteway for the Conveyance of 550 acres of land Proven in Open Court by Jesse Atteway and Ordered to Ly for further proof.

A Lease and Release for the Conveyance of 150 acres land from Rob't Ross to Robt Hannah acknowledged in Open Court and Ordered to be Recorded.

A Deed from John Burn & John Norris to And'w Cunningham for the Conveyance of 50 acres of land Acknowledged in open Court and Ordered to be Recorded.

A Lease and Release for the Conveyance of 135 acres of land from William Neil to Samuel Neil Acknowledged in open Court and Ordered to be Recorded.

A Lease and Release for the Conveyance of 300 acres of land from Thomas Gorden & Elizabeth his wife to Aaron Harlan proven in Open Court by James Hanna & Wm Hanna and ordered to be recorded.

A Lease and Release for the Conveyance of 280 acres of land from Hugh McVay & Martha his wife to Danl Martin Proven in Open Court by Mansel Crips & Robert Culberton and Ordered to be recorded.

Ordered that Letters of Administration of all & Singular the Goods & Chattels of William Drew Dec'd be Granted to Sarah Roberts widow of [**Page 211**] of the said Wm Drew dec'd, she being Duly Qualified as the Law Directs. Whereupon she the s'd Sarah Roberts Together with Tandy Walker and Daniel Ozburn her Securities Entered into and Acknowledged their Bonds in the sum of £500 pounds with Condition according to Law.

Ordered that a warrant of Appraisement Issue to Thomas Dendy, Wm. Dendy, Saml Powel & Zachariah Bailey, free holders, who being first Sworn before some one Justice of the peace of this County to Appraise the Estate of the s'd Wm Drew dec'd and Make a Return to the s'd Administratrix within forty days.

On Application of John Simpson, merchant, he is Licenced, allowed, & Admitted to Retail all kinds of Spirituous Liquors at his Store in this County in any less Quantity than Three Gallons for the Term of One Year from the Date hereof, He complying with the act of Assembly in that case made and provided.

On application of John A. Elmore he is Admitted to keep a Publick Tavern at his house where he now lives for the Term of One Year from this Date he Complying with the act of Assembly &C, Whereupon he the s'd John A.

Elmore Together with James Saxon and Saml Saxon his Securities entered into & acknowledged their bond according to Law.'

[11 March 1788]

A Lease and Release for the Conveyance of 200 acres of land from John Shirley & Rebecca his wife to William Mitchell Proven in Open Court by Stephen Wood and Wm. Goodman and Ordered to be Recorded.

Ordered that Letters of Administration of all & Singular the Goods and Chattels of John Furguson Dec'd be Granted to James Furguson, he being duly Sworn as the Law directs, Whereupon he the s'd James Furguson Together with Rob't Ross and Saml Lemon his Securities Entered into and Acknowledged their bonds in the sum of £500 with Condition according to Law.

Ordered that a warrant of Appraisement Issue to four freeholders, who being first Sworn to Appraise the Goods and Chattells of the s'd John Furgurson Dec'd and Return the Appraisement to the s'd Adm'r within forty days.

Page 212: Charles Smith vs Charles Sullivant. In Debt. Sumry Process. This day Came the parties by their Attys, Gave Judgment for Plft for the sum of £3 s7 with Intrest & Cost.

Charles Smith vs Charles Sullivant. In Debt. Sumery Process. This day came the parties by their Attys and the Court after hearing the same Decreed that the Plft Recover against the s'd Deft the sum of £2 s12 d2 with Intrest and that the Plft pay Cost of Suit.

James McNees vs Goyn Gibson. In Trover. By Consent of the Partys it is ordered that a Commission Issue to three Justices of the peace in the state of Virginia to Examined William Hutcheson on the part of the Defendant, Giveing Notice to the Plt ten days of the time & place of such Examination previous to the said Examination that they return the Commission Together with a Certificate of their proceedings to Next Court. There to read in evidence.

James McNees vs Goyn Gibson. In Trover. Continued by Consent till Next Court.

Peter Carnes vs Reubin Pyles. In Debt. Summery Process. Came the parties by their Attorney and the Matter being Dabated by the Attos on both sides, the Court Decreed that the Plft recover against the s'd Deft the sum of £4 s7 with Intrest and Cost.

Joseph Burton vs John McElroy. In Debt. Summery Process. Came the parties by their Attorneys and after the Matter being Debated the Court

Decreed that the Plft recover against the s'd Deft the sum of £3 s5 with Intrest & Cost.

[11 March 1788]

Fielding Woodroof vs Thomas Elliott. S. Process in Debt. Dismist by Consent of the parties at the Defts Cost.

Page 213: Daniel Brown vs Robt Cooper. In Debt. Sumry Process. The Court after hearing the parties by their attorneys Decreed, that Plft Recover against the s'd Defts the sum of £9 with Intrest & Cost.

Fielding Woodroof vs Shadrach Martin & Michael Waldrop. In Debt. Sum'r Process. Continued by Consent till Next Court.

John Walker vs Charles Sullivant. Sumr Process in Debt. The Court after hearing the parties by their Attorneys Decreed that the Pltf Recover against the s'd Deft the sum of £4 with Cost of Suit.

James Dourough vs Flanders Thompson. In Debt. Sumr Process. The Court after hearing the Parties by their Attorneys Decreed that the Plft Recover against the s'd Deft. the sum of ----- with Intrest & Cost.

Peter Carnes vs Reubin Pyles. Sumr Process In Debt. The Court after hearing the parties by their attorneys Decreed that the Plft recover against the s'd deft the sum of s20 d4 and that the Pltf pay Cost of Suit.

Francis Wafer vs Saml Magness. Sumr. Process. Continued by Consent till Next Court.

Benjamin King & Co. vs Amry Day. Sumr Process in Debt. The Court after hearing the Parties by their Attorneys Decreed that the Pltf recover against the s'd Deft the sum of ------ according to Note with Intrest & Cost.

Page 214: Jones & Smith vs William Thomason. Sumr Process. In Debt. The Court after hearing the Parties by their Attorneys Decreed that the Pltf recover against the s'd Deft the sum of £7 s14 d10 with Intrest & Cost.

Daniel Brown vs William Jackson & Wm. Gilbert. Sumr Process in Debt. By Consent of the parties this Suit is Ordered to be dismist at Pltf. Cost.

George Barnes vs Reubin Pyles. Sumr Process in Debt. The Deft Came into Court and Confessed Judgment for the sum of ---- according to Note. Whereupon it was Considered by the Court that Pltf recover against the s'd Deft. The s'd sum of ----- with Intrest & Cost.

Ordered that Letters of Administration of all & Singular the Goods & Chattels of Reason Rutledge Dec'd be Granted to John Rutledge, He being

Duly Sworn as the Law Directs. Whereupon he the s'd John Rutledge Together with Russel Rutledge and Thomas Williamson his Securities Entered into and Acknowledged their Bonds in the sum of £500 pounds with Condition according to Law.

[11 March 1788]

Ordered that a warrant of Appraisement Issue to four free holders, who being first Sworn before some one Justice of the peace of this County to Appraise the Estate of the s'd dec'd and Make a Return of the s'd Appraisement to the s'd Administrator within forty days.

Ordered that Letters of Administration of all & Singular the Goods & Chattels of Charles Edwerds Dec'd be Granted to Wm Craig, He being Duly Sworn as the Law Directs. Whereupon he the s'd Wm Craig together with Duncan Obryan and Thos Boyce his Securities Entered into and Acknowledged their Bonds in the sum of £500 pounds with Condition according to Law.

Ordered that a warrant of Appraisement Issue to four free holders, who being first Sworn before some one Justice of the peace of this County to Appraise the Estate of the s'd dec'd and Make a Return of the s'd Appraisement to the s'd Administrator within forty days.

Page 215: A Lease and Release for the Conveyance of 184 acres of land from Patrick Obryan to James Underwood Acknowledged in Open Court and Ordered to be Recorded.

George Barnes vs Andrew Anderson. S. Process. In debt. The Court after hearing the Parties by their Attorneys Decreed that the Pltf Recover against the s'd Deft the sum of ---- according to Note with Intrest and cost of Suit.

On application of Duke Williams He is Licens'd allowed and admitted to keep a Publick Tavern at his house where he now lives for the full space & Term of One year, he complying with the late act of Assembly in that Case made an provided. Whereupon he the s'd Duke Williams Together with John Williams & John Williams Jun'r his Securities Entered into & Acknowledged their bonds according to law.

Thos Cunningham vs David Bailey. In Debt. By Consent of the Parties this Suit is ordered to be Dismist at Defts. Cost.

A Deed from Andrew Cunningham to Abraham Gray proven heretofore by John Lindsey and now proven by Henry Hambleton and Ordered to be Recorded.

A Power of Att'o from James Templeton to James Adair proven in Open Court by the oath of John Lindsey and Ordered to Ly for further proof.

LAURENS COUNTY SC COURT MINUTES 1786-1789

[11 March 1788]

A Lease and Release for the Conveyance of 150 acres of land from Isaac Hollingsworth to Nathl Rooks proven according to the former act and ordered to be Recorded.

John Gray vs Samuel Ewing. The Parties mutually Submitted the Determination of this Suit to Robt McCrary, James Montgomery, & Jonth'n Downs Esq'r and agreed that their Award thereupon should be made a Judgment of this Court And that the s'd Arbitrators should return the s'd Award to next Court Whereupon it was ordered accordingly.

Page 216: John Walker vs Saml Ewing. In Trover. The parties mutually Submitted the Determination of this Suit to Cager Bennett and John Roland and Agreed their Award thereupon should be made a Judgment of this Court And that the s'd Arbitrators should return the s'd Award to next Court Whereupon it was ordered accordingly.

On application of Angush Campbell for Jonathan Johnston, Ordered that Jonathan Johnston be Licens'd allowed & Admitted to Sell all kinds of Spirituous Liquors at his store in this County in any Less Quantity than three Gallons for the Term of On year, he complying with the Late act of Assembly in that Case made & provided.

Thos Cunningham vs George Barnes & Wm. Barksdale. In Debt. By Consent of the parties this Suit is Ordered to be Dismist at Defts Cost.

A Power of Attorney from Joseph Riding to Saml Saxon Proven in Open Court by David Meglathery & ordered to be Recorded.

Court adjourned till tomorrow Morning Nine OClock. James Montgomery, John Rodgers, Danl Wright, Esquires.

Court met according to Adjournment the 12th March 1788. Present Jonathan Downs, James Montgomery, George Anderson, Danl Wright, Angus Campbell, John Rodgers.

Ordered that Letters of Administration of all & Singular the Goods and Chattels of Robert Page Dec'd be Granted to Wm Rooks, he being duly Sworn as the Law directs, Whereupon he the s'd Wm Rooks Together with ------------ his Securities Entered into and Acknowledged their bonds in the sum of £500 with Condition according to Law.

Page 217: Ordered that a warrant of Appraisement Issue to four freeholders, who being first Sworn to Appraise the Goods and Chattells of the s'd Dec'd and Return the Appraisement to the s'd Adm'r within forty days.

LAURENS COUNTY SC COURT MINUTES 1786-1789

[12 March 1788]

Wm Gilbert vs Rich'd Harper. Trover. By Consent of the parties this suit is Ordered to be Dismist at Defts Cost.

A Lease and Release for the Conveyance of 100 acres of land from Thomas Allison to James Adair Acknowledged in Open Court and Ordered to be Recorded.

Francis Wafer vs Saml Magness. S. Process. Ordered (by Consent of the parties) That a Commission Issue to three Justices of the peace in Rutherford County in the State of No Carolina to Examine and take the Deposition of Wallace Batey a Witness in behalf of the plaintiff and return the said Commission Together with a Certificate of your proceedings to that Court, Giveing the adverse party ten days notice of the time and place of their meeting.

Hugh McVay vs Robert Maxwell. In Trover. New Trial ordered, by mutual Consent of the parties.

Ambrose Hudgins Junr is appointed overseer of that part of the highway leading from Michael Waldrop's to James Young's in the place of Wm Harris. Ordered that he cause the several free male inhabitents & slaves Contiguous to & Convenient to s'd road to work thereon & to cause the same to be kept in good Repair for One year as the law directs.

A Letter from Wm Sims directed to Wm Williamson dated 25th January 1778 presented in Open Court by Angus Campbell & Ordered to be Recorded.

A Note of hand from Wm Williamson to Thos Woodard and [Page 218] Indorsed by Thos Woodard to Wm Sims Dated the 29th July 1772 presented in Open Court by Angus Campbell & Ordered to be Recorded.

A bond from Wm Sims to Angus Campbell Dated the 13th December 1776 Conditional to make Titles to a Certain Tract of 250 acres of land the s'd bond presented in Court the [by] s'd Angus Campbell and Ordered to be Recorded.

William Shaw vs William Jackson. In Debt. Came the Pltf and the Deft. being Solemnly Called but came not to Defend his Suit whereupon it was Ordered that Judgment by Default be entered against him.

William Shaw vs William Jackson. In Debt. Came the Pltf and the Deft. being Solemnly Called but came not thereupon Came also a Jury to wit Rich'd Jowel, John Dendy, Asa Turner, James Anderson, Lewis Graves, John Powers, Jas Sample, James Parks, Claburn Sims, Saml Franks, And'w Parks & James Parks who being Sworn well & Truly to Inquire of Damages in this Suit On their Oath find for the Pltf the sum of £15 with Cost of Suit. Whereupon It was Considered by the Court that the Pltf Recover against the s'd Deft the s'd sum of £15 and his Cost by him in this behalf Expended.

[12 March 1788]

James Pucket vs Joseph Adair. In Slander. The Parties Mutually Submitted the Determination of this Suit to John Hunter & Saml Saxon with Liberty to Choose a Third man in Case of Disagreement, And agreed their award thereupon should be made a Judgment of this Court the s'd Arbitrators to return their award to next Court.

William Moore vs Joseph Parsons. In Trover. Came the Deft by Wm Shaw his Atty and the Pltf. being Solemnly Called but came not [Page 219] but made default nor is his Suit further prosecuted therefore on the Motion of the Deft by Attorney aforesaid it is Considered by the Court that he Recover against the said Pltf five shillings besides his Cost about his Defence in this behalf Expended according to the form of the Act of Assembly in this Case made and provided.

Wadsworth & Turpin vs Sarah Cargill. Attachment. By Consent this suit is ordered to be Continued till Next Court.

John Simpson vs Sarah Cargill. Attachment. Continue by Consent till Next Court.

John Hunter & George Anderson vs Andrew Rodgers. Attachment. Ordered to be Gazetted.

Martin Williams vs Richard Bullock. Attachment. Holloway Power appeared in Open Court and Entered himself Special Bail in this Action and undertakes for the s'd Rich'd Bullock That he the s'd Holloway Power will pay the Cost and Condemnation of the Court or render his body in Discharge thereof to prison, Whereupon on the motion of the Deft by his atto it is Ordered that the Officer Deliver to the s'd Richard Bullock the property by him attacht in behalf of the s'd Pltf from the s'd Deft.

A Lease and Release for the Conveyance of 200 acres of land from John Goodwin and Rachel his wife to Reubin Pyles Acknowledged in open Court she being first privily examined apart from her husband as the Law Directs and Ordered to be Recorded.

On application of John D. Kern, he is Licence'd Allowed and Admitted to Sell and Retail Spirituous Liquors at his Store in this County in any Less Quantity than three Gallons for the Term of One Year &c.

Page 220: Pyles & McNees vs John Boyd. Sum'r Process. In Case. Continued by Consent till Next Court.

[12 March 1788]

Henry Myers vs Jonathan Gilbert. Ordered to be Discontinued at Pltfs Cost.

Saml Ewing vs Boling Bishop. In Trespass. The Parties Mutually Submitted the Determination of this Suit to John Hunter, Saml saxon, James Montgomery & Robert Hanna as Arbitrators and Agreed their Award thereupon should be made a Judgment of this Court, the same was Ordered accordingly.

Edwerd Garrett vs Charles Puckett. In Debt. Discontinued at Pltfs Cost by Consent.

Saml Dilrumple vs Saml Bydston. In Detinue. Discontinued at Pltfs Cost.

Nathan Camp vs Joseph Mayhon. In Debt. Ordered (by Consent of the Parties) that a Commission Issue to three Justices of the Peace in the State of No Carolina to examine and take the Deposition of James Brock a Witness for the Plaintiff and Make a return, the s'd Commission Together with a Certificate of their proceedings Sealed up to next Court Giveing the Adverse party Legal Notice of the time & place of their meeting and examination of the s'd James Brock &c.

Thomas Elliott vs David Burn. In Debt. Discontinued by Consent at Plfts Cost.

Wm Bailey vs John Cargill. Attachment. Discontinued by Consent at Pltfs Cost.

John Blackwell vs John Milam. Trespass. By Consent this Suit is Ordered to be Dismist. Each party paying their own Cost.

Page 221: Wadsworth & Turpin vs Abraham Neighbours. In Case. By Consent this suit is Ordered to be Discontinued at Pltfs Cost.

Wadsworth & Turpin vs Memucan[?] Walker. In Case. Discontinued by Consent at Pltfs Cost.

William Anderson vs Hugh Brown. Attachment. Discontinued by Consent at Pltfs Cost.

On application of Thos Wadsworth, he is Licence'd Allowed and Admitted to Sell and Retail all kinds of Spirituous Liquors at his Store in this County in any Less Quantity than three Gallons for the Term of One Year &c.

A Lease and Release for the Conveyance of 100 acres of land from George Adams & Sarah Adams to Rich'd Turner proven heretofore by Rich'd Watts and now proven by John Caldwell & Ordered to be Recorded.

LAURENS COUNTY SC COURT MINUTES 1786-1789

[12 March 1788]

Whereas John Elmore obtaind yesterday an order to Obtain Licence to keep a Publick Tavern where he now lives for one year the s'd John Elmore came into Court and pray that the s'd Order might be set aside & be Void, which Was ordered accordingly.

Mary Williams vs Joseph Goodman. Continued till Next [court] by Consent.

Ordered that the old road Leading from Hugh ONeal's Mill to Mudlick Creek be Considered and Established as the Publick Road and that John Neiley be appointed Overseer of the s'd Road & that he Cause the several free Male Inhabitents and Slaves Contiguous to & convenient to s'd Road to work thereon & cause the same to be kept in Good repair for one year as the Law Directs.

Page 222: Jean Tolds vs Joseph Goodman. Continued till Next Court by Consent.

Ordered that Jacob R. Brown be and is hereby appointed Overseer of that part of the highway Leading from Mill Creek to Little River Bridge in the place of Anthoney Golden & that he Cause the Several free Male Inhabitants and Slaves Contiguous to & convenient to s'd Road to work thereon & cause the same to be kept in Good repair for one year as the Law Directs.

Lidall Allen Infant Orphan of Charles Allen Dec'd with the approbation of the Court made Choice of Lewis Saxon as his Guardian Whereupon he the s'd Lewis Saxon Together with Joshua Saxon and Charles Allen his Securities entered into and Acknowledged their bonds in the sum of £200 with Condition for Securing the s'd Orphans Estate and Indemnifying the Court.

Court Adjourned till Tomorrow Mourning Nine OClock. Minets Signed by Jonathan Davis, John Hunter, George Anderson, Esquires.

Court met according to adjournment the 13th March 1788. Present James Montgomery, George Anderson, Charles Saxon, Wm Mitchusson, Jonathan Downs, John Hunter.

Wm Gilbert vs Martin Williams. On Motion made on oath by George Flanagan a Witness for the Pltf against the s'd Deft, Ordered that the Plft pay him the sum of 25/ Ten days attendance at 2/6 P'r Day.

Page 223: Robert Farris vs William Austin. In Debt. By Consent of the Parties this Suit is Ordered to be Continued till next Court at Defts Cost.

James Russell vs Patrick Riley. In Case. This day came the Deft by his Atty and the Pltfs being Solemnly Calld came not but made Default nor is his Suit further prosecuted. Therefore on Motion of the Deft by his Atto it is

Considered that he Recover against the s'd Pltf five shillings Damages besides his Cost about his Defence in this behalf Expended according to an Act of the Genl Assembly in that Case made & provided.

[13 March 1788]

John Blalock vs Thos McDanald. Attachment. Ordered to be Gazetted.

Edwerd Pugh vs Andrew McWilliams. In Trover. Discontinued at Defendants Cost.

Henry Myers vs Clem't Davis. Continued till Next Court.

Robert McCrary vs James Jones. Attachment. This day came the Plft by James Yancey his Attorney and the Defendant being again Solemnly called came not, and thereupon came also a Jury to wit Rich'd Jowel, John Dendy, Asa Turner, James Anderson, Lewis Graves, John Powers, James Sample, James Parks, Claburn Sims, Zachariah Sims, Saml Franks, & Andrew Parks who being Sworn well & Truly to Inquire of Damages in this Suit On their Oath find for the Pltf the sum of £8 s13 d6 with Intrest & Cost. Whereupon it was Considered by the Court that the Pltf Recover against the s'd Deft the s'd sum of £8 s13 d6 together with Intrest & Cost and the s'd Deft in Mercy &c.

Page 224: Mary Williams vs Robert Toombs. Continued till Next Court by Consent.

William Young vs James McNees & Hugh Young. Continued till Next Court by Consent.

Jacob Newman vs Robert Cooper. In Case. Came the Deft by Charles Goodwin his Atty and the Pltf being Solemnly Calld Came not nor is his Suit further prosecuted, therefore on Motion of the Deft by his Atto afores'd it is Considered by the Court that the Pltf be Nonsuited & that the Deft recover against him five shillings besides his Cost about his Defence in this behalf Expended according to the form of the Act of Assembly in this Case made and Provided.

Elijah Taylor is appointed Overseer of that part of the highway Leading from Little river near the Courthouse to Michael Waldrop's in the Place of William Tweedy. And that he Cause the Several free male Inhabitents & Slaves Contiguous to and Convenient to s'd Road to work thereon & to cause the same to be kept in Good Repair for One year as the Law directs.

Wm Hanna vs Benjamin Rainey. In Trover. Continued by Consent till Next Court.

Robert Ritchey vs William Goodman. Detinue. This day came the parties by their atto's & thereupon came also a Jury to wit, Rich'd Jowel, John Dendy,

LAURENS COUNTY SC COURT MINUTES 1786-1789

Asa Turner, James Anderson, Lewis Graves, John Powers, James Sample, James Parks, Claburn Sims, Zachariah Sims, Saml Franks, & Andrew Parks who being Elected, Tried & Sworn the Truth to Speak upon the Issue Joind upon their Oaths do find for the Pltf the sum of £10 with Cost of Suit. Whereupon it was Considered by the Court that the Pltf Recover against the s'd Deft the s'd sum of £10 together with his Cost by him in this behalf expended and the s'd Deft in Mercy &c.

Page 225: [13 March 1788]

John Stewart vs James Cannon & John Smith. Attachment. Continued till Next Court by Consent.

A Lease and Release for the Conveyance of 400 acres of land from Nebo Gant to Jonath'n Downs proven by Robert Cooper before John Hunter Esquire and Ordered to be Recorded.

James Pucket vs Joseph Adair. In Slander. On application of Ayres Gorely on oath a Witness for the Defendant against the s'd Pltf Ordered that the Deft pay him the sum of Ten Shillings for 4 days attendance @ 2/6 P'r day with Milage Coming & Going 70 Miles from the State of Georgia £1 4 2 Together with Mileage coming & returning 3/6.

John D. Kern vs Charles Hutchings. In Case. John Elmore Comes into Court and undertakes for the Deft as Special Bail, that in Case he the s'd Charles Hutchings should be cast in this Suit now depending &to be Tried between the s'd John D. Kern and the s'd Charles Hutchings That he the s'd John Elmore will pay the Cost and Condemnation of the Court or render his body in Discharge thereof to prison.

Ordered that the Sheriff of this County Receive the body of Charles Hutchings in Discharge of John Elmore's Special Bail in the above action John D. Kern vs the s'd Charles Hutchings.

Ordered that Letters of Administration of all & Singular the Goods & Chattels of John Simmons Dec'd be Granted to Nancy Simmons widow of the s'd John Simmons Decd dec'd, she being Duly Qualified as the Law Directs. Whereupon she the s'd Nancy Simmons Together with Charles Simmons and Robert Ross her Securities Entered into and Acknowledged their Bonds in the sum of £500 pounds with Condition according to Law.

Ordered that a warrant of Appraisement Issue to four free holders, who being first Sworn before some one Justice of the peace of this County to Appraise the Estate of the s'd dec'd and Return an Inventory thereof to the s'd Administratrix within forty days.

Page 226: On application of Lewis Banton for Letters of Administration of all and singular the goods & Chattells of Peter Wood Decd, Ordered that a

LAURENS COUNTY SC COURT MINUTES 1786-1789

Citation Issue citing and admonishing the kindred & Creditors of the said Peter Wood decd to appear at the Next Court to be held for this County to Shew Cause if any they have Why Letters of Administration should not be Granted as aforesaid.

[13 March 1788]

Joseph Griffen & Mary Griffen vs Thos Edghill Senr. Attachment. Ordered to be Gazetted.

Robert Ritchey vs Wm Goodman. On Application of John Ritchey on Oath a Witness for the Pltfs against the Deft. Ordered that the Deft pay him the sum of 52 shillings and 6 pence for 21 days Attendance at this Court at 2/6 P'r day.

Thomas Dugan vs John Madding. In Trover. Continued till Tomorrow.

Mary Burns vs David Allison. Continued by Consent till Next Court.

Reuben Pyles vs James McNees. Case. Continued by Consent till Next Court.

Charles Harvey vs William Goodman. In Debt. Continued till Tomorrow.

James McLaughin vs Benjamin Killgore. In Case. Continued till Next Court by Consent.

Edward Mitchusson vs John Arnald. In Debt. Continued till Next Court by Consent.

Court adjourned till tomorrow Morning 9 OClock. Minets Signed by Jonathan Downs, James Montgomery, John Hunter, George Anderson, Esquires.

Page 227: Court met according to adjournment the 14th March 1788. Present Jonathan Downs, Wm Mitchusson, Danl Wright, Esquires.

Silvester Hogan vs Nathan Camp. Assault & Battery. The Parties Mutually Submitted the determination of this Suit to Ayres Gorely & John Bush & agreed their Award thereupon should be made a Judgment of the Court, which s'd Arbitrators now returned this award, to wit, that the Suit should be Dismist at Pltfs Cost, Whereupon it was ordered accordingly.

Lewis Banton vs John Ritchey. Assault & Battery. This day came the parties by their attos and thereupon came also a jury to wit, Rich'd Jowel, John Dendy, Asa Turner, James Anderson, Lewis Graves, John Powers, Ja's Sample, James Parks, Claburn Sims, Zachariah Sims, Saml Franks, & And'w Parks who being Sworn well the Truth to Speak upon the Issue Joined upon their Oaths do say that the Pltf [sic] is Guilty of the Trespass, Assault & Battery in the Declaration mentioned, and they do assess the Pltf Damages by accation there of to £5 besides his Cost. Whereupon it was Considered by the Court that the Pltf Recover against the s'd Deft his Damages aforesaid & his Cost by him in the behalf expended And the s'd Deft in Mercy &c.

[14 March 1788]

Pursuant to an Act of the Gen'l Assembly of this State passed the 29th day of February AD 1788 The Court proceeds to appoint Constables for Laurens County when the following persons were appointed to wit, Edw'd Gidien, John Owins, John Entrekin, Thos Cahoon, Elijah Stephens, John Wright, Stephen Wood, John Coker, John Milam, John Coal and Saml Parsons. Ordered that the Justices administer the oath of Office to the Above Mentioned Persons previous to entering into the Execution [of] their Respective Offices.

Thos Dugan vs John Madding. Trover. This is Ordered to be Continued till Next court.

Page 228: Charles Neal vs Jeremiah Webb. Attachment. Discontinued at Pltfs Cost.

Charles Harvey vs Wm Goodman. In Debt. John Ritchey here in Court becomes Security for the Pltf that in Case he should be Cast in this Suit he will pay unto the Deft all such Cost of Charges as by accation thereof be awarded by the Court.

Fielding Woodroof vs William Thomason. Sum Process. In Debt. The Deft comes into Court and confessed Judgment for ----- according to Note with Intrest & Cost. The Pltf agreed to Stay execution till the first of August next.

Court Adjourned till Tomorrow Morning Nine OClock. Minets Signed by Jonathan Downs, Joseph Downs, George Anderson, Esquires.

Court met according to adjournment the 15th March 1788. Present Jonathan Downs, James Montgomery, John Rodgers, Joseph Downs, George Anderson, Esquires.

William Rodgers vs Wm Jackson. Attachment Discontinued at Plfts. Cost.

ordered that following Estrays be exposed to Publick Sale by the Sheriff for Cash or paper medium at a Credit of Two Months Taking bond with Sufficient Security payable to the Country Treasurer to wit.

A Sorrel Horse Taken up by Rob't Coker the 26th Sept 1787 and Told before Joseph Downs Esq'r.

A White Mare Taken up by Tho's Cason 17th Octr 1787 told before Angus Campbell.

LAURENS COUNTY SC COURT MINUTES 1786-1789

Page 229: [15 March 1788]

A Sorrel Mare in the Possession of John Rodgers taken up the 24th Novr 1787 & told before John Rodgers, Esqr.

Sixteen head of hogs Taken up by John Garret 10th Octr 1787 & told before James Montgomery.

A Dark Bay Mare Taken up by Danl Wright & Told before the s'd Danl Wright, Esqr.

A Dark Bay horse Taken up by Joseph Allison & Told before the s'd Danl Wright, Esqr.

A Sorrel Mare Taken up by Jonathan Downs the 24th Novr 1787 & Told before the Joseph Downs, Esqr.

Ordered that the Sheriff Call upon the Several Takers up of Estrays that are above mentioned, of such as are not Delivered to the s'd Sheriff this day and expose the same to publick sale after being advertised ten days at Two Months Credit as the above.

Ordered that the Justices of this County do Meet at the Court house on Fryday the 18th of April Next in Order to Settle & Adjust the Publick Business of this county, and that Copys of the above Order Issue to the Several Justices of this County Purporting the same, and that the s'd Copys be Delivered in to the hands of the Sheriff in order to be Served on the Justices aforesaid.

Danl Brown Esq'r Came into Court & beged Leave to Resign the Office of County Treasurer for this County. Ordered that the s'd Resignation of Daniel Brown Esq'r be Received accordingly And that the Court return him the s'd Danl Brown their thanks for this Faithfull Discharge of his Duty as Country Treasurer which was Returned accordingly.

Wm Hall Infant orphan of Acquilla Hall Dec'd with the approbation of the Court made choice of Jonathan Downs Esq'r his Guardian, Whereupon the s'd Jonathan Downs Together with Nehemiah Franks & John Rodgers his Securitys entered into & acknowledged their bonds in the sum of £150 for Securing the s'd Orphans Estate & Indemnifying the Court.

Page 230: Reubin Pyles vs Joseph Downs, James Montgomery, John Rodgers, commissioners. In Debt. Discontinued at Defts Cost.

Court Adjourned till Court in Course. Minets signed by Jonathan Downs, Joseph Downs, James Montgomery, George Anderson, John Rodgers, Esqr.

LAURENS COUNTY SC COURT MINUTES 1786-1789

At a court held for the County of Laurens at the Courthouse on the 9th day of June 1788. Present Joseph Downs, Silvanus Walker, Charles Saxon, Angus Campbell, Esquires.

The following persons were Drawn to serve as Pettit Jurours at the next Court to be held for this County on the Second Monday in September next.

1. Joseph Waldrop	11. Silas Garret	21. Joseph Hollingsworth
2. James Higgins	12. John Gray	22. Joseph Williams
3. Rob't Taylor	13. Rob't Smart	23. John Cammock
4. Wm Gallagla	14. Rob't Scott	24. Mich'l Waldrop
5. James Pucket	15. Jas Strain	25. John Lindsey
6. Joseph Whitmore	16. Stokes Edwards	26. Wm Suter
7. John Todd	17. Saml Lard	27. James Gamel
8. Wm Willson	18. John Willson	28. Simpson Warren
9. John Saxon Sen'r	19. Rob't Cuningham	29. Sam'l Powell
10. Solomon Langston	20. John Hall	30. Roger Brown

Page 231: The following persons were Drawn to Serve as Grand Jurours at December Court next.

1. James Young	11. William Harris
2. Robert Cuningham	12. Arthur Durham
3. John Brown Sen'r	13. Wm Griffin
4. Reubin Pyles	14. Ed'w Mitchusson
5. John McClintock	15. Tandy Walker
6. James Craig	16. Lewis Banton
7. Thomas McCrary	17. George Hollingsworth
8. Thomas Fakes	18. George Young
9. Joshua Saxon	19. Rich'd Pugh
10. Shadrach Martin	20. Nehemiah Franks

George Walker Esq'r Produced in Open Court a Credential signed by the Hon'ble John Rutledge, Edanus Burke and Henry Pendleton, Esq'r, Judges of the Court of Common pleas of this State admitting him the said George Walker to practice as an attorney at Law in any of the courts of Law or Equity in this State, Whereupon it was Ordered that he the said George Walker be enroled as such in this County.

The Last will and Testament of James McCain Dec'd was presented in open Court by Elizabeth McCain the Executrix therein named & proven by John Hollingsworth one of the Witnesses thereto and ordered to be Recorded.

On Motion of the said Elizabeth McCain Executrix afores'd it was Ordered that Letters Testamentary Isue in form she being first Duly Qualified according to Law.

LAURENS COUNTY SC COURT MINUTES 1786-1789

[9 June 1788]

Ordered that a Warrant of Appraisement Issue to four freeholders who being first Sworn before some on Justice of the peace of this County to praise the Estate of the s'd Jas McCain and Return a copy of the s'd Appraisment to the s'd Ext'rx within forty days.

Page 232: Solomon Langston is Appointed Overseer of that part of the high way Leading from Aron Lynch's to the Charleston Road in the place of Aron Lynch. Ordered that he cause the several free male Inhabitants and Slaves Contagious [sic] to & convenient to said Road to Work thereon & keep the same in Good repair for one year as the Law Directs.

David Bailey is Appointed Overseer of that part of the high way Leading from Taylor's path to Cargill's Path in the place of Hugh Young. Ordered that he cause the several free male Inhabitants and Slaves Contagious [sic] to & convenient to said Road to Work thereon & keep the same in Good repair for one year as the Law Directs.

The following persons were Drawn to serve as Constables at this Court To wit John Milam, Jno Owins, John Entrekin.

A Deed of Gift from Mary Edwards to James & John Edwards proven heretofore by the oath of John Neily & now proven by the oath of Joseph Nealy & Ordered to be Recorded.

A Deed from And'w Cuningham to Spencer Bobo for the Conveyance of 100 acres of land proven in open Court by James & Elizabeth Cuningham & Ordered to be Recorded.

Whereas there was formerly a Deed of Conveyance of 190 acres of land from David Allison to Thomas Palmore presented in open Court and proven by the oath of Sam'l Whorton & ordered to ly for further proof. Declared that the s'd Order be Receeded from.

An account of the Administration of the estate of Cha's Edwards dec'd was Returned in open Court by William Craig the Administrator of the s'd Estate & Ordered to be Recorded.

Page 233: Court adjourned till Tomorro morning nine Oclock. Minets Signed by Joseph Downs, Silvanus Walker, Angus Campbell, Esq'rs.

Court met according to Adjournment the 10th day of June 1788. Present James Montgomery, Charles Saxon, Joseph Downs, Esq'rs.

Jacob Manor is appointed Overseer of that part of the highway leading from Durbins Creek to the Beverdam Creek in the place of Martin Williams; Orderd that he the s'd Jacob Manor cause the several free male Inhabitents contagious [sic] to & Convenient to said Road to work thereon & keep the same in good Repair for one year as the Law Directs.

[10 June 1788]

A Lease and Release for the Conveyance of 247 acres of land from Hasting Dial & Rebekah his wife to John Swearings acknowledged in open Court & Ordered to be Recorded.

John Gray vs Saml Ewing. Special action on the Case. The parties mutually submitted the Determination of this Suit to Robert McCrary & James Montgomery & agreed that their award thereupon should be made a Judgm't of this Court. The said Arbitrators now Returning their Award in these words; to wit, that the s'd Saml Ewing pay to him the s'd John Gray at or before the first day of October Ensuing the Date hereof the sum of £10 s17 sterling money, and also to pay all the Lawfull Court Charges that has Occurred upon the said Suit Conserning a Negro wench Whereupon it was Considered by the court that the s'd Plft Recover against the said Deft the s'd sum of £10 s17 & his Cost in his behalf Expended.

Silv's Walker vs Jo's Griffin & Mary Griffin. In Debt. On Motion of the pltf this suit is Ordered to be Dismist at his Cost.

Page 234: Here present Angus Campbell, Esq'r.

Sarah Jones Infant orphan of John Jones dec'd with the approbation of the Court made Choice of John Adair as her Guardian, who Together with Joseph Adair his Security entered into & acknowledged their Bonds in the sum of £100 conditional to secure the said Orphans Estate & Indemnify the Court.

Joseph Adair vs Wm Dean. Sum'r. Trover. Continued by Consent till next Court.

Patrick Cuningham vs Sarah Ward. In Debt. Continued by Consent Till next Court.

Anthony Griffin is appointed Overseer over that part of the highway Leading from Mill Creek to Little River Bridge in the place of Jacob R. Brown. Ordered that he the said Anthony Griffin cause the several free male Inhabitants and Slaves Contagious [sic] to & convenient to said Road to Work thereon & keep the same in Good repair for one year.

William Boyce vs John Watts. T. A. Battery. Discontinued at Mutual Cost.

John Walker vs Saml Ewing. Trover. The parties mutually Submitted the Determination of this suit to Reubin Roland & Micajah Bennet and agreed that there award thereupon should be made a Judgment of this Court. the said

Arbitrators now Returned their Award upon Which it was Considered that the said Suit be Dismist at the Plts Cost.

[10 June 1788]

Pyles & McNees vs John Boyd. Sum'r Process. Discontinued at Plfts. Cost.

Page 235: James McNess vs Reubin Pyles. Detinue. Continued by Consent till next Court.

Fielding Woodroof vs Shadrach Martin & Michael Waldrop. S. Process. Debt. Judgement according to Specialty with Cost.

Reubin Pyles vs James McNees. Case. Continued by Consent till next Court.

A Bond from Wm. Sims to James Waldrop bearing date the 13th day of Novr 1773 Conditioned to make titles to a tract of 550 acres of land proven in Open Court by the oath of Chas Griffin and Ordered to be Recorded.

Peter Carnes vs Joseph South. S. Process Debt. Continued by Consent at Plfts Cost.

Thomas Murphey adm'r of Greer vs John Williams. S. Process Case. The Deft. Comes into Court & pleads payment which he proves to the Court. Whereupon it was Considered by the Court that the S'd Pltf Taking nothing by his bill but for his false Clamour be in mercy & that the Deft go hence without Day & Recover against the s'd pltf his cost in his behalf expended.

Isaac Crowther assignee of Yancey vs William Pugh. The Deft Comes into Court & Confesses Judgement for the sum of £16 s6 d3 with Stay of Execution till the first Day of December next.

Page 236: A Deed from Mary Williams to Elizabeth Tinsley for the Conveyance of Several Negroes therein named proven according to Law & Ordered to be Recorded.

A Deed of Gift from Joseph Griffin & Mary his wife to James and Washington Williams Acknowledged in open Court & Ordered to be Recorded.

A Deed of Gift from Joseph Griffin & Mary his wife to John Williams Acknowledged in open Court & Ordered to be Recorded.

A Bill of Sale from Mary Williams to John Williams acknowledged in Open Court and Ordered to be Recorded.

An account of the administration of the Estate of John Simmons dec'd was Returned into Court by Nancy Simmons the Adm'rx of said Estate & was Received by the Court & Ordered to be Recorded.

LAURENS COUNTY SC COURT MINUTES 1786-1789

[10 June 1788]

James Pucket vs Joseph Adair. Slander. The Parties mutually Submitted the Determination of this Suit to the award of Saml Saxon, John Hunter & Samuel Ewing & Agreed their Award thereupon should be made a Judgem't of this Court the said Arbitrators now Returning their Award to wit, that the s'd James Pucket Pltff & the said Joseph Adair Deft pay Each one their own Cost, Whereupon it was ordered to be Dismis'd accordingly.

Saml Ewing vs Boling Byshop. Trover. The Parties mutually Submitted the Determination of this Suit to the award of Ja's Montgomery, Robert Hanna, John Hunter & Samuel Saxon & Agreed their Award thereupon should be made a Judgem't of this Court the said Arbitrators now Returning their Award in these words, to wit, that the s'd Saml Ewing Do Discontinue the Action brought against the said Roling Bishop in the County Court of Laurens at the Cost of him the said Saml Ewing &c, Whereupon it was ordered accordingly.

Page 237: Martha Boyd vs Andrew Rodgers Junr. In Debt. Abraham Boyd comes into Court & undertakes for the Pltf that in Case she should be Cast in this Suit that he will pay the whole of the Cost of s'd Suit.

On application of James Thurston a blind man & on Examination was found to be a proper Object of Charity in Consideration whereof it is ordered that the County Treasurer pay unto him the s'd James Thurston as soon as any Publick money shall come into his office the sum of £5.

William Hanna vs Benjn Rainey. In Trover. This day came the Parties by their Atto's and Thereupon came also a Jury to wit, Joshua Nobles, Charles Brodey, Joel Burgess, Jacob Right, John Sims, David Allison, Saml Hall, John Hughes, Roger Murphey, Abel Boling, Wm. Sims & Wm Donnahoe who being Elected tried and Sworn the truth to speak upon the Issue Joined upon their Oaths do Say that the Deft is Guilty of the Trover & Conversion in the Declaration mentioned & they do assess the Plts Damages by Occation thereof to £20, Whereupon it was Considered by the Court that the Plt Recover against the said Deft his Damages aforesaid in form afores'd assest & his Cost by him in this behalf Expended.

On application of Roger Brown on oath a Witness for the Pltf against the said Deft Ordered that the sum of 27 shillings & 6 pence for Eleven days attendance at 2/6 P'r day be Taxed in the Bill of Cost against the Deft.

Also that the sum of 32 shillings & 6 pence be taxed in the bill of Cost for Robert Hanna Junr a Witness for the Pltf against the s'd Deft for 13 Days Attendance at 2/6 P'r Day.

Also the sum of 40 shillings for John Hall a witness for the Pltf against the s'd Deft for Sixteen days attendance at 2/6 P'r Day.

LAURENS COUNTY SC COURT MINUTES 1786-1789

Page 238: [10 June 1788]

Robert McCrary vs James Jones. Attachment. The Pltf formerly Obtained a Judgement of this Court Against the said Defendant, On application of the said Robert McCrary Pltf it is ordered that a tract of land attached by the said Robert McCrary the property of the s'd James Jones Deft be by the Sheriff Exposed to Publick Sale after being Duly Advertised for Cash or paper medium & the money arising from such sale pay unto the said Robert McCrary Towards Satisfaction of the Judgment obtained as afores'd for the sum of ------ the Overplus if any there be Return to the Deft.

A Lease & Release for the Conveyance of 114 acres of land from Saml Neighbours to Abraham Box acknowledged in open Court and Ordered to be Recorded.

Martha Boyd vs Andrew Rodgers Junr. Sumr Process in Debt. This day came the parties by their attorneys and after Several Witnesses being Sworn & Examined upon the premises & the Council heard on both sides the Court Decreed that the Pltff take nothing by her bill but for her false Clamour be in Mercy &c. & that the Deft go hence without Day & Recover against the s'd Deft his Cost by him in the behalf Expended.

On motion made on oath by Abraham Neighbours a Witness for the Deft against the said Pltf Ordered that the sum of five shillings be taxed in the bill of Cost against the s'd Pltf for Two Days Attendance at @ 2/6 P'r Day.

Court Adjourned till Tomorrow Mourning Eight OClock. Minets singed by John Hunter, Joseph Downs, Charles Saxon, Angus Campbell, Esquires.

Page 239: Court met according to Adjournment the 11th day of June 1788. Present John Hunter, James Montgomery, Angus Campbell, George Anderson, Esq'rs.

Wadsworth & Turpin vs Sarah Cargill. Attachment Case. This day came the Pltf by T. H. P. Carnes his Attorney and the Deft being against Sollomly called but Came not and thereupon came also a Jury to wit, Joshua Nobles, Charles Brodey, Joel Burgess, Jacob Wright, David Allison, Saml Hall, John Hughes, Roger Murphey, Abel Boling, Wm. Sims, Abraham Neighbours, James Wells & Joel Burgess who being Elected tried and Sworn well and truly to Inquire of Damages in this Suit upon their Oaths do Say that the Pltf hath Sustained Damages by Occation of the nonperformance of the promises & Assumptions in the Declaration mentioned to the sum of £29 s2 together with his Cost, Therefore it is Considered by the Court that the Plt Recover against the said Deft his Damage afores'd in form afores'd assest & his Cost by him in this behalf Expended.

LAURENS COUNTY SC COURT MINUTES 1786-1789

[11 June 1788]

John Simpson vs Sarah Cargill. Attm't Case. This day Came the Plft by his Attorney & the Deft tho Solemnly [called] Came not Whereupon it was Considered by the Court that a Judgement be entered Against the s'd Deft for what Damages the s'd Pltf hath Sustained by Occation of the nonperformance of the promises & Assumptions in the Declaration mentioned to be Inquired of by a Jury unless the said Deft appear & plead to Issue Immediately.

Page 240: John Simpson vs Sarah Cargill. Attm't Case. This day came the Pltf by James Yancey his Att'o & the Deft being against Solemnly called but came not & thereupon came also a Jury to wit, Joshua Nobles, Charles Brodey, Jacob Wright, David Allison, Saml Hall, John Hughes, Roger Murphey, Abel Boling, Wm. Sims, Abraham Neighbours, James Wells, & Joel Burgess who being well & Truly to Inquire of Damages in this suit upon their Oaths do Say that the Pltf hath sustained Damages by Occation of the nonperformance of the promises & assumptions in the Declaration mentioned to £15 s12 d1 besides his cost, Whereupon it was Considered by the Court that the Plt Recover against the said Deft his Damages aforesaid in form afores'd assest & his Cost by him in this behalf Expended.

Ordered that the property of Sarah Cargill late of this County attached at the Suit of Wadsworth & Tirpin & John Simpson be by the Sheriff Exposed to publick sale being first Duly Advertised for Cash or paper medium & The money arising from such sale pay unto the said Wadsworth & Tirpin & John Simpson Towards Satisfaction of the Judgements which they the s'd Wadsworth & Tirpin & John Simpson lately in this County Court obtained against the s'd Sarah Cargill & the overplus if any there be Return to the s'd Sarah Cargill.

Thomas Black vs Wm Ragsdale. In Debt. This day came the parties by their attorneys & the Defendant Sayeth that he cannot gainsay the Plfts action for the sum of £5 with Cost & Stay of Execution six months therefore with the assent of the s'd pltf it is Considered by the Court that s'd Pltf Recover against the s'd Deft the said sum of £5 & his Cost by him in his behalf Expended & the s'd Deft in Mercy &c.

Angus Campbell vs John Kellet. Trover. Continued by Consent till next Court.

Page 241: Martin Williams vs Howloway Power. Sumr Process. In Debt. The Court after hearing the parties by their attorneys decreed that the Pltf recover against the s'd Deft the sum of £12 Virginia money dollars at six shillings and six pence each & that the above Judgement be paid according to the Installment act.

Robert Cooper vs Rich'd Carrol. Sum'r Process. Case. Continued by Consent till next Court.

LAURENS COUNTY SC COURT MINUTES 1786-1789

[11 June 1788]

William Shaw vs Bartholomew Craddock & Sarah Craddock. Sum'r Process. Debt. This day came the parties by their attorneys & Plts action for the sum ----- according to note with Stay of execution three months, Therefore with the assent of the Plts it is Considered by the Court that the said Pltf Recover against the said Deft the afores'd sum of ----- & his Cost by him in this behalf Expended.

A Lease & Release for the Conveyance of 80 acres of Land from George Berry to Wm Berry acknowledged in open Court and Ordered to be recorded.

Robert Fariss vs William Austin. In Debt. Continued by Consent till next Court.

Page 242: Henry Myers vs Clem't Davis. Trespass. Assault & Battery. This day came the Parties by their Attorneys & thereupon came also a Jury to wit Joshua Nobles, Charles Brodey, Joel Burgess, Jacob Wright, John Sims, David Allison, Saml Hall, John Hughes, Roger Murphey, Abel Boling, Wm. Sims & Wm Donnahoe who being Elected tried and Sworn the truth to speak upon the Issue Joined upon their Oaths do Say that the Deft is Guilty of the Trespass Assault & Battery in the Declaration mentioned & they do assess the Plts Damages by Occation thereof to £10 besides his cost, Whereupon it was Considered by the Court that the Plt Recover against the said Deft his Damages aforesaid in form afores'd assest & his Cost by him in this behalf Expended and the s'd Deft in Mercy &c.

Whereas James McNees This Day Applied for Letters of Administration of all & Singular the goods & Chattles Rights & Credits of John McNees Dec'd. Ordered that a Citation Isue Siting & Admonishing the kindred and Creditors of the said John McNees to appear at the next Court to be held for this county on the second Monday in September next to shew Cause if any they have why Letters of Administration should not be Granted as afores'd.

State vs John Hutson & Saml McClurkin. Indictment. Assault. The Grand Jury Returned a true Bill.

Page 243: The State vs Ann Owins & Mary Mehaffy. Indictment Larceny. The Grand Jury Returned a True Bill.

Patrick Riley vs Wm Thomason. The parties mutually submitted the Determination of this suit to the award of Cha's Sullivan, Nathan Camp, Saml Boling & Wm. Fariss & agreed that their award thereupon should be made a Judgement of this Court the s'd Arbitrators now Returning their Award in these words To wit, that each party pay their own Cost only one half Guinea paid from s'd Riley to s'd Wm Thomason for the Guinea cost payed by Thomason Whereupon it was Ordered Accordingly.

LAURENS COUNTY SC COURT MINUTES 1786-1789

[11 June 1788]

Henry Myers vs Clem't Davis. On Motion made on oath by Josiah East a Witness for the Pltf against the s'd Deft Ordered that the sum of 37 shillings & 6 pence be taxed in the Bill of Cost against the s'd Deft for 15 days attendance at 2/6 p'r day. Also the sum of 37 shillings & 6 pence for Daniel Davis for 15 days Attendance at 2/6 P'r Day.

Andrew Rodgers, Jas Saxon, Wm. Twedy, Zachariah Bailey, David Bailey, Cha's Simmons, Cha's Allen, John Carter, Abner Babb, Wm Dendy, Dan'l Ozburn, Edmond Learwood, Absolam Bobo & Thomas Boyce were Sworn Grand Jurours of Inquest for the Body of the County after having Received their Charge retired from the Bar to Consult of their Verdict & after some time Returned into Court & presented as follows. [blank]

Page 244: The State vs Ann Owins & Mary Mehaffy. William Rodgers & Saml Saxon comes into Court & Undertakes as Security for the appearance of the s'd Defts at the next Court & Acknowledged themselves Indebted to the State in the sum of £50 to be levied of their Respective Goods & Chattles, provided the s'd Defts do not appear as afores'd Wm. Rodgers, Saml Saxon, So. B. The s'd Defts by Thos P. Carnes their Attorney traversed the Indictment till next Court.

The State vs John Hutson & Saml McClurkin. Indictment. The Defts Traversed the Indictments till next Court Ordered that the Recognizance be Cont'd till then.

State vs Edmond Dickes. Indictment. Ordered that a Scire facias Issue on the Recognizance.

Wm Young vs James McNees & Hugh Young. Continued by Consent till next Court.

Nathan Camp vs Joseph Mahon. In Debt. Continued by Consent till next Court.

Mary Williams vs Jos Goodman. Continued by Consent till next Court.

James Dillard vs Clem't Davis. Slander. Continued by Consent till next Court.

Page 245: Thomas Duggan vs John Madden. In Trover. This day came the parties by their attorneys & thereupon came also a Jury to wit, Joshua Nobles, Cha's Brodey, Joel Burgess, Jacob Wright, John Sims, David Allison, Saml Hall, John Hughes, Roger Murphey, Abel Boling, Wm. Sims & Will'm Donnahoe who being Elected tried and Sworn the truth to speak upon the Issue Joined upon their Oaths do Say that the Deft is Guilty of the Trover & Conversion in the Declaration mentioned & they do assess the Plts Damages by Occation thereof to £15 besides his cost, Whereupon it was Considered by the Court that the Plt Recover against the said Deft his Damages aforesaid in form afores'd assest & his Cost by him in this behalf Expended and the s'd Deft in Mercy &c.

[11 June 1788]

On motion made on oath by George Akins a Witness for the Pltf against the s'd Deft. Ordered that the sum of 27 shillings & 6 pence be Taxed in the bill of Cost at this Court also the sum of 25 shillings for Milage for Going & Coming three times 25 miles out of Newberry County. Also the sum of five shillings for Wm Gray for Two days attendance at 2/6 p'r Day. Also for milage for Going & Coming 25 miles the sum Eight shillings & four pence at 2d p'r mile. Also the sum of 25 shillings for John Entrekin a witness in s'd suit for 6 Days attendance at 2/6 p'r Day.

Also the sum of 27 shillings & 6 pence for Benj'n Kilgore a Witness in s'd suit for 11 days attendance at 2/6 P'r Day. Also the sum of 22 shillings & 6 pence for Robt McCrary a Witness in s'd suit for 9 days attendance at 2/6 P'r Day.

Ordered that process Isue against the Several persons presented by the Grand Jury at this Court to appear at the next Court to answer the same.

Page 246: State vs Wm Duke. Indictment. Bastardy. The said Wm Duke Deft Comes into Court & Confessed himself to be the father of a Bastard Child begotten on the body of Jane McDavid & Throw'd himself upon the mercy of the Court. After Due Deliberation had on the premises it was ordered that the Deft Wm Duke be find in the sum of £3 s11 & pay the Cost of prosecution.

Lewis Duvall & James Parks Comes into Court & Undertakes for the Def't Wm Duke as Security to pay the above five of £3 s11 &c.

Ordered that the s'd Wm Duke enter into bonds with two Sufficient Securities in the sum of £20 to save harmless & Indemnify the County of Laurens for the maintainance of the s'd Bastard Child.

Wm Duke, Lewis, Duvall & James Parks Comes into Court and acknowledged themselves indebted to the County in the sum of £20 to be Levied of their Respective goods & Chattles, Lands and Tenements. Yet upon Condition that the s'd Wm Duke shall & Will save harmless and Indemnify the Justices of the County Court of Laurens from the maintainance of a Bastard child begotten by the s'd Wm Duke on the body of Jane McDavid. William Dukes, Lewis Duvall. Test: Lewis Saxon, C. C.

The state vs John Penington. Indictment. Ambrose Hudgins & John Penington comes into Court & Acknowledged themselves indebted to the State in the sum of £50 to be Levied of their Respective goods and Chattles, lands & tenements. Yet upon Condition that the s'd John Penington shall & do appear

LAURENS COUNTY SC COURT MINUTES 1786-1789

at the next Court and abide by & [Page 247] perform the same & shall not depart the same till Discharg'd. John Penington, Ambrose Hudgins. Test: Lewis Saxon, C. C.

[11 June 1788]

State vs Saml Parsons. Indictment. Joseph Parsons & Saml Parsons comes into Court & Acknowledged themselves indebted to the State in the sum of £50 to be Levied of their Respective goods and Chattles, lands & tenements. Yet upon Condition that the s'd Saml Parsons shall & do appear at the next Court and abide by & Perform the same & shall not depart the same till Discharg'd. Saml Parsons, Joseph Parsons. Test: Lewis Saxon, C. C.

Jones & Smith vs Wm Thomason. Ordered that a Venditioni Exponas be Issued for the property of the said Wm. Thomason be Issued for the property of the said Wm Thomason now under execution Returned unsold for the want of Buyers.

James Yancey Esq'r was Duly Elected County attorney for one year for the County of Laurens. Ordered that he be enrol'd as Such in Record of this Court.

Joseph Gaigee vs Lewis Banton. Sum'r Process. Discontinued at Plfts. Cost.

On Application of Joseph Griffin, Executor in Right of his wife of the Estate of James Williams Dec'd, Ordered that a Warrant of Appraisement Issue to four freeholders to appraise the Estate of the said Dec'd & Return an Account of the Same to next Court.

Page 248: Ordered that all the Estrays that was Entered upon the Toal Book Before Last Court that have not been proven be by the Sheriff Exposed to publick sale after being advertised Twenty Days for Three months credit, notes to be Given with Sufficient Security.

Court Adjourned till Court in Course. Minutes Sign'd by John Hunter, Joseph Downs, Angus Campbell, Ja's Montgomery, John Rodgers, Geo: Anderson.

At a Court held for the County of Laurens on the 8th Day of September 1788. Present Jonth'n Downs, Silv's Walker, John Rodgers, John Hunter, Esq'rs.

The following persons were Drawn to serve as Pettit Jurours at the next Court to be held on the Second Monday of December next.

1. Joseph South	11. Wm Burk	21. Joseph Allison
2. Wm Higgins	12. John Grier	22. Thos Chapman
3. Joseph Blakely	13. Wm Burton	23. Joseph Hollingsworth Senr
4. Ab'm Box	14. Joseph Pinson	24. Wm Rainey
5. Saml Saxon So Chs	15. John Williams	25. George Wigginton

LAURENS COUNTY SC COURT MINUTES 1786-1789

6. Micheal Box
7. Wm Davis
8. Memk'n Walker
9. John Garret
10. Jno Cuningham Junr

16. Tho's Logan
17. Rich'd Dixon
18. Stephen Plant
19. Rob't Faris
20. Hardy Canant

26. Angus Campbell Sen'r
27. John Rainey
28. Wm Boyd
29. And'w Owins
30. Joseph Rammage

[8 September 1788]

Ordered that John Coker & Saml Parsons attend as Constables at this Court.

A Power of Attorney from Ebenezer Starns to Jacob Bowman Acknowledged in open Court & Ordered to be Recorded.

Page 249: A Deed from John Henderson to Mary Henderson for the Conveyance of 150 acres of land Acknowledged in open Court & Ordered to be recorded.

Thomas Murphey vs Wm Thomason. In Debt. Dismist at Defts Cost.

John Walker adm'r of Pamplin dec'd vs Thos Cargill & And'w Rodgers Junr. In Debt. And'w Rodgers one of the Defts Comes into Court & Confessed Judgement for the sum of £17 Virginia currency equal to £13 4 10½ Sterling together with Cost. The Pltf agrees to stay execution six months.

An Account of the Estate of James McCain Dec'd was presented in open Court by Elizabeth McCain the Executrix & ordered to be recorded.

A Lease & Release for the conveyance of 100 acres of land from John Waldrop to Seth Petty Pool Acknowledged in open Court & Ordered to be Recorded.

Charles Saxon vs John Cargill Sen'r. S. Process. Debt. The Court after hearing the Parties Decreed that the Deft pay unto the Pltf the sum of £4 s4 d8 with Interest from the 15th day of Jan'y last & Cost of Suit.

A Power of Attorney from George Hollingsworth to Benj'n Grubbs Acknowledged in open Court and Ordered to be recorded.

A Copy of Wm Drew's will was presented in Open Court & Ordered to be Recorded

James McNees vs John Cargill & Wm Rodgers so And'w. S. Process in Debt. The Court after hearing the parties Decreed that the Defts pay unto the Pltf the sum of £5 s12 d10 with Interest & Cost of Suit.

A Lease & Release from Abijah Oneal to Jonth'n Johnston for the Conveyance of 75 acres of Land proven heretofore to Jo's Armstrong now ordered to be Recorded.

LAURENS COUNTY SC COURT MINUTES 1786-1789

Page 250: Court adjourned till Tomorrow 9 OClock. Minets singed by Johnth'n Downs, Charles Saxon, John Rodgers, Angus Campbell, John Hunter, Esquires.

Court met according to Adjournment the 9th of Sept'r 1788. Present Jonth'n Downs, John Hunter, Cha's Saxon, John Rodgers, Esq'rs.

A Quit Claim from John Bowles to Thomas Rodgers acknowledged in open Court & ordered to be recorded.

A Lease & Release for the Conveyance of 130 acres of Land from Luke Waldrop & Mary his wife to Wm East Jun'r Proven in open Court by Wm. East & Shadrach East & Ordered to be Recorded.

Robert Faris vs Nathaniel Austin. In Debt. This Day came the parties by Their Attorneys & therefore came also a Jury to wit: Joseph Waldrop, James Higgins, James Pucket, John Todd, Wm. Willson, John Saxon, Solomon Langston, Silas Garret, John Gray, James Strain, Stokes Edwards & John Willson who being Elected Tried & Sworn the Truth to Speak upon the Issue Joined upon their oaths Do find for the Pltf the sum of £14 with Interest & Cost; Whereupon it was considered by the Court that the s'd Pltf recover against the Deft the s'd sum of £14 with Interest & Cost of Suit.

On application of Clabourn Sims for Letters of Administration of all & Singular the Estate of Wm Sims Dec'd, ordered that a Citation Issue Siting & Admonishing all the kindred & Creditors of the said Wm Sims dec'd to appear at our next Court to be [Page 251] held on the second Monday in Decm'r next, to shew cause if any that have why Letters of Administration should not be granted as afores'd.

John Blalock vs Thos McDanald. Attachment. Ordered to stand Over.

Jean Tolds vs Joseph Goodman. Continued by Consent till next Court.

Mary Williams vs Robert Tombs. Continued by Consent till next Court.

Wm Young vs Jas McNees & Hugh Young. In Debt. Continued till next Court.

A Power of Attorney from Mary Babb to Peter Ruble acknowledged in open Court & Ordered to be Recorded.

Nathan Camp Pltf vs Joseph Mahon Deft. In Debt. This day came the Parties by their Attorneys & Thereupon Came also a Jury to wit, Jo's Waldrop, James Higgins, James Pucket, John Todd, Wm. Willson, John Hall, Solomon Langston, Silas Garret, John Gray, James Strain, Stokes Edwards & John Willson who being Elected Tried & Sworn the Truth to Speak upon the Issue Joined upon their oaths Do find for the Pltf the sum of £120 old currency with

Interest & Cost of Suit; Whereupon it was considered by the Court that the s'd Pltf recover against the Deft the s'd sum of £120 old Currency with Interest & Cost of Suit.

[9 September 1788]

Robert Retherford vs Robt H. Hughes & John Archer Elmore. In Debt. The Defendants Comes into Court & Confesses Judgment for the sum of £44 s18 d8, Whereupon it was Considered by the Court that [**Page 152**] the said Pltf Recover against the s'd Defts the s'd sum of £44 s18 d8 Together with Interest & Cost of Suit.

Mary Williams Extx of J. Williams Decd. vs Joseph Goodman. In Trover. This day came the Parties by their Attorneys & Thereupon Came also a Jury to wit, John Saxon, Jo's Hollingsworth, Jo's Williams, John Cammock, Michael Waldrop, John Lindsey, Wm. Suter, Ja's Gammel, Sam'l Powell, Roger Brown, Joseph Parsons & David Allison who being Elected Tried & Sworn the Truth to Speak upon the Issue Joined upon their oaths Do say that the Deft is not Guilty of the Trover & Convertion in the Declaration mentioned & that the Pltf Take Nothing by his Bill but for his false Clamour be in mercy &C & that the Deft. Go hence without Day & recover against the said Pltf his Cost in this Suit in his behalf expended & C.

On application of Moriah Goodman a Witness for the said Deft against the said Plts ordered that the Pltf Pay her the sum of 15 shillings for 6 days Attendance at 2/6 P'r Day.

Also the sum of 27/6 for Thos Duggin for 11 Days Attendance at 2/6 p'r Day with mileage for Going & Coming 25 Miles 4 Times at 2d pr Mile.

Also to Capt. John Wallace the sum of 32/6 for 13 Days Attendance at 2/6 Pr. Day with Mileage for Going & Coming 25 Miles 7 times at 2d pr Mile.

On Motion of affidavit filed, Ordered that an attachment Issue Returnable Immediately to Compell the Attendance of Gracy Bailey, Charity Bailey & Martha Stean for Disobedience to a Subpoena Issued at the Instance of Ann Owins & Mary Mehaffy at the suit of the State.

Page 253: Curtis Moore vs John Conner & Martin Martin. In Debt. The Defendants Comes into Court & Sayeth that they cannot Gainsay the Plfts action for 2000 weight of Tobacco at Two Dollars & a half Pr Hundred which Doth amount to £11 s13 d4 with Interest from the Date of the note. Whereupon it was Considered by the court that the said Plft recover against the said Defts the said sum of £11 13/4 Together with his Cost by him in his behalf Expended.

An account of the Estate of James Williams Dec'd was presented into Open Court by Joseph Griffin the adm'r & ordered to be Recorded.

LAURENS COUNTY SC COURT MINUTES 1786-1789

[9 September 1788]

Nathan Camp be Joseph Mahon. In Debt. On application of James Brock a Witness for Pltf against the Deft Ordered that the Deft pay him the sum of Ten shillings for 4 days Attendance at 2/6 Pr Day with Milage for Going & Coming 40 Miles 3 times.

Also to John Saxon the sum of £13 s17 d6 for 31 Days Attendance at 2/6 Pr day.

Also to Rich'd Collins the sum of £3 s5 for 26 Days Attendance at 2/6 Pr day with Mileage for Going & Comeing 30 Miles 6 times at 2d Pr mile.

The Last will and testament of Haunce Miller Dec'd was proven in Open Court by the oaths of Thos Ewing & Joseph Adair & ordered to be Recorded.

Peter Carnes vs Joseph South. S. Process. Debt. The court after hearing the parties decreed that the Deft Pay unto the Pltf the sum of £3 s5 d3 Together with his cost by him in his behalf Expended & the s'd Deft in Mercy &c.

Page 254: Peter Carnes vs Joseph South. On Motion made on oath by Benj'n Clarday a Witness for the Deft against the s'd Pltf Ordered that the s'd Deft pay him the sum of 7/6 for 3 days Attendance at 2/6 Pr day.

Also the sum of 12/6 to John Saxon for 5 Days Attendance at 2/6 Pr Day.

Court Adjourned till Tomorrow morning Nine Oclock. Minets Signd by James Montgomery, John Rodgers, Wm. Michusson, Angus Campbell, Esq'rs.

Court met according to Adjournment the 10th September 1788. Present Jonth'n Downs, Ja's Montgomery, John Hunter, Angus Campbell, Esquires.

Rosanna Glen vs Reubin Flanagan. In Debt. Continued by Consent till next Court.

John Chapman vs Wm. Lowery. Attm't. Wm Goodman & James Goodman came into Court & undertakes for the Deft as Special Bail that in Case the s'd Deft should be cast in this suit, that they will pay the cost & Condemnation of the Court: or render their Bodys in Discharge thereof to Prison or they will Pay the Cost & Condemnation of the Court for him &c.

Page 255: Charles Harvey vs Wm Goodman. In Debt. This day came the Parties by there Attorneys & Thereupon came also a Jury to wit: Joseph Waldrop, James Higgins, James Pucket, John Tod, Wm. Willson, John Hall, Solomon Langston, Silas Garret, John Gray, Ja's Strain, Stokes Edwards & John Willson who being Elected Tried & Sworn the Truth to Speak upon the Issue Joined went out of court to Consult of their Verdict & being Return'd into Court to Render the same; the Plft were solemnly calld but came not

Neither is his suit further Prosecuted, Whereupon motion of the Deft it is considered by the Court that the Jurours from Rendering their Verdict be Discharged & that the Pltf be nonsuited & c & that the said Deft go hence without Day & recover his Cost by him in his behalf expended in s'd Suit.

[10 September 1788]

On motion made on oath by Margaret Proctor a Witness for the Plft against the s'd Deft, Ordered that the Plft pay her the sum of Ten Shillings for 4 days attendance at 2/6 Pr Day with Mileage for Going 20 Miles twice at 2d pr mile.

Also to Robt Gillam the sum of 5/ for 2 Days attendance at 2/6 Pr da with Mileage for Going & Comeing 20 Miles one at 2d Pr Mile.

The Last Will & Testament of Wm Millwee Decd was proven in open Court by the oaths of George Ross & James Henderson & Ordered to be recorded.

James Dillard vs Clement Davis. In Slander. This day Came the Parties by their attorneys & thereupon came also a Jury to wit: John Saxon, Joseph Hollingsworth, Robert Taylor, John Cammock, Micheal Waldrop, John Lindsey, Wm. Suter, James Gammell, Saml Powell, Roger Brown, Joseph Parsons, David Allison, who being Elected Tried & Sworn the Truth to Speak upon the Issued Joined upon their oaths do say that the Deft is Guilty of the Slander in the Declaration mentioned **[Page 256]** in manner & form as the Plft against him has Declared & that the Plft hath Sustained Damages by Occation thereof to the amount of £4 besides his Cost, Whereupon it was Considered by the Court that the s'd Pltf recover against the s'd Deft his Damages afores'd in form afores'd Asses'd & her cost by him in this behalf Expended & The s'd Deft in Mercy &c.

On application on oath of Saml Ewing a Witness for the Pltf against the said Deft Ordered that the Deft Pay him the sum of £2 s12 d6 for 21 Days attendance at 2/6 Pr day.

Also to John Walker the sum of £3 s2 d6 for 25 days attendance at 2/6 Pr day.

Also to Wm Hunter the sum of 25 shillings for 10 days attendance at 2/6 Pr Day.

Mary Burns vs David Allison. In Trover. This Day Came the Deft by James Yancey & Wm. Shaw his Attorneys & moved for a nonsuit for that as this action was Commenc'd by the Plft as Adm'rx of John Burns decd & upon Craving oyer of the Letters of Administration it appears that James Burns was a Joint admr; the Court then overruled the pleas & ordered the Defts Atto' to plead the Gen'l issue. The reason of the Court refusing to let the Deft Plead Specialty was that upon the Oath of Mary Burns admr'x of John Burns dec'd it appeared that James Burns mentioned in the Letters of adm'n was never Qualafied as an Admr nor Gave Security as such; but that he was a

LAURENS COUNTY SC COURT MINUTES 1786-1789

Minor & the Def'ts att'o sayd he would likewise Take advantage if the Action was brought in both their names' The deft then Pled the Gen'l Issue. & Thereupon came a Jury to wit. Joseph Waldrop, James Higgins, James Pucket, John Todd, Wm. Willson, John Hall, Solomon Langston, Silas Garret, John Gray, James Strain, Stokes Edwards & John Willson who being Elected Tried [Page 257] & Sworn the Truth to Speak upon the Issue Joined upon their oaths Do say that the Deft is Guilty of the Trover & Convertion in the Declaration mentioned & they do assess the Plft Damages by occation thereof to the sum of £10 s20 together with his cost; Whereupon it was considered by the Court that the s'd Pltf recover against the Deft the Damages afores'd in form assessed & her Cost by her in her Behalf expended and the s'd Deft in Mercy &c.

James Dillard broke the Peace in the Court Yard by Assaulting Clement Davis; the said James Dillard comes into Court & throws his self upon the mercy of the same. Ordered that the s'd James Dillard pay a fine of five shillings.

Court adjourned till tomorrow morning 9 OClock. Minets signed by Jonth'n Downs, John Hunter, John Rodgers, Angus Campbell, Esq'rs.

Court met according to Adjournment the 11th day of Sept'r 1788. Present Ja's Montgomery, Jonth'n Downs, John Hunter, Charles Saxon, Silv's Walker, Esq'rs.

Thomas Chappell vs James Peterson. Writ Case. Discontinued at Plft. Cost.

Ditto vs Ditto. S. Process Case. Discontinued at Deft. Cost.

Page 258: Dan'l Jackson vs Benj'n Kilgore & Ed'w Mitchusson, exor of Drury Tue. In Debt. The Defts Comes into Court & Says that they Cannot Gainsay the Plft Action for the sum of £300 old currency. Whereupon it was considered by the Court that the said Pltf recover against the Deft the s'd sum of £300 old Currency & his Cost by him in his behalf Expended & the s'd Deft. in Mercy &c.

Lancelot Armstrong vs Benj'n Kilgore. In Debt. Continued by Consent Till next Court.

Susanna Man vs Isia Greer, Jas Greer & Jno Jones. In Trespass. Continued by Consent Till next Court.

James Little vs Esabella Hancock. In Trover. By Consent this Suit is Ordered to be Dismist at Plfts Cost.

Thos Lewis vs Wm Murphey. Attm't. On application of the Pltf. it is ordered that a Commission Issue to Two or more of the Justices in Greenville County to Examine & Take the Deposition of Wm. Choice & George Martin

Witnesses in this suit in behalf of the Plft. & That They return the said Commission of Deposition to our next Court there to be Read in Evidence in this Suit. The Pltf is ordered to Give the Deft ten Days notice of the time & Place of Such Examination.

[11 September 1788]

Page 259: Susanna Man vs John Rammage. In Trover. The Parties Mutually Submitted the Determination of this suit to the award of James Craig, Bazzle Prator & Thos Ewing & Agreed their Award thereupon should be made a Judgement of this Court. Ordered that the s'd Arbitrators return their award to next court.

Ch'as Bradey vs Thos Allison. In Slander. The Parties Mutually Submitted the Determination of this suit to the award of Silv's Walker, Sam Whorton, James Abercrumbie & George Hollingsworth with Leave of Impirage & Agreed their Award thereupon should be made a Judgement of this Court. Ordered that the s'd Arbitrators return their award to next court.

Reubin Pyles vs Jas McNees. In Case. Continued by Consent till Next Court.

James McNees vs Reubin Pyles. Slander. Continued by Consent till Next Court.

Same vs Same. Detinue. Continued by Consent till Next Court.

The State vs Ann Owins & Mary Mehaffy. Indictm't. Larceny. This day came the Parties by their Attorneys & thereupon came also a Jury to wit Robt Hanna, Robt Taylor, Joseph Williams, John Cammock, Micheal Waldrop, John Lindsey, Wm. Suter, Chas Brodey, Hugh Young, Roger Brown, Joseph Parsons & Solomon Langston, Who being Elected Tired & Sworn the truth to speak upon the Issued Joined upon their oaths do say that the Deft is not Guilty as in the Indictment alledged, Whereupon it was Considered the Court that the [**Page 260**] Pltf recover against the said Deft her Cost by her in her Behalf Expended in this Suit & the Deft in Mercy &c.

State vs John Pennington. Indictm't. Assault & Battery. Continued till next Court at Deft Cost & the former Recognizance Continued by the Court.

State vs Saml Parsons. Indictm't. Continued till next Court at Deft Cost & the former Recognizance Continued by the Court.

Shadrach Martin vs Saml Farrow. In Trover. This day came the Parties by their Attorneys & thereupon Came also a Jury to wit, Joseph Waldrop, James Higgins, James Pucket, John Tod, Wm. Willson, John Hall, John Saxon, Silas Garret, John Gray, James Strain, Stokes Edwards & John Willson who being Elected Tried & Sworn the Truth to Speak upon the Issue Joined upon their Oaths Do say that the Deft is Guilty of the Trover & Conversion in the

LAURENS COUNTY SC COURT MINUTES 1786-1789

Declaration mentioned & they do assess the Plft Damages by Occation thereof the sum of £15 besides his Cost, Whereupon it was Considered by the Court that the s'd Plft recover against the s'd Deft his Damages afores'd in form afores'd assessed & his Cost by him in his behalf expended in s'd Suit & the s'd Deft in Mercy &c.

[11 September 1788]

The Defts att'o moved for a new Trial. Ordered to be Taken into Consideration in the Morning.

In the suit Shadrach Martin vs Saml Farrow; John Gray on his oath as a Witness in s'd suit say'd that at the holding of the first court held at Ninety Six after the avacuation of the same he heard Landon Farrow a Witness in s'd suit say that if his brother was Sued for any thing Done During the War that rather than he should suffer he would swear false & that he Could prove it.

Page 261: Shadrach Martin vs Saml Farrow. On motion made on oath by Caner Hudson a Witness for the Plft against the said Deft, Ordered that the Deft pay him the sum of 7/6 for 3 days Attendance at 2/6 Pr Day also Mileage for Coming & Going 25 Miles once at 2d pr Mile. Also to Sarah Hudson the sum of 7/6 for 3 days Attendance at 2/6 Pr Day with Mileage for Coming & Going 25 Miles once at 2d pr Mile. Also to Benj'n Kilgore the sum of 30/ for 12 Days Attendance at 2/6 Pr Day.

Wadsworth & Turpin vs Reubin Pyles. In Case. The Deft Comes into Court & Says that he Cannot Gainsay the Plft action for the sum of £12 s18 d5, Whereupon if was Considered by the Court that the s'd Pltf recover against the s'd Deft the s'd sum of £12 s18 d5 & his cost by him in his behalf Expended; the Pltf agrees to stay execution till the first day of Decem'r next.

Mary Burns vs David Allison. On motion made on oath by Absolem Johnston a Witness for the Pltf against the said Deft, Ordered that the Deft pay him the sum of 25/ for 10 Days attendance at 2/6 Pr Day.

A Power of Attorney from Sarah Right to Jacob Bowman acknowledged in open Court & Ordered to be Recorded.

David Allison vs James McNees. In Trover. The Parties Mutually Submitted the Determination of this suit to James Abercrumby, Hasting Doyall, Benjn Rainey, Saml Whorton & Lewis Duvall & Agreed their Award thereupon should be made a Judgement of this Court. Ordered that the s'd Arbitrators return their award to next court. The Pltf agrees to pay the Clerks & Sheriffs fees.

Page 262: Court Adjourned till Tomorrow morning Nine Oclock. Minets Signd by Silv's Walker, Ja's Montgomery, John Rodgers, Esq'rs.

LAURENS COUNTY SC COURT MINUTES 1786-1789

Court met according to Adjournment the 12th Sept'r 1788. Present George Anderson, Jas Montgomery, Angus Campbell, John Rodgers, Wm Mitchusson, Esq'r.

James McLaughlin vs Benj'n Kilgore. This day Came the Parties by their atto's & thereupon came also a Jury, to wit: Joseph Waldrop, James Higgins, James Pucket, John Todd, Wm. Willson, John Hall, Solomon Langston, Silas Garret, John Gray, James Strain, Stokes Edwards & John Willson who being Elected Tried & Sworn the Truth to Speak upon the Issue Joined upon their oaths Do say that the Deft is Guilty of the Trover & Convertion in the Declaration mentioned & they do assess the Plft Damages by occation thereof to the sum of £20. Whereupon it was considered by the Court that the s'd Pltf recover against the said Deft the said sum of £10 & his Cost by him in his Behalf expended.

On motion made on oath of Matthew McMillion a Witness for the Pltf against the Deft ordered that the Deft pay him the sum of 17 shillings & 6d for 7 Days Attendance at 2/6 Pr Day With Milage for Going & Coming 33 Miles twice at 2d pr mile.

Also to Alex'r McMillian the sum of 10/ for 4 Days Attendance at 2/6 Pr Day with Milage for Going & Coming 33 Miles once at 2d pr mile.

Page 263: On application of Capt. Edward Mitchusson Ordered that the Tax of £3 Due to the County from s'd Mitchusson for Tavern Licence Granted to him at Decm'r Court Last be reduced to Thirty shillings according to the rate of the act of Assembly in that case made & provided.

Edward Mitchusson vs John Arnald. Dismist at Plft Cost.

The State vs Joseph South. Indictm't. Keeping a Tavern without License. Ordered to be Dismist at Deft Cost & that he be Discharged from his recognizance.

Clement Dial vs Thos Edgehill. Continued by Consent Till next Court.

James Sullivant vs Thos Portswood. Attachm't. This day came the Pltf by his Att'o & the Deft being Solemnly Call'd but came not; Whereupon it was considered by the Court that Judgement by Default be Entered against him: to be Inquiry of by a Jury unless the s'd Deft Shall appear & plead to Issue at next Court.

John Martin vs John Wallace. In T. A. & Battery. This day came the parties by their Attorneys & Thereupon came also a Jury to wit John Saxon, Joseph Hollingsworth, Rob't Taylor, John Cammock, Micheal Waldrop, John Lindsey, Wm. Suter, James Young, Sam'l Powell, Roger Brown, Joseph Parsons & Wm Gilbert, who being Elected Tried & Sworn the Truth to Speak upon the Issue Joined upon their oaths Do say that the Deft is Guilty of the T. A. & Battery in the Declaration mentioned & they do assesst the Pltf Damages by Occation thereof to the amount of £3, Whereupon it was Considered by the Court that the s'd Pltf recover against the said Deft his Damages afores'd in form asses'd & his Cost in this Suit in his behalf expended & the s'd Deft in mercy &c.

[12 September 1788]

Page 264: John Martin vs John Wallace. On Motion made on oath by Abr'm Neighbours a Witness for the said Plft against the said Deft Ordered that the Deft pay him the sum of £3 s4 for 26 days Attendance at 2/6 Pr Day. Also to Nathaniel Hill the sum of £2 10 for 20 Days Attendance at 2/6 Pr Day.

Shadrach Martin vs Saml Farrow. In Trover. Verdict for Plft for £15 & Cost from which s'd Judgement the Deft pray'd an Appeal to the Court of Common Pleas to be held at Cambridge on the 26th day of Nov'r next which was Granted him the said Deft. Whereupon the said Deft Together with Benj'n Kilgore & Sam'l Saxon his Securities Entered Into & Acknowledged their bonds with Condition to Prosecute the said appeal with Effect.

Wm Shaw vs Wm Pugh. In Debt. This day came the Deft into Court & says that he Cannot Gainsay the Plfts action for the sum of £16 s16 d3 with Interest, Whereupon it was Considered by the Court that the said Pltf Recover against the said Deft the s'd sum of £16 s16 d3 & his Cost by him in his behalf Expended. The Plft agrees to Stay Execution till the 26th of Nov'r next.

John D. Kern vs Tho's Hutching. In Case. Continued by Consent till next Court.

Ordered that a Commission Issue to any three Justices of the peace in Charleston to Examine & take the Deposition of Tho's Singleton a Witness in this suit in behalf of the Pltf & that the return the said Deposition & Commission to our next Court there to be red in Evidence in this suit. Also a Commission to any Three Justices in Lexington County to Examine and **[Page 265]** take the Deposition of Hargrove Arthur a Witness in this Suit in behalf of the Pltf & that they return the said Deposition & Commission to our next Court there to be red in Evidence in this suit, Giving the Deft the usual Notice.

Mary Boyd vs Bat: Craddock & Mary Craddock. In Debt. This day came the Deft & the Pltf being Solemnly Call'd but came not nor is her motion of the Deft it is Considered by the court that the s'd Defts recover against the s'd Pltf five shillings Damages besides their Cost by them about their Defence Expended According to the form of the act of Assembly in that case made & provided.

On motion made on oath by Thos Dendy a Witness for the Deft against the Plft Order that he Pltf pay him the sum of 17/6 for 7 Days Attendance at 2/ Pr Day.

[12 September 1788]

John Gorely Vs Ed'w Mitchusson. Continued by Consent till next Court.

Wm Terry vs Lewis Duvall & Wm. Brown. This Day came the Defts & the Plft tho Solemnly Call'd Came not: nor is his suit further Prosecuted. Therefore on motion of the Deft it is Considered by the Court that the s'd Deft Recover against the s'd Plft five Shillings Damages besides their Cost by them about their Defence in this behalf Expended.

On motion made on oath by Roger Brown a Witness for the Plft against the said Deft Ordered that the said Plft pay him the sum of 30/ for 12 Day attendance at 2/6 P'r Day.

Page 266: Wm Gilbert vs Martin Williams. In Case. This day came the Parties by their Attorneys & thereupon Came also a Jury to wit Joseph Waldrop, James Higgins, James Pucket, John Todd, Wm. Willson, John Hall, Solomon Langston, Silas Garret, John Gray, James Strain, Stokes Edwards & John Willson who being Elected Tried & Sworn the Truth to Speak upon the Issue Join'd upon their oaths Do say that the Deft is Guilty of the nonperformance of the promises & assumsions in the Declaration mentioned & they do assess the Plft £20 by occation thereof. Whereupon it was considered by the Court that the s'd Pltf recover against the said Deft his Damages in form afores'd assest & his Cost by him in his Behalf expended.

The Deft moved for a new Trial; ordered to be Taken up in the morning.

On motion made on oath by James Gilbert a Witness for the Plft against the said Deft Ordered that the Deft pay him 35 Shillings for 14 Days attendance at 2/6 P'r Day.

Also to John Chesser the sum of 35/ for 14 Days attendance at 2/6 P'r Day.

Frances Wafer vs Saml Magniss. Sum'r Process. Debt. The Court after the parties on both sides Decreed that the Pltf Recover against the said Deft the sum of £4 s14 d4 besides his Cost by him in his behalf Expended.

Wm Harris vs Lewis Duvall. Continued till Next Court.

Charles Findley vs Elizabeth Brigs. This day came the Deft & the Plft tho Solemnly Call'd Came not; nor is his suit further prosecuted; therefore on motion of the Deft it is Ordered by the Court that the said Deft Recover **[Page 267]** against the said Plft five shillings Damages Besides his Cost by him about his Defence in this behalf Expended &the s'd Plft in mercy &c.

Lewis Duvall vs Sarah Cargill. Attachment. Whereas the Deft in this action Did on the 12th day of Sep'r 1788 file his Declaration in the Clerks Office of this Court against the Deft who is absent & hath no att'o known within this

LAURENS COUNTY SC COURT MINUTES 1786-1789

State upon whom a copy of the Declaration with a Rule to plead thereunto with a year & a Day might be served, it is Therefore ordered in pursuance of an act of the Gen'l Assembly in that Case made & provide. That the Deft do Appear & plead to the s'd Declaration on or before the Second Monday in Sep'r next otherwise Final & Absolutely Judgement will be Given & Awarded against her.

[12 September 1788]

Rich'd Duty vs Chas Jones. Continued by consent Till next Court.

James Floyd vs John Martin. Appeal. ordered that the Judgement Of John Rodgers Esq'r Obtained by the said John Martin against the s'd James Floyd be Reversed with Cost.

James Cook vs James Young. This day came the Deft & the Plft Tho Solemnly Call'd Came not nor is his suit further prosecuted; Therefore on Motion of the Deft it is Considered by the Court that the said Def't Recover against the Plft the sum of five shillings Damages Besides his Cost by him about his Defence in this Behalf Expended.

Court Adjourn'd till Tomorrow morning 9 Oclock. Minets Signd by Jonth'n Downs, Wm Mitchusson, Dan'l Wright, Joseph Downs, Esq'rs.

Page 268: Court met according to Adjournment the 13th Sep'r 1788. Present Jonth'n Downs, John Rodgers, George Anderson, Esq'r.

Ordered that Letters of Adm'n of all & Singular the Goods and Chattles of John McNees dec'd be Granted to James McNees he being Duly Qualified as the Law Directs; Whereupon he the said James McNees Together with John Rogers his Security Entered into & acknowledged their bonds in the sum of £500 with Condition according to Law.

Ordered that a Warrant of appraisement Issue to four freeholders To appraise the Estate of the said John McNees Dec'd & return an Account of their proceedings to this Court.

Joshua Downs Presented in open Court an appointment from Lewis Saxon, Clerk of Laurens county, appointing him the s'd Joshua Downs Deputy Clerk of the County afores'd, he the said Joshua Downs being by the court approved of as Deputy Clerk of s'd County & thereupon was admitted to Take the oath of office, which he Took accordingly.

Ordered that the following Estrays be by the Sheriff of this County Exposed to Publick sale at a credit of Three months Taking Sufficient notes payable to the County Treasurer.

LAURENS COUNTY SC COURT MINUTES 1786-1789

[13 September 1788]

To wit: A Black Mare taken up by Thos Revill & Tol'd before Dan'l Wright Esq'r the 8th of Ap'l 1788.

Also a horse Taken up by John Chapman & Toled before John Hunter Esq'r the 27th of March 1788.

Also a Sorrol horse Taken up by Jas Willson & Toled before Silv's Walker Esq'r the 3d of May 1788.

Also a bay mare Taken up by Joel Burgess & Toled before George Anderson the 2d Day of May 1788.

Also 22 head of hogs Taken up by Abner Babb & Toled before Silv's Walker the 17th of May 1788.

Page 269: Also a Gray horse Taken up by John Linch & Toled before James Montgomery Esq'r the 17th of May 1788.

Also a black mare Taken up by Isia Vines & Toled before Joseph Downs the 16th of May 1788.

Also a Strawberry Roan mare taken up by John Campbell & toled before Jas Montgomery Esq'r the 24th of May 1788.

Also a Chesnut sorrel mare Taken up by John Jones & Toled before Ja's Montgomery Esq'r the 26th of May 1788.

Also a bay mare Taken up by James Anderson & Toled before George Anderson the 20th of May 1788.

Also a bay mare Taken up by Robert Pollard & Toled before Angus Campbell, Esq'r.

Also a small roan horse Taken up by Jno Hall & Toled before John Rodgers Esq'r the 4th day of June 1788.

Ordered that all Estrays not present To be sold this day must be by the Sheriff previous to the sale [be] Advertized Ten Days.

Ordered That the County Treasurer pay unto Lewis Saxon, Clerk of this Court, the sum of £5 the sallery due him for his publick Services in said Office.

Court adjourn'd Till Court in Course. Minets Sign'd by Jonth'n Downs, Geo: Anderson, John Rodgers, Esq'rs.

LAURENS COUNTY SC COURT MINUTES 1786-1789

Page 270: At a court held for the County of Laurens on the Eighth day of Decem'r AD 1788. Present Silvanus Walker, Angus Campbell, John Rodgers, Esq'rs.

The following persons were Drawn to serve as pettit Jurours at our next Court to be held on the Second Monday in March next, To wit.

1. John Copelin
2. Rob't Templeton Jun'r
3. Drury Boyce
4. Abner Teague
5. James Watson
6. John Gunter
7. Tho's Wilks
8. Rob't Freeman
9. John Fields
10. John Swearings
11. Sam'l Neighbours
12. James Neiley
13. Rob't Hambleton
14. George Taylor
15. Joshua Arnald
16. Wm Ragsdale
17. Wm Niccles
18. Joseph Holcome
19. Boling Byshop
20. George Whitmore
21. Wm Stone
22. John Blackley Jun'r
23. Benj'n Griffin
24. Tho's Blackley
25. Ambrose Hugins
26. Wm Norris
27. Dan'l Methany
28. Argile Shirley
29. Wm South
30. Wm Hughes

Ordered that Wm Bailey be Appointed Overseer of that part of the Highway Leading from the Cross Road Between Tho's Dendy's & John Cargill's to Hugh Neal's Mill in the place of the s'd Tho's Dendy. Ordered that he cause the Several Free male Inhabitants & Slaves Contagious [sic] to & Convenient to s'd Road to work thereon & keep the same in Good Repair for one year.

James Dohertie Esq'r Produced in Open Court a Credential signed by the Hon'ble Henry Pendleton, Aedanus Burk, and Tho's Heyward, Esq'rs, Judges of the Court of Common pleas of this State admitting him the s'd James Dohertie to practice as an att'o at Law or Equity of this State, which s'd Credentials being publickly read in open court, it was Thereupon Ordered that he be enroled as such in this Court.

A Lease & Release from John Chesnut to Saml Akins for the Conveyance of 150 Acres of Land proven according to Law Before a single Magistrate & ordered to be recorded.

Page 271: On application made by Clabourn Sims, Ordered that Letters of Adm'n of all & Singular the goods & Chattles of Wm Sims Dec'd be granted to him he being first Duly Sworn as the Law Directs, Whereupon he together with John Hall & John Rogers his Securities entered into & acknowledged their Bonds in the sum of £55 with Condition according to Law.

Ordered that a Warrant of Appraisement Issue to four freeholders of this County to Value & appraise the Estate of the s'd Wm Sims & return a True inventory thereof to the s'd Adm'r within Sixty days from this Date.

On application of Harley Attoway for Letters of Administration of all & Singular the Estate of Wm McDole Dec'd. Ordered that a Citation Issue Siting & Admonishing all & singular the kindred and Creditors of the s'd

Dec'd to appear at our next Court to shew Cause if any they have why Letters of Administration should not be Granted as afores'd.

[8 December 1788]

Curtis Moore vs Wm Boyce. In Slander. Dismist at Plfts. Cost.

Court adjourn'd Till Tomorrow morning Ten OClock. Minets Sign'd by Silv's Walker, John Rodgers, Angus Campbell, Esq'rs.

Court met according to Adjournment the Ninth Day of Decem'r 1788. Present Cha's Saxon, Angus Campbell, Dan'l Wright, Joseph Downs, Esq'rs.

John D. Kern vs Charles Hutching. In Case. John Elmore formerly Special Bail for the Deft. in Discharge of the s'd Bail. Ordered that he be Discharg'd from s'd Bail.

James McNees & John Montgomery comes into Court & Undertakes for the s'd Deft Charles Hutchings that in case **[Page 272]** the s'd Deft should be Cast in this suit now Depending between John D. Kern Plft & the s'd Charles Huchings Deft that they will pay the Cost & Condemnation of the Court in s'd Suit or otherwise render his body in Discharge Thereof to prison.

A Deed from John Fields & his wife to Roger Murphy for the Conveyance of 125 acres of Land proven in open Court by the oaths of Ebenezer Murphey & George Maddin & Ordered to be Recorded.

The State vs Eliz. Wood. Bastardy. The said Elizabeth Wood came into Court Having a bastard Child & Refused to Declare on oath who is the father of s'd Bastard Child. Whereupon it was Ordered that the s'd Elizabeth Wood be Committed to the common Joal of this County & there to Remain until next Court.

Nevertheless if the s'd Eliz. Wood shall any time between this & the next Court to be held in this County on the Second Monday in March next Declare on oath before some one Justice of the peace for this County who is the father of s'd Bastard Child or pay a fine of £40 proclamation money &*Cost of Prosecution Then to be Discharg'd from prison.

Wm Head vs John Williams. In Slander. Dismist at Defts Cost.

A Lease & Release from Dunkin Campbell & Mary Campbell to James Gammel for the Conveyance of 70 acres of Land proven in open Court by the oath of John Gammel & Ordered to be Recorded.

Page 273: Jean Tolds vs Joseph Goodman. Dismist at Mutual Cost.

LAURENS COUNTY SC COURT MINUTES 1786-1789

[9 December 1788]

Mary Williams vs Robert Tombs. In Case. Continued by Consent till next Court

On application of John F. Wolf Ordered that Licence be Granted him to Sell & Retail all kinds of Spirituous [Liquors] at his Store in this County near Thomason's Mill in any Less Quantity than three Gallons for one year from the Date hereof.

A Lease & Release from Wm Donnahoe to Cornelius Donnahoe for the Conveyance of 150 acres of Land Proven according to Law before a Single Magistrate and ordered to be recorded.

Sam'l Scott vs Wm Grims. In T. A. & Battery. Dismist at Plfts. Cost.

The Grand Jurors Return'd into Court the following Bills of Indictment, To wit.

The State vs James Cunningham. Indictm't Assault. The Grand Jury Return'd a True Bill.

The State vs John Jones. Indictm't Assault. The Grand Jury Return'd a True Bill.

The State vs And'w Rogers. Indictm't Assault. The Grand Jury Return'd a True Bill.

Court adjourn'd till 9 Oclock Tomorrow morning. Minets sign'd by Angus Campbell, John Rodgers, Dan'l Wright, Charles Saxon, Esq'rs.

Page 274: Court met according to Adjournment the Tenth Day of Decem'r 1788. Present Angus Campbell, John Rodgers, Dan'l Wright, Charles Saxon, Esq'rs.

Peter Carns vs Martin Pugh. Sum'r Process. Debt. Continued Till next Court.

Peter Carns vs Clement Davis. S. Process. Debt. Continued by Consent till next Court.

Peter Carns vs J. Williams. Sum'r Process. Debt. Continued Till next Court.

Peter Carns vs John McElroy. Sum'r Process. Debt. The Court after hearing the Parties Decreed that The said Peter Carnes Recover Against the said John McElroy the sum of £54 s8 d9 with Interest & Cost of suit.

[10 December 1788]

Susanna Man vs John Rammage. The parties mutually Submitted the Determination of this Suit to the Award of Tho's Ewing and Wm Price and agreed their Award thereupon should be made a Judgement of this Court. The s'd Arbitrators now Returning their award in these words: to wit: that the said John Rammage pay unto the s'd Susanna Man all Cost of Suit accruing thereon & Two Barrels of corn on the 25th day of Decem'r next. Whereupon it was Considered by the Court that the s'd Plft Recover against the s'd Def the s'd Two Barrels of Corn Together with her Cost in s'd Suit Expended & The s'd Def't in mercy &c.

Page 275: Wm Young vs Jas McNees & Hugh Young. In Debt. This day came the parties by their attorneys & thereupon came also a Jury, To wit: James Blackley, Abraham Box, Wm Higgins, Tho's Chapman, Micheal Box, Stephen Plant, Rob't Faris & Joseph Allison who being Elected Tired & Sworn the Truth to speak upon the Issue Join'd Retired out of Court to Consult of Their Verdict & being Return'd into Court in order to Render the same, the Plft being Three Times Solemnly Called & Came not nor is his suit Further prosecuted. Whereupon on motion made by the Defts It was Considered by the Court that the Jurours from rendering their Verdict be Discharg'd and that the Plft be nonsuited & C & that the said Defts go hence without Day & recover against the s'd Plft five shillings Damages Besides his Cost by him in this behalf Expended in the suit &C.

Charles Harvey vs Wm Floyd. Assault & Battery. By Consent of the Parties this suit is ordered to be Continued till next Court.

Johnth'n Johnson vs Benj'n Rainey. Att'mt. Debt. Dismist at Plaintiffs Cost.

The State vs Benj'n Rainey. Bound in Recognizance. Ordered that he be Discharg'd from the Same on payment of Cost.

Hugh Crumbless vs Curtis Moore & others. In Slander. This day Came the Parties by their Atto's of the Plfts Att'o says that the action is brought wrong. Thereof he suffers a Nonsuit: Whereupon it was Considered by the Court that the s'd Defts Recover against the s'd Plfts the sum of five shillings Damages besides their Cost by them in this behalf Expended &c.

Page 276: Joseph Brown vs John Neiley. Attm't. The property reprived. Benj'n Carter Comes into Court & undertakes for the Deft John Neiley that in case he should be Cast in this suit that he will pay the Cost & Condemnation of the Court in s'd suit or render his body in Discharge thereof to prison.

Wm Head vs M. Williams & John Williams. In Trover. On application of David Childres a witness in s'd Suit ordered that the Defts pay him the sum of 27/6 for 11 Days Attendance at 2/6 P'r Day.

LAURENS COUNTY SC COURT MINUTES 1786-1789

[10 December 1788]

John Chapman vs William Lowery. Attm't. On application of the Plfts, Ordered that a Commission Issue to Theoderick Carter, Jeremiah Pate and --- Devenport, Esquires, in y'e state of Virginia to Examine & take the Deposition of Matthew Solmon a Witness in this Suit in behalf of the Plft & that they return the Commission & Deposition by them take to out next Court to be Held on the Second Monday in June next. There to be read in Evidence in this suit, the Plft Giving the Deft ten Days Notice of the time & place of the s'd Examination.

Benj'n Rainey vs Philip Wells. ordered that Wm. Head formerly Special bail for the Deft be Discharg'd from the same. John House Comes into Court & undertakes for the Deft P. Wells as Special Bail that in case he should be cast in this suit that he will pay the Cost & Condemnation of the Court in s'd suit or render his body in Discharge thereof to prison.

John Loftin vs Sam'l Ewing. Continued By Consent Till next Court.

Joseph Akins vs Philip Wells. John Adams Comes into Court & undertakes for the Plft that in case he should be Cast in this suit that he will pay the Cost & Condemnation in s'd suit or render his body in Discharge thereof to prison.

Page 277: Wm Young vs Ja's McNees & Hugh Young. On application made on oath by Micheal Waldrop a witness in s'd suit, Ordered that the Plft pay him the sum of 35/ for 14 days Attendance at 2/6 P'r day. Also to John Montgomery the sum of 25/ for 10 Days Attendance at 1/6 P'r Day with Mileage for Going & Coming 30 miles 3 times out of Union County.

The State vs Elizabeth Wood. Bastardy. The s'd Elizabeth Wood after being Committing to Joal was ordered into Court and being Brought into Court Swore that Elisha Carter son of Thomas Carter is the father of a Bastard Child Begotten on the body of the said Elizabeth Wood. Ordered that she the s'd Elizabeth Wood be Continued in the Custody of the Sheriff untill she Gives to the Court further satisfaction Relative to the Getting of the s'd Bastard Child.

The State vs Martin Martin. Indictm't. Assault & Battery. The Grand Jury Return'd a True Bill. Whereupon P. Carnes Traversed the s'd Indictment till next Court. Ordered to be Continued till next Court.

The State vs Wm. Dunlap. Indicm't. Assault & Battery. Returned into Court by the Grand Jury a True Bill. Whereupon James Dohertie Traversed the s'd Indictment till next Court. Ordered to be Continued till next Court.

Reuben Pyles foreman, Nehemiah Franks, Rich'd Pugh, John McClintock, Arthur Durham, John Brown, Shadrach Martin, Lewis Banton, Wm. Griffin, Robert Cuningham, George Young, Joshua Saxon & James Young, were sworn as Grand Jurours of inquest for the body of this County. Having Received their Charge Retired from the Bar to Consult of their Verdict & After some time Return'd into Court & presented as follows to wit

Page 278: [10 December 1788]

We the Grand Jurours for the County afores'd Present that
1st a Certain Road Laid out by an order of Court Runing from Where John Goodwin formerly Lived between Redy River & Saluday is now so out of Repair & destitute of any overseer; that it becomes a great Grievance to all that part of the County; Which s'd Road ought to be Repaired the Best & Directest way to Cason's Ferry.

2d. Also we present as a Grievance that a Certain road Leading from John McClintock's to Hugh Oneal's Mill is out of repair & Destitute of any overseer.

3d. We also present that a Certain Sam'l Weathers Living on Cane Creek hath without Doubt This several Years Lived a most Adulterated & Scandalous Life with Mary Wood & Elizabeth Wood Daughter of the said Mary Wood & Also that the s'd Eliz. Wood hath a Bastard Child without any Lawfull father & that the s'd Saml Weathers Lives the Life aforesaid with the said Mary Wood & Eliz. Wood To the Scandal of the family & Evill Example of all others. This we present as one of the Greatest Nusances Immaginable.

4th. We also present that a Road Leading form James Young's on Bush River to the fishdam Road is Greatly out of Repair & Destitute of any overseer as they Believe & for want thereof is a Great prejudice.

5th. We also present that there is no place nor Room provided for the protection of the Grand Jury in time of their publick services for the County afores'd. This we present as a very Great Grievance.

6th. We also present as a very Great Grievance that a Certain woman by the name of Ann Mosse or otherwise known by the name of Ann Burns by the best Information & our own Knowledge the s'd Ann Masse or otherwise Ann Burn with three Children & has been upon Sufference (viz) at times without Bread for Three days & that she Lives a Lazy loose Scandalous Life & is a Nusance of the County accord'g & Further that her Children hath & is like to suffer. Do Recommend that our presentment to be Worshipful Court for their Consideration.

1. Reuben Pyles foreman
2. Nehemiah Franks
3. Rich'd Pugh
4. John McClintock
5. Arthur Durham
6. John Brown
7. Shadrach Martin
8. Lewis Banton
9. Wm. Griffin
10. Robert Cuningham
11. Geo Young
12. Joshua Saxon
13. James Young

LAURENS COUNTY SC COURT MINUTES 1786-1789

Page 279: [10 December 1788]

John Stewart vs James Cannon & John Smith. Attm't. Dismist at Plft Cost.

On application of Ezekiel Roland he is Licensed allowed & Admitted to sell & retail all kinds of Spirituous Liquors at the Cross Road near Rich'd Hia's in any Less Quantity Than Three Gallons for the Term of One Whole year from the Date hereof.

On application of Paul Phindley for Letters of Adm'n of all and Singular the Goods & Chattles rights & Credits of the Estate of James Pollard dec'd. Ordered That a Citation Issue Citing and Admonishing all & singular the kindred & Creditors of the said Dec'd To appear at the next Court to shew Cause if any they have why Letters of Adm'n should not be Issued as afores'd.

Joseph Adair vs Wm Dean. Sum'r Process. Discontinued at Defts Cost by his Consent.

Court adjourn'd Till Tomorrow morning Ten OClock. Minets sign'd by Charles Saxon, Danl Wright, Angus Campbell, Esquires.

Court met According to adjournment the 11th Day of Decem'r 1788. Present Angus Campbell, John Rodgers, Daniel Wright, Esquires.

A Deed for the Conveyance of 354 Acres of land from Wm Milwee to Wm Dobson Acknowledged in open Court & Ordered to be Recorded.

State vs Sam'l Weathers. Bound in Recognizance to keep the peace. Ordered that he the s'd Sam'l Weathers be Discharged therefrom on payment of Cost.

Page 280: State vs Mary Wood & Elizabeth Wood. Bound in Recognizance to keep the peace. Ordered that they be Discharged therefrom on payment of Cost.

State vs John Hudson & Sam'l McClurkin. Indicm't. Assault & Battery. Ordered that Sam'l McClurkin be Struck out of the Indictment.

State vs J. Hudson. Indictment Assault & Battery. This day came The Parties by their Attorneys, and thereupon came also a Jury to wit, James Blackley, Abraham Box, William Higgins, Thomas Chapman, Micheal Box, John Garret, John Greir, John Williams, Joseph Ramage, Stephen Plant, Robert Faris & Joseph Allison who being Sworn well & truly to Try the Issue Joined, upon their oaths do say that the Deft is not Guilty of the Assault as in the Indictment Alledged. Therefore, it was Considered by the Court that the s'd John Hudson be Discharg'd from his Recognizance on payment of Cost.

LAURENS COUNTY SC COURT MINUTES 1786-1789

[11 December 1788]

Alex'r Simpson is Appointed overseer of that part of the Highway Leading from Hugh Oneal's Mill down to the Cross road near John Hunters in the place of Sam'l Eakins. Ordered that the following persons be assigned him the said Alex'r Simpson to work on s'd road & keep the Same in Good Repair for one year: (To wit) Sam'l Eakins, James McDanald, Joseph Motes, Robert Simpson, James Simpson, Tho's Davis, James Little, Peter Hitt, John Simpson, Tho's Wadsworth, Patk McDowall, Danl Sims & Silv's Walker hands.

Peter Carnes vs John Williams. Sum'r Process Debt. Dismist at Plfts Cost.

The State vs Elizabeth Wood. The said Elizabeth Wood comes into Court and Sayeth that she is Guilty of having a bastard Child Begotten on her by d & that Elisha Carter is the father of the said Bastard Child & throws herself upon the mercy of the Court, Whereupon it was Considered by the Court that she be fine the sum of £5 proclamation [**Page 281**] money & pay cost of prosecution. Ordered that the said Eliz. Wood enter into Security to pay the Above fine next Court.

The State vs John Jones. Indictm't Assault & Battery. Newton Higgins & Joseph Brown comes into Court & acknowledged themselves Indebted to the County in the following sums To wit, The said John Jones in the sum of £20 and the s'd Newton Higgins & Joseph Parsons in the sum of £10 each to be Levied of their Respective Goods & Chattels Lands & Tenements yet upon Condition that if the said John Jones shall appear at our next Court to Answer to a Bill of Indictment Exhibited against him by the Grand Jury t& shall not Depart the same Court untill Discharg'd Therefrom the above obligation to be Void otherwise to Remain in full force Power & Virtue.

Arthur Durham is appointed overseer of that part of the Highway Leading from John Goodwin's old place Down the road Leading to Cason's ferry as far as Reaburns Creek. Ordered that he the said Arthur Durham cause the several Free male Inhabitants & Slaves Contagious to & Convenient to said Road to work thereon & keep the Same in Good Repair for one year for one year from this Date.

Tandy Walker is appointed overseer of that part of the Highway Leading from James Sullivant's Down Against And'w Rodgers's Mill & Robert Young D'o from Against And'w Rodgers's Mill to Little River. Ordered that they the said Tandy Walker & Robert Young cause the several Free male Inhabitants & Slaves Contagious to & Convenient to said Road to work thereon & keep the Same in Good Repair for one year for one year from this Date.

The State vs Elizabeth Wood. Bastardy. The Deft fined by the Court £5, Wm. Goodman Comes into Court & Undertakes as Security for the Deft to pay the above fine of £5 at or before next Court. Ordered that the s'd Elizabeth Wood be Discharg'd from her Recognizance on payment [**Page 282**] of prosecution.

LAURENS COUNTY SC COURT MINUTES 1786-1789

[11 December 1788]

State vs John Penington. Indictment. Assault & Battery. The Deft. came into Court & Confessed himself Guilty of the Assault as on the Indictment alledged & Threw himself upon the Mercy of the Court: Whereupon the Court fined him one shilling. Ordered that he be Discharged from his Recognizance on payment of Cost.

Joseph Brown vs John Neiley. Attachment. Continued at Plfts Cost till next Court.

State vs John Hudson, Sam'l McClurkin, John Henderson. Sc. Fa forfeited Recognizance. The Defts Fined by the Court one shilling which was paid in Court to the Sheriff. Ordered that the Defts be Discharg'd from their Recognizance on payment of Cost.

State vs Elisha Carter. Bastardy. John Carter saltspring comes into Court and Acknowledged himself indebted to the County in the sum of £10 to be levied of his Goods & Chattles Lands & Tenements: yet upon Condition that if the said Elisha Carter shall appear at our next Court to Answer to an Indictment Exhibited against him & shall not Depart The same untill Discharged therefrom than the above obligation to be void.

Court adjourn'd Till Tomorrow morning 9 OClock. Minets sign'd by Silv's Walker, Wm Mitchusson, Angus Campbell, Esq'r.

Court met According to adjournment the 12th of Decem'r 1788. Present Angus Campbell, John Rodgers, Wm Mitchusson, Esquires.

Page 283: Reubin Pyles vs James McNees. In Case. The Parties Mutually Submitted the Determination of this Suit to Thomas Wadsworth & Thomas Garner with Liberty for the s'd Arbitrators to Chose an umpire in Case they Cannot agree. The said parties Agrees that their Award should be made a Judgement of this Court. Ordered that the s'd Arbitrators Return their Award to Next Court.

James McNees vs Reubin Pyles. In Slander. The Parties Mutually Submitted the Determination of this Suit to Thomas Wadsworth & Thomas Garner with Leave for the said Arbitrators to Chose an umpire in Case they Cannot agree & the s'd parties Agrees that their Award should be made a Judgement of this Court. Ordered that the s'd Arbitrators Return their Award to Next Court.

Angus Campbell vs John Kellet. In Trover. Judgment by Default. The Plfts Att'o agrees to wave the Advantage of this Default.

Thos Lewis vs Wm Murphey. Attachment. Ordered to be Dismist at Plfts Cost their being no Legal Bond Tiled.

[12 December 1788]

Clement Deal Plft vs Thos Edgehill Deft. Attm't. Continued by Consent till next Court.

Ordered that a Road be Cleared the nearest & Best way from Allison's Mill on Durbins Creek (by M. Wolf's) to Downs's Shoals on Reaburns Creek & that Wm. Thomason be appointed Overseer thereof And to Continue from **[Page 284]** s'd Downs's Shoal to the Tumbling Shoals on Redy River & that John Thomason be appointed Overseer thereof & From thence to Continue to Rutledge's ford on Salluda & that Robert Box be appointed Overseer thereof. Ordered that they the s'd Wm Thomason, John Thomas, & Robert Box cause the several free male Inhabitants & Slaves Contagious to & Convenient to s'd roads to work thereon & keep the same in Good Repair for one year from the Date hereof.

State vs Sam'l Parsons. Indictment. This day came the Parties by their Attorneys & thereupon came also a Jury to wit James Blackley, Ab'm Neighbours, Wm Higgins, Thomas Chapman, Micheal Box, John Garret, John Greir, John Williams, Joseph Ramage, Stephen Plant, Robert Faris & Joseph Allison who being Elected Tried & Sworn the Truth to Speak upon the Issued Join'd upon their oaths do say that the Deft is Guilty of the Neglect of Duty as in the Indictment Alledged. Whereupon, it was Considered by the Court that the s'd Deft be fine one shilling which he paid in Court to the Sheriff. Ordered that he be Discharg'd from his Recognizance on payment of Cost.

Ordered that the County Treasurer pay out of The publick money in his hands unto David Anderson Sheriff of this County The sum of £7 s10 for his Extra Services this Last Year.

Ordered that the Road Leading from the Courthouse to Swancey's Ferry on Saluday be Cleared out the way it was formerly Established by the Commissioners.

Ordered that The following Defaulters of the Grand Jury (to wit) WM Harris & Tandy Walker be Notified to Appear at next Court to Shew Cause why they Did not Appear at this Court Also that the following persons Defaulters for the Petty Jury to wit Joseph South, Memucan Walker, Joseph Pinson & Angus Campbell be Notified the same way.

[Page 285]: Ordered that Letters of Adm'n of all & singular the Goods & Chattles Rights & Credits of Peter Wood dec'd be granted unto Leis Banton he being first duly sworn as the Law Directs, whereupon he the s'd Lewis Banton Together with John Richey & And'w Rodgers Jun'r Entered into & acknowledged their Bonds in the sum of £500 with Condition According to Law.

LAURENS COUNTY SC COURT MINUTES 1786-1789

[12 December 1788]

Ordered that a Warrant of Appraisement Issue to four freeholders in This County to Value & Appraise the Estate of the s'd Pet'r Wood Decd & Return the appraisement to the Adm'r within forty days from this date.

Andrew Parker is appointed overseer of that part of The highway leading from Copeland's to John McClintock's in the place of Lewis Devall. Ordered that he the s'd And'w Parkes cause the several free male Inhabitants & Slaves Contagious to & convenient to s'd Road to work thereon & keep the same in Good repair for one year from the date hereof.

Ordered that all the Estrays Liable to be sold this Court be by the Sheriff Tomorrow Exposed to publick sale at a Credit of Ten months. Giving Notes with approved Security.

Edw'd Mitchusson vs Ja's Allison adm'r of John York decd. Ordered that a Scire Facias Issue citing the s'd James Allison to appear at our next court to Shew cause if any he has why Execution may not issue against him on a Judgement formerly obtain'd by the s'd Plft against the s'd Deft.

Court Adjourn'd till Court in Course. Minets Sign'd by Joseph Downs, Silv's Walker, Wm Mitchusson, Esq'rs.

Page 286: At a Court held for the County of Laurens at the Courthouse on the Ninth day of March AD 1789. Present Jonth'n Downs, Geo: Anderson, Joseph Downs, John Rodgers, Jas Montgomery, Esq'rs.

The following persons were Drawn to serve as Grand Jurours at next Court to be held for this County on the second Monday in June next. To wit

1. Robert Lard
2. John Carter S. Spring
3. Joseph Adair
4. Robert McCrery
5. Nathan Barksdale
6. Clement Deal
7. John Richey
8. James Henderson
9. Sam'l Saxon
10. James Little
11. Sam'l Henderson
12. William Hunter
13. John Brown Jun'r
14. Thos Cunningham
15. Rich'd Griffin
16. David Dunlap
17. Alex'r Harper
18. Wm Barksdale
19. Philip Day
20. Kitt Smith

The following persons were drawn to serve as Petty Jurours at next Court (to wit)

1. Mark Moore
2. P. Riley
3. Rich'd McDanald
11. Wm Hellams
12. Wm Benson
13. George Watts
21. Gilbert Monary
22. Joseph Mason
23. Dan'l Rodgers

LAURENS COUNTY SC COURT MINUTES 1786-1789

[9 March 1789]

4. Nicholas Brown	14. Thos Elliott	24. Thos Lindsey
5. Rich'd Turner	15. John Attoway	25. George Neeley
6. James Young L. River	16. Peter Hitt	26. James Moore
7. James Poole	17. Benj'n Carter	27. Thos Rodgers
8. Thos Springfield	18. Jonth'n Childs	28. John Hollingsworth
9. Thos Ducket	19. Saml McClurkin	29. Benj'n Stone
10. Geo Morgan R. River	20. David Templeton	30. Holloway Power

Page 287: Wm Sims is appointed overseer of the highway Leading from Thos Carter's old place to Jas Sullivant's in the place of John Fields; Ordered that he the said Wm Sims cause the several free male Inhabitants & Slaves Contagious to & Convenient to s'd Road to work thereon & keep the same in good repair for one whole Year from this Date.

Danl Parrot Infant Orphan Came into Court & Chose Thos Ship as his Guardian, whereupon Lewis Saxon Comes into Court & undertakes as Security in the sum of £100 for Securing the said Orphan's estate & Indemnifying the County.

Lewis Banton vs Thos Boyce. In Slander. Dismist at Defts. Cost.

On application of Wm. Thos Rodgers he is admitted to keep a public Tavern at the Courthouse of this County for the time of one year, whereupon he the s'd Wm Thos Rodgers together with George Anderson & John Rodgers Esq'r are to enter into Bond with the Clerk as the Law Directs.

Patrick Cuningham vs Rich'd Robinson. Att'mt. Ordered to be Continued till Tomorrow.

Danl McLain vs John Hutson. This action abates by the Death of the plft.

Danl McClain vs John Hutson. In Trover. This action abates by the Death of the plft.

John Hunter & Geo: Anderson Esq'r vs And'w Rodgers Jun'r. Attm't. Dismist at Plfts Cost.

Thos Springfield vs Joshua Cates. Attm't. Discontinued at Plfts. Cost.

Robt Hall vs Chas Merill. Attm't. Dismist at Defts Cost Except the atto fee.

Ordered that the Clerk of this County be & is hereby authorized to Issue Citations at any time when applied for Returnable to the Succeeding[?] Court in Cases of Administration. Provided Test of the said Citation be Twenty days before the s'd Court.

LAURENS COUNTY SC COURT MINUTES 1786-1789

Page 288: [9 March 1789]

Wm Shaw Esq'r vs Wm Jackson. The Sheriff having Return'd a writ of Fi Fi in this suit in the following words, to wit: By Virtue of the within Execution I have &C, ordered that an alias Fi Fa Issue on Motion of James Yancy Esq'r Returnable to next court.

The Last will & Testament of Wm Hellams Dec'd was presented in open Court & proved by the oath of Rich'd Owens a witness thereto and Ordered to be Recorded & whereas no Executor named in the will, Ordered that John Hellams & Richard Childres be and is hereby appointed Executors to the s'd Estate.

Ordered that a warrant of appraisement Issue to four freeholders To view & appraise the s'd Estate & Return an account of the said appraisement to next Court.

John Boyd is appointed overseer of that part of the highway Leading from Little River near the Courthouse to Micheal Waldrop's in the place of Elijah Taylor. Ordered that the said John Boyd Cause the Several free male Inhabitants & slaves Contagious to and Convenient to s'd Road to work thereon & keep the same in Good Repair for one y ear.

The Last will and Testament of James Allison Dec'd was presented in open Court by James Allison Jun'r The Executor Therein Named & proven by the oath of Rolley Bowen a Witness thereto & ordered to be Recorded.

Ordered that Letters testamentary Issue in Due form to the said James Allison he being first Duly sworn as the Law Directs.

Ordered that a warrant of appraisement Issue to four freeholders in this County To view & appraise the Estate of the said James Allison Dec'd & Return an Inventory & account of the said appraisement to next Court.

Page 289: Danl McLain vs John Huston. On application of Wm Obannion a Witness in this suit for the Deft against the said Plft, Ordered that the Deft pay him the sum of 35 shillings for 14 days attendance at 2/6 P'r Day.

Elizabeth Allison Infant orphan of James Allison Dec'd came into Court and made Choice of Nancy Allison as her Guardian, whereupon the said Nancy Allison together with Joseph Allison her Security Came into Court and acknowledged their Bonds in the sum of £200 for the securing of the s'd orphan's Estate & Indemnifying the County.

Mary Allison Infant orphan of James Allison Dec'd came into Court and made Choice of James Allison Jun'r as her Guardian, whereupon he the s'd James Allison together with Joseph Loyn his Security Came into Court and acknowledged their Bonds in the sum of £200 for the securing of the s'd orphan's Estate & Indemnifying the County.

[9 March 1789]

On application of John Quin he is hereby Licenced, allowed and admitted to Sell & Retail all kinds of Spirituous Liquors in any Less Quantity than three Gallons at his house where he now lives for the term of one year.

Court adjourned Till Tomorrow Morning. Minets signed by John Rodgers, Ja's Montgomery, George Anderson, Jonth'n Downs, Joseph Downs, Esquires.

Court met according to Adjournment the 10th of March 1789. Present George Anderson, John Rodgers, Charles Saxon, Angus Campbell, Esquires.

Page 290: John Pitts vs Peter Griffin. Sum'r process. This day Came the deft by his Attorney & the Plft tho Solemnly Called came not but made Default Nor is his suit further prosecuted, therefore on Motion of the Deft it is Considered by the Court that he Recover against the s'd Plft five shillings Damages Besides his Cost about his Defence in This Behalf Expended according to the form of the Act of Assembly in that Case made & provided.

John Pitts vs Peter Griffin. Sum'r process. Debt. This day Came the deft by his Attorney & the Plft tho Solemnly Called came not but made Default Nor is his suit further prosecuted, therefore on Motion of the Deft it is Considered by the Court that he Recover against the s'd Plft five shillings Damages Besides his Cost about his Defence in This Behalf Expended according to the form of the Act of Assembly in that Case made & provided.

Peter Carnes vs Martin Pugh. Sum'r Process. Debt. The Court after hearing the parties Decreed that the Plft Recover against him the s'd Martin Pugh the sum of £5 s8 d9 with Interest & his Cost by him in this Behalf Expended. The Plft agrees to stay execution till April next.

Peter Carnes vs Clem't Davis. Sum'r Process. Debt. The Court after hearing the parties Decreed that the Plft Recover against the s'd Def't the sum of £1 s1 d9 with Interest & his Cost by him in this Behalf Expended.

Martin Williams vs Holloway Power. Sum'r Process. Debt. James Saxon Comes into Court & undertakes for the Plft that if he should be Cast in this Action that he will pay all Cost and Damages awarded by the Court or Render his body in Discharge thereof to prison.

Martin Williams vs Holloway Power. Sum'r Process. Debt. Continued by Consent till Next Court.

Page 291: Mary Williams vs Robert Toombs. In Case. This day Came the Deft by his Attorney and the Plft tho Solemnly Called Came not But made Default nor is her suit further prosecuted. Therefore on motion of the Deft it is Considered by the Court that he Recover against the s'd Plft the sum of five shillings Damages & his cost by him in this behalf Expended.

[10 March 1789]

Reuben Pyles vs James McNees. In Case. Continued under Reference till next Court.

James McNees vs Reuben Pyles. Slander. Continued under Reference till next Court.

James McNees vs Reuben Pyles. Detinue. Continued under Reference till next Court.

Clement Dial vs Thos Edgehill. Attm't. This day came into Court the Deft by his atto & the Plft tho Solemnly Called came not but made Default Nor is his suit further prosecuted, therefore on Motion of the Deft it is Considered by the Court that he Recover against the s'd Plft five shillings Damages Besides his Cost about his Defence in This Behalf Expended according to the form of the Act of Assembly in that Case made & provided.

James Sullivant vs Thos Portswood. Attm't. This day Came the Plft by Thos P. Carnes his Attorney and the Deft tho Solemnly Cal'd came not & Thereupon came also a Jury (to wit) John Copeland, Drury Boyce, Thos Wilks, John Fields, John Swearings, Sam'l Neighbours, Joshua Arnald, Wm. Ragsdale, Boling Byshop, George Whitmore, Wm Stone & John Blackley who being sworn well & Truly To Enquire of Damages in this Suit upon their oaths do find for the Plft the sum of £17 s11 d10¼, Whereupon it was Considered by the Court that the s'd Plft Recover against the s'd Deft & Charles Riley[?] Garnishee the s'd sum of £17 s11 d10¼ Together with his Cost by him in this Behalf expended & the s'd Deft in Mercy &c.

Page 292: Mary Flanagan vs Benjamin Rainey. Discontinued at Plfts Cost.

P. Cuningham vs Rich'd Robertson. Attachment. Wm Donnohow being Summoned as a Garnishee Came into Court and Swore that he was Justly Indebted to Rich'd Robinson Twenty four hundred weight of Tobacco (Altho his note was made payable for the same to Amus Anderson) whereupon it was Considered by the Court that the Plft Recover against the said Wm Donnohow on Tobacco priced in Hogsheads at $3 P'r Hundred Weight according to the Plft Note & his Cost by him in this behalf expended & the s'd Deft in Mercy &c.

State vs Elisha Carter. On a charge of Bastardy on the oath of Eliz. Wood. The Court after hearing the Evidence on the part of Deft. Ordered that he be Dismist on payment of Cost of prosecution.

LAURENS COUNTY SC COURT MINUTES 1786-1789

[10 March 1789]

Mary Williams vs Robert Tombs. On Motion made on oath by Danl Megin a witness in s'd suit ordered that the s'd Pltf pay him the sum of 25/ for 10 Days attendance at 2/6 Pr Day also to Anthony Golding the sum of 15/ for 10 Days Attendance at 2/6 P'r Day

Rich'd Daly vs Charles Jones. In Slander. The parties Mutually Submitted the Determination of their suit to the Award of James Duncan, Rob't Whitton, George Young, James Dillard & Thomas Ewing, & agreed that their Award thereupon should be made a Judgment of this Court. The said arbitrators now returning their Award in these Words (to wit) That this suit be Dismist at Mutual Cost Whereupon it was ordered accordingly.

On application of Wadsworth & Turpin, Ordered that they be and are hereby Licenced, allowed & admitted to sell & retail all kinds of Spirituous Liquors at their store in this County in any less Quantity than three Gallons for the Term of one whole year.

Page 293: Mary Ferguson Infant orphan of John Ferguson Dec'd came into Court & made Choice of George Anderson Esq'r at her Guardian, Whereupon he the said George Anderson together with Angus Campbell Esq'r his Security did enter into Bond with the Clerk in the sum of £100 for the Securing the said orphan's Estate & Indemnifying the County.

Clem't Davis vs Thos Evans. Assault & Battery. This day Came the parties by their Attorneys & thereupon came also a Jury to wit John Copeland, Drury Boyce, Thos Wilks, John Fields, John Swearings, Sam'l Neighbours, Joshua Arnald, Wm. Ragsdale, Boling Byshop, George Whitmore, Wm Stone & John Blackley who being Elected, Tried, & sworn the Truth to speak upon the Issue Joined upon their oaths say that the Deft is not Guilty of the Assault & Battery as in the Declaration mentioned That the Pltf recover nothing by his bill but for his false Clamour be in Mercy &c & that the s'd Deft go hence without Day & recover against the said Plft his Cost by him in this Behalf Expended.

On application of John Martin on oath a witness for the Plft against the s'd Deft, Ordered that the Plft pay him the sum of 50 shillings for 20 days attendance at 2/6 p'r day.

Also to Manuel Crisp the sum of 12 shillings & 6 pence for 5 days attendance at 2/6 p'r Day.

On application of Claburn Sims adm'r of Wm Sims decd who made on oath that he never had obtain'd a warrant of appraisement, ordered that a warrant of appraisement Issue in Due form & that Letters of adm'n be renewed.

LAURENS COUNTY SC COURT MINUTES 1786-1789

[10 March 1789]

Mary Flanagen vs Benj'n Rainey. Case. Ordered that this suit be Dismist at John Williams' Cost, he being the person who brought the action.

George Morgan vs Wm Mitchell & Geo Anderson Esq'r. Continued by Consent till next Court.

Henry Mondith vs John Journey. Attachment. Ordered to be Dismist at Plfts Cost.

Page 294: On application of James McClintock Ordered that he be Licenced, allowed & admitted to sell & retail all kinds of Spirituous Liquors at his house where he now lives in any less Quantity than three Gallons for the Term of one year from this date.

James McNees vs Goyn Gibson. In Trover. This da Came the Deft by his Attorney & the Plft Tho Solemnly call'd came not but made Default nor is his suit further prosecuted, therefore on Motion of the Deft it is Considered by the Court that he Recover against the s'd Plft five shillings Damages Besides his Cost about his Defence in This Behalf Expended according to the form of the Act of Assembly in that Case made & provided.

Ordered that Letters Testamentary Issue to Wm Goodman & Mary his wife the executors of Rob't Richey dec'd they being duly sworn as the Law Directs & ordered that the same be Recorded.

Ordered that a Warrant of Appraisement Issue to four freeholders in This County to Value & Appraise the Estate of the s'd Robert Richey Decd & Return an account of their Appraisement to the Ex'rs within sixty days from this date.

Daniel McCarty vs Clement Davis. Assault & Battery. This day came the parties by their attorneys & thereupon Came also a Jury (to wit) John Copeland, Drury Boyce, Thos Wilks, John Fields, John Swearings, Sam'l Neighbours, Joshua Arnald, William Ragsdale, Boling Byshop, George Whitmore, Wm Stone & John Blackley who being Elected, Tried, & sworn the Truth to speak upon the Issue Joined upon their oaths say that the Deft is Guilty of the Assault as in the Declaration alledged: and they do assess the Plfts Damages by Occation thereof to the amount of £10. Therefore it was Considered by the Court that s'd Plft Recover against the s'd Deft his Damages afores'd in form afores'd assest & his Cost by him in this Behalf Expended & the s'd Deft in Mercy &c.

On application of Danl Davis on oath a witness in s'd suit, Ordered that the Deft pay him the sum of 30/ for 12 day attendance at 2/6 p'r day.

LAURENS COUNTY SC COURT MINUTES 1786-1789

Page 295: [10 March 1789]

On application of John Simpson he is hereby Licenced, allowed and admitted to Sell & Retail all kinds of Spirituous Liquors in any Less Quantity than three Gallons at his store where he now lives for the term of one year from this date.

On application of John Dan'l Kern he is hereby Licenced, allowed and admitted to Sell & Retail all kinds of Spirituous Liquors in any Less Quantity than three Gallons at his store for the term of one year.

Ordered that Letters of adm'n of all and Singular the Goods & Chattles of Wm Midole dec'd as granted unto Harley Attoway he being first duly Sworn as the Law directs. Elisha & John Attaway Security £500 [stricken]. Ordered Warrant of Appraisement Issue to four freeholders in This County to appraise the Estate of the s'd Wm Midole Decd & Return their Appraisement to the s'd Adm'r within sixty days.

Court adjourn'd till tomorrow morning 9 OClock. Minets sign'd by Jonth'n Downs, James Montgomery, Joseph Downs, Esq'r.

Court met according to adjournment the 11th day of March 1789. Present Jonth'n Downs, Ja's Montgomery, John Rodgers, Joseph Downs, Charles Saxon, Esquires.

David Bailey vs Thos Rodgers. Assault & Battery. Continued by Consent till next Court.

Benj'n Rainey vs Wm Jackson. Attachm't. Continued till next court

Benj'n Rainey vs Mary Babb. Continued by Consent till next Court.

James Yancey vs John Garner. In Debt. Continued by Consent till next Court.

Wm Brown adm'r of Brown dec'd vs Anthony Golding. In Trover. Continued by Consent till next Court.

Page 296: Benj'n Brown vs Anthony Golding. In Trover. Continued by Consent till next Court.

Lewis Banton adm'r of Wood dec'd vs Joseph Williams. Trespass. Continued by Consent till next Court.

Lewis Banton adm'r of Wood dec'd vs Thomas Boyce & Owen Brady. In Trover. Cont'd by Consent till next Court.

Lewis Banton adm'r of Wood dec'd vs Rich'd Pugh. In Trover. Continued by Consent till next Court.

LAURENS COUNTY SC COURT MINUTES 1786-1789

[11 March 1789]

Thomas Murphey adm'r of Greer decd vs Wm Thomason. In Debt. Continued by Consent till next Court.

Lewis Banton adm'r of P. Wood dec'd vs Tho's Wood Jun'r. In Trover. Continued till next Court.

Lewis Banton adm'r of Wood dec'd vs Tho's Wood Sen'r & James Wood. In Trover. Continued till next Court.

Tho's Garner vs Benj'n Rainey. Att'mt. Dismist at Defts Cost Except the Attorneys fee.

Edm'd Mitchusson vs James Allison. Si. Fa. Continued by Consent till next Court.

Martin Williams vs Rich'd Bullock. Attm't. This day Came the Deft by his Attorney & the Plft tho Solemnly call'd came not but made Default nor is his suit further prosecuted, therefore on Motion of the Deft it is Considered by the Court that he Recover against the s'd Plft five shillings Damages Besides his Cost by him in this Behalf Expended.

Page 297: Joseph Downs vs John Ripley. Case. This day Came the Deft by his Attorney & the Plft tho Solemnly call'd came not but made Default nor is his suit further prosecuted, therefore on Motion of the Deft it is Considered by the Court that he Recover against the s'd Plft five shillings Damages Besides his Cost by him in this Behalf Expended according to the form of the act of assembly in that Case made & provided.

Joseph Downs vs John Ripley. In Case. This day Came the Deft by his Attorney & the Plft tho Solemnly call'd came not but made Default nor is his suit further prosecuted, therefore on Motion of the Deft it is Considered by the Court that he Recover against the s'd Plft five shillings Damages Besides his Cost by him in this Behalf Expended.

Wm Jackson vs Benj'n Kilgore. This day Came the Deft by his Attorney & the Plft tho Solemnly call'd came not but made Default nor is his suit further prosecuted, therefore on Motion of the Deft it is Considered by the Court that he Recover against the s'd Plft five shillings Damages Besides his Cost by him in this Behalf Expended according to the form of the act of assembly in that Case made & provided.

John Martin vs Wm Harris. Assault & Battery. This day came the parties by their Attorneys & thereupon came also a Jury to wit John Copeland, Drury Boyce, John Watson, Thos Wilks, Tho's Blackley, John Swearings, Sam'l Neighbours, Joshua Arnald, Wm. Ragsdale, Boling Byshop, George Whitmore, & Wm Stone who being Elected, Tried, & sworn the Truth to speak upon the

Issue Joined upon their oaths say that the Deft is not Guilty of the Assault as in the Declaration mentioned & that each party pay their own Cost Whereupon it was Considered by the Court that it be Dismist accordingly & the s'd Deft in Mercy &c.

[11 March 1789]

Page 298: On application of John A. Elmore Ordered that he be hereby Licenced, allowed & admitted to sell & Retail all kinds of Spirituous Liquors at his house where he now lives in any less Quantity than three Gallons for the Term of one year.

Mary Flanagin vs Benj'n Rainey. Ordered thare may be Summonses Issued to Summons any Garnishee that shall be known to have any of John Williams's property in his hands, in order to Satisfy the Cost of this Suit.

Joseph Dossett vs Ambrose Ripley. Attm't. Discontinued at Plfts Cost.

Ordered that a note Given to the County Treasurer by James Thurston for the sum of Eleven shillings be Discounted in the finis.

John Entrikin vs Clement Davis. Attm't. Discontinued at Plfts Cost.

Saml Ewing vs Clement Davis. Attm't. Discontinued at Plfts Cost.

Joseph Brown vs John Neily. Attm't. This day came the parties by their Attorneys & after hearing each party by their attorney it was ordered by the Court that the Attachment be Dismist at Plfts Cost.

On application of Jacob R. Brown on oath as a witness for the Deft against the s'd Plft Ordered that the Plft pay him the sum of 5/ for 2 days attendance at 2/6 P'r day with Milage for Coming & Going 20 Miles out of Newberry County at 2d p'r mile.

Also for Abia Griffin a witness for the Deft against the s'd Plft the sum of 12/6 for 5 days attendance at 2/6 P'r day.

Also to Wm Cummins the sum of 12/6 for 5 days attendance at 2/6 P'r day.

Also to John Griffin the sum of 5/ for 2 days attendance at 2/6 P'r day.

On application of Duke Williams it is Ordered that he be hereby Licenced, allowed & admitted to keep a public Tavern at his house where in this County for [**Page 299**] the Term of one year. Whereupon he the said Duke Williams Together with John Coal & Reuben Pyles his Securities is previous to his obtaining s'd Licence to Enter in a bond with the Clerk as the Law Directs.

LAURENS COUNTY SC COURT MINUTES 1786-1789

[11 March 1789]

John Lofton vs Saml Ewing. In Trover. This day came the parties by their attorneys & thereupon Came also a Jury (to wit) John Copeland, Drury Boyce, Thomas Wilks, John Fields, John Swearings, Sam'l Neighbours, Joshua Arnald, Wm Ragsdale, Boling Byshop, George Whitmore, & Wm Stone who being Elected, Tried, & sworn the Truth to speak upon the Issue Joined upon their oaths say that the Deft is Guilty of the Trover & Convertion as in the Declaration mentioned: & they do assess the Plfts Damages by Occation thereof to the amount of £15. Therefore it was Considered by the Court that s'd Plft Recover against the s'd Deft his Damages the aforesaid sum of £15 besides his Cost by him in this Behalf Expended. The Defendant Pray'd anew Trial which was Granted by the Court on his payment of Cost.

Clement Davis vs Ann Madden. In Trover. This day came the Deft by her attorney & the Plft tho Solemnly call'd came not but made Default nor is his suit further prosecuted, therefore on Motion of the Deft it is Considered by the Court that she Recover against the s'd Plf't five shillings Damages Besides her Cost by her in this Behalf Expended.

On application of Elizabeth Wright a Witness in s'd suit, ordered that the Plft pay her the sum of 10/ for 4 days attendance at 2/6 p'r day.

Danl McCarty[?] vs Clem't Davis. Assault & Battery. On application made on oath by Josiah East as a witness for the Deft against the s'd Plft Ordered that the Deft pay him the sum of 30/ for 12 days attendance at 2/6 P'r day.

Court adjourn'd till tomorrow morning 9 OClock. Minets sign'd by Jonth'n Downs, Joseph Downs, James Montgomery, George Anderson, Esquires.

Page 300: Court met according to adjournment the 12th day of March 1789. Present Jonth'n Downs, James Montgomery, John Rodgers, Daniel Wright, Esquires.

John Jones vs Rich'd Childres. In Slander. Dismist each party paying their own Cost.

State vs Jas Cuningham. Indictm't. Assault & Battery. The Deft comes into Court & Confesses himself Guilty of the Assault as in the Indictment alledged and throws himself upon the mercy of the Court, Whereupon it was Considered by the Court that he pay a fine of one shilling & Cost of prosecution.

The State vs John Jones. Assault. This day came the parties by their attorneys & thereupon Came also a Jury (to wit) John Copeland, Drury Boyce, John Blackley, Tho's Wilks, John Fields, John Swearings, Sam'l Neighbours, Joshua Arnald, Wm Ragsdale, Boling Bishop, George Whitmore, & Wm Stone who being Elected, Tried, & sworn the Truth to speak upon the Issue Joined upon their oaths say that the Deft is not Guilty of the Assault as in the Indictment alledged. Whereupon it was ordered that he be Discharged therefrom on payment of Cost.

[12 March 1789]

Wm Hall is appointed Overseer of that part of the highway Leading from Dunkins Creek to Enoree River in the place of Nicholas Brown. Ordered that he cause the several free male Inhabitants & Slaves Contagious to & convenient to said Road to work thereon & keep the same in Good repair for one year from this date.

State vs Martin Martin. Indictment. Assault & Battery. Dismist on Martin Martin paying Cost of prosecution.

John D. Kern vs Charles Hutchings. In Case. This day came the parties by their attorneys & thereupon Came also a Jury (to wit) John Copeland, Drury Boyce, John Blackley, Tho's Wilks, John Fields, **[Page 301]** John Swearings, Sam'l Neighbours, Joshua Arnald, Wm Ragsdale, Boling Bishop, George Whitmore, & Wm Stone who being Elected, Tried, & sworn the Truth to speak upon the Issue Joined upon their oaths say that the Deft is not Guilty of the Nonperformance of the promises & assumptions in the Declaration mentioned & that he go hence without day and Recover against the s'd Plft his Cost by him in this behalf expended, Whereupon it was ordered accordingly.

On application made on oath by James Adair a witness in said suit, ordered that the Plft pay him the sum of 35/ for 14 days attendance at 2/6 P'r day.

Also Joseph Adair the sum of 32/ for 13 days attendance at 2/6 P'r day.

Also Tho's Ewing the sum of 30/ for 12 days attendance at 2/6 P'r day.

Also Jas Johnson the sum of 7/6 for 3 days attendance at 2/6 P'r day.

Also James Young the sum of 35/ for 14 days attendance at 2/6 P'r day.

Also Saml Dillard the sum of 30/ for 12 days attendance at 2/6 P'r day.

Margaret Jones vs Abraham Adams. In Slander. Dismist at Defts Cost.

Court adjourn'd till tomorrow morning 9 OClock. Minets sign'd by Joseph Downs, James Montgomery, Daniel Wright, Esquires.

Court met according to adjournment the 13th day of March 1789. Present James Montgomery, Charles Saxon, Dan'l Wright, Wm Mitchusson, Angus Campbell, George Anderson, Esquires.

LAURENS COUNTY SC COURT MINUTES 1786-1789

[13 March 1789]

Wm Goodman & Mary Goodman vs John Richey. Case continued till next Court at Plfts Cost.

John Gorely vs Edw'd Mitchusson Adm'r of D. Chew decd. Discontinued at Plfts Cost.

A Deed for the Conveyance of 100 acres of Land from Hugh McVay to Robert Culbertson proven in open Court by the oath of James Culbertson and ordered to be recorded.

Page 302: William Thos Rodgers vs Philip Wells & Benj'n Rainey. In Debt[?]. The Court after hearing the parties decreed that the Plft recover against the s'd Defts the sum of £10 besides his cost by him in this behalf Expended. Ordered that the Plft stay Execution Three Months. Capt. Edw'd Mitchusson comes into Court & undertakes for the Defts that he will be Security for his paying the above Judgment.

Ordered that Lewis Banton adm'r of Peter Wood decd have three months time Given him to Return an account of the s'd Administration.

Charles Sullivan vs John Donnahow & Wm Donnahow. In Trover. This day came the parties by their attorneys & thereupon Came also a Jury (to wit) John Copeland, Drury Boyce, John Blackley, Thomas Wilkes, John Fields, John Swearings, Sam'l Neighbours, Joshua Arnald, Wm Ragsdale, Boling Byshop, George Whitmore, & Wm Stone who being Elected, Tried, & sworn the Truth to speak upon the Issue Joined upon their oaths say that the Defts are Guilty of the Trover & Conversion as in the Declaration mentioned & they do assess the Plfts Damages by Occation thereof to the amount of £50 besides his Cost. Whereupon it is Considered by the Court that said Plft Recover against the s'd Defts his Damages the aforesaid in form afores'd assest & his Cost by him in this Behalf Expended & the s'd Defts in Mercy &c.

On application made on oath by Mary McFagin a Witness in s'd suit, ordered that the Defts pay her the sum of 20/ for 8 days attendance at 2/6 p'r day.

Also to Mary Mitchell the sum of 25/ for 10 days attendance at 2/6 p'r day.

Also to Eliz'a Kennedy the sum of 17/6 for 7 days attendance at 2/6 p'r day.

Also to Wm Thomason the sum of 45/ for 18 days attendance at 2/6 p'r day.

Also to Sarah Dunklin the sum of 17/6 for 7 days attendance at 2/6 p'r day with Going & Coming 20 miles at 2d p'r mile.

Also to John Thomason the sum of 20/ for 8 days attendance at 2/6 p'r day.

[13 March 1789]

Also to Stephen Sullivant the sum of 22/6 for 9 days attendance at 2/6 p'r day.

Also to James Filpot the sum of 7/6 for 3 days attendance at 2/6 p'r day.

Page 303: John Gocher vs Thomas Mars. Ordered that a Firi Facias Issue for to lett him the s'd Thomas Mars to be and appear at our next Court to be held on the second Monday in June next to shew cause if any he has why an Execution may not be Issued against him on a judgment formerly obtain'd against him by the s'd John Gocher.

John Smith vs Wm Davis. Continued by Consent till next Court.

Joseph Dunklin & Sarah Dunklin vs Wm Donnahow & John Donnahow. In Trover. This day came the parties by their attorneys & thereupon Came also a Jury (to wit) John Copeland, Drury Boyce, John Blackley, Thomas Wilks, John Fields, John Swearings, Sam'l Neighbours, Joshua Arnald, Wm Ragsdale, Boling Bishop, George Whitmore, & Wm Stone who being Elected, Tried, & sworn the Truth to speak upon the Issue Joined upon their oaths say that the Defts are Guilty of the Trover & Conversion as in the Declaration mentioned & they do assess the Plfts Damages by Occation thereof to the amount of £50 besides his Cost. Whereupon it was Considered by the Court that s'd Plfts Recover against the s'd Defts their Damages afores'd in form afores'd assest & their Cost by them in this Behalf Expended & the s'd Defts in Mercy &C.

Walter Roberts vs Wm Mitchusson. In Trover. The parties mutually submitted the Determination of this suit to the award of Thomas Perkins & David Smith with Leave to Chuse am Umpire in Case they cannot agree. Ordered that the s'd Arbitrators Return their award to next Court.

Mary Dunklin & David Brown vs Hugh Brown. This day came the Deft by his attorney & the Plft tho Solemnly Called came not but made Default Nor is their suit further prosecuted, therefore on Motion of the Deft it is Considered by the Court that he Recover against the s'd Plfts five shillings Damages Besides his Cost about his Defence in This Behalf Expended.

Page 304: Martin Williams vs Holloway Power. Continued till next Court.

Wm Griffin vs John Jones. Continued by Consent till next Court.

John Mitchell is appointed overseer of that part of the highway leading from the Tumbling shoal on Redy River to Rutlege's ford on Saluday in the place of Robert Box. Ordered that he cause the several free male Inhabitants & Slaves Contagious to & convenient to s'd Road to work thereon & keep the same in Good repair for one year.

LAURENS COUNTY SC COURT MINUTES 1786-1789

[13 March 1789]

George Caldwell vs John Richey. In Debt. Continued by Consent till next Court.

Charles Brady vs Thos Allison. Slander. Continued under Compromise.

Clement Davis vs Reubin Pyles. Continued by Consent till next Court.

Ordered that the County Treasurer settle with Joseph Griffin for Building a Publick Bridge & the balance if any there be Due pay unto him the said Joseph Griffin.

Thomas Elliott vs David Burns, Barnes Chandler, & David Burns Junr. In Debt. Continued by Consent till next Court.

Ordered that Robert Bell be appointed Constable in the place of John Owing the s'd Owins resigning his office.

John Danl Kern vs Charles Hutchings. In Case. On application made on oath by John Jones a witness in s'd suit, Ordered that the s'd Plft pay him the sum of 7/6 for 3 days attendance at 2/6 P'r day.

Ordered that Dickason Austin be appointed Constable in the place of John Wright.

Page 305: Robert Culbertson is appointed overseer of that part of the highway leading from Theopholis Goodwin's to Little River near the Courthouse in the place of Robert Ross. Ordered that he cause the several free male Inhabitants & Slaves Contagious to & convenient to s'd Road to work thereon & keep the same in Good repair for one year.

Court adjourned till Court in Course. Minits sign'd by James Montgomery, Dan'l Wright, George Anderson, Wm Mitchusson, Esquires.

At a Court held for the County of Laurens at the Courthouse The Eighth day of June AD 1789. Present Joseph Downs, George Anderson, Angus Campbell, Silv's Walker, John Rodgers, Ja's Montgomery, Esq'rs.

Ordered that James Pucket be appointed Constable in the place of Robt Bell.

The following persons were Drawn to serve as Pettit Jurours for next Sept'r Court (to wit)

1. Lewis Graves	11. James McClain	21. James Miller
2. John Powell	12. John Carter Jun'r	22. John Benson
3. Wm Blackley	13. Charles Jones	23. Benj'n Malden
4. James Clardy	14. John Jones	24. Wm McClure

5. Joseph Burton	15. Ja's Blackley	25. Hugh Abernath [*sic*]
6. Wm Brown	16. Martin Martin L.	26. James Taylor
7. Jeremiah Daniel	17. Anthony Griffin	27. John Prude Jun'r
8. Wm Rodgers	18. John Murphey	28. Wm Gilbert
9. Tho's Jones	19. George Madden	29. Edw'd Box
10. Cha's Pucket	20. Sam'l Dunlap	30. John Henderson

[8 June 1789]

Page 306: A Lease & Release for the Conveyance of 200 acres of land from Wm. Cooper to Solomon Langston Proven in open Court by John Campbell & Agnes Couch & Ordered to be Recorded.

A Lease & Release for the Conveyance of 225 acres of land from Charles Simmons to James Templeton acknowledged in open court & Ordered to be Recorded.

An Account of the appraisement of the Estate of Wm Hellams dec'd was presented into open Court by John Hellams adm'r of the said Estate & Ordered to be Recorded.

Ordered that Lewis Saxon pay unto Joseph Griffin the sum of £2 it being the ballance due him for building the County bridge over Little River.

An Account of the appraisement of the Estate of Wm Medole dec'd was presented into open Court by Harley Attoway adm'r of the said Estate & Ordered to be Recorded.

Ordered that Letters of adm'n of all & singular the Goods & Chattles of George Moore Dec'd be Granted to Nathan Barkesdale he being duly Qualifyed as the Law Directs. Whereupon he the said Nathan Barkesdale together with Charles Allen his Security entered into & Acknowledged their bonds in the sum of £100 with Condition according to law. Ordered that a Warrant of appraisement Issue to four freeholders in this County to View & appraise the Estate of the s'd Dec'd & Return an Inventory of their proceedings to the said adm'r within sixty days.

Ephraim Ramsey is hereby Admitted to practice as an atto' in this County he having satisfy'd the Court of his obtaining Licence as the law Directs.

John Meek is appointed overseer of that part of the highway leading from Mill Creek to the Island ford on Saluday in the place of Clement Dial. Ordered that he cause the several free male Inhabitants & Slaves Contagious to & convenient to s'd Road to work thereon & keep the same in Good repair for one year from this date.

Page 307: Martin Doyal is appointed overseer of that part of the highway leading from Thomason's mill to the bridge above Cornelius McMahan's in

LAURENS COUNTY SC COURT MINUTES 1786-1789

the place of James Downen. Ordered that he cause the several free male Inhabitants & Slaves Contagious to & convenient to s'd Road to work thereon & keep the same in Good repair for one year from this date.

[8 June 1789]

The Last will & testament of Wm Prather Dec'd was presented in open Court & proven by the oath of John Lindsey & ordered to be Recorded.

An account of the appraisement of the Estate of James Allison Dec'd was Return'd & presented in open Court by Ja's Allison Jun'r ex'tr of the said Estate & the same was ordered to be Recorded.

Wm Dendy is appointed Constable by the Court. Ordered that he be Enroll'd as such.

On the petition of the Inhabitants of this County, ordered that a publick bridge be built over Little River where the publick Road leading from Hammons's old store to the Island ford on Saluday Crosses s'd Little River near to Hugh Oneal's mill & that Silvanus Walker & Angus Campbell Esq'rs be & is hereby appointed Commissioners to let the building of said bridge Either at publick or private contract, which ever they may find most of the advantage of the publick.

James Puckett is appointed overseer of that part of the highway leading from Thomas Carter's old place to Swanceys ferry on Saluday in the place of Lewis Banton. Ordered that he cause the several free male Inhabitants & Slaves Contagious to & convenient to s'd Road to work thereon & keep the same in Good repair for one year from this date.

Court adjourn'd till Tomorrow morning 8 Oclock. Minits sign'd by John Hunter, Geo. Anderson, Angus Campbell, James Montgomery, Silvanus Walker, Esquires.

Page 308: Court met according to Adjournment the 9th day of June 1789. Present Jonathan Downs, James Montgomery, John Hunter, Silvanus Walker, Esq'rs.

Geo: Morgan vs Wm Mitchell & George Anderson. In Debt. Dismist by Consent at Defts Cost.

State vs Ann Hall. Bastardy. The s'd Ann Hall swore before James Montgomery Esq'r that Wm Dean of this County is the father of s'd Bastard Child, which she also acknowledged in Court. Whereupon it was considered that the said Ann Hall pay a fine of £3 s11 d8 together with Cost. The Court agreed to give her Twelve months for the payment of the said Fine.

[9 June 1789]

An Inventory of the Appraisement of the Estate of Wm. Sims Dec'd was presented into open court by Clabourn Sims Adm'r of the s'd Estate & was ordered to be Recorded.

Susanna Man vs Josiah Grier, James Grier & John Jones. In Trover. Refer'd to the Award of John Hunter Esq'r, John Owins & Joseph Adair. Ordered that they Return their award to Next Court.

John Lofton vs Samuel Ewing. In Trover. This day Came the parties by their Attorneys & thereupon came also a Jury (to wit) Benj Stone, James Young, Thomas Springfield, Geo: Morgan, Wm. Hellams, John Attoway, Ben: Carter, Sam'l McClurkin, Joseph Mahorn, Tho's Rodgers, Jonathan Hollingsworth & Holloway Power who being sworn the Truth to speak upon the Issue Joined upon their oaths do say that the Plft hath Sustained Damages by Occation of the Trover & conversion as in the Decl'n mentioned to the Amount of £12. Whereupon it was considered by the Court that the said Plft Recover against the said Deft his Damages afores'd in form afores'd assest & his Cost by him in this Behalf Expended & the s'd Deft in Mercy &c.

Page 309: On application of Thomas Loften a witness for the Plft in said suit, Ordered that the Deft pay him the sum of 32/6 for 13 days attendance at 2/6 P'r day.

Ordered that Robert Young be appointed Constable for this County.

On application of John Carter Jun'r, Ordered that Letters of adm'n of all & singular the Goods & chattles Right & Credits of Geo: Carter Dec'd be granted him the s'd John Carter, he being first duly sworn according to Law. Whereupon he the s'd John Carter Together with John Carter Sen'r & David Green Entered into and Acknowledged their Bond in the sum of £500 with Condition according to Law.

Ordered that a Warrant of appraisement Issue to four freeholders in this County to Value & appraise the Estate of the s'd Dec'd & Return an account of the same to the said adm'r within sixty days from this date.

Lewis Saxon assinee of D. Brown vs. Charles Sullivant. S. Process in Debt. This day came the Parties by their attorneys & the Deft proving payment the sum of £5 s5. Whereupon it was Considered by the Court that the s'd Pltf recover against the s'd Deft the ballance of his note amounting principal Interest to £2 s9 together with his cost by him in this behalf Expended.

An account of the adm'n of Robert Richey Dec'd was Return'd into open Court by Wm Goodman the Executor & Ordered to be Recorded.

LAURENS COUNTY SC COURT MINUTES 1786-1789

[9 June 1789]

On application of Abigal McNight for Letters of adm'n of all & singular the Goods & chattles Right & Credits of And'w McNight Dec'd. Ordered that a Citation issue Citing & Admonishing all & Singular the Kindred & Creditors of the s'd Dec'd to appear at our next court to shew cause if any they have why Letters of adm'n may not be Issued as afores'd.

Ordered that Letters of adm'n of all & singular the Goods & chattles Right & Credits of Wm Parker Dec'd be granted unto Geo: Anderson, he being first duly sworn according to Law. Whereupon he the s'd Geo: Anderson Together with Wm Anderson & John Rodgers Esq'r his Securities is to Enter into and Acknowledge their Bond with the clerk in the sum of £500 with Condition according to Law.

Ordered that a Warrant of appraisement Issue to four freeholders in this County to Value & appraise the Estate of the s'd Dec'd & Return an account of the same to the said adm'r within sixty days from this date.

James Yancey vs John Garner. In Debt. The Deft Came into Court & says that he cannot Gainsay the Plfts action for the sum of £15 **[Page 310]** with Interest & Cost Whereupon it Was considered by the Court that the s'd Plft Recover against the said Deft the sum of £15 with Interest 7 his Cost by him in this behalf Expended.

Reuben Pyles vs Clement Davis. In Debt. Discontinued at Plfts Cost.

Wm Martin son of Shadrach Martin is hereby appointed Constable.

In the suit John Loftin vs Saml Ewing, the Jury is ordered to bring in their verdict, sealed up next Court. They being retired to Consult of the same.

Court adjourn'd till Tomorrow morning Eight Oclock. Minits sign'd by Geo. Anderson, John Rodgers, Dan'l Wright. Esq'rs.

Court met according to Adjournment the 10th of June 1789. Present Geo: Anderson, James Montgomery, John Rodgers, Daniel Wright, Esq'rs.

The State vs Ann Hall. Bastardy. Ordered that Wm. Dean the father of her Bastard Child pay unto her weekly the sum of two shillings for the Term of Ten years for the Maintainance of s'd Bastard child.

On application of Jacob Bowen he is admitted to sell & Retail all kinds of Spirituous Liquors at his mother's house on Durbins Creek in any Less Quantity than three Gallons for the term of one year.

Richard Collins vs Reubin Stone. In Debt. Continued by Consent till next Court.

LAURENS COUNTY SC COURT MINUTES 1786-1789

[10 June 1789]

David Pedan vs Holloway Power. Att'a. Dismist at Plfts. Cost.

Marshall Franks & Patty Franks vs Joshua Arnald & Leanna Arnold. In Slander. Dismist at Mutual Cost.

Edw'd Garret vs Charles Puckett. In Debt. Dismist at Defts Cost.

Page 311: Lewis Saxon vs Charles Sullivant. On application made on oath by James Russell a witness for the Plft in said suit, Ordered that the Deft. Pay him the sum of 5/ for 2 days attendance at 2/ P'r Day.

Lancelot Armstrong vs Benjamin Kilgore. In Debt. The Deft. Comes into Court & Says that he Cannot Gainsay the Plfts action therefore he Confessed Judgem't according to the Note with Interest & Cost. Whereupon it was Considered by the Court that the s'd Plft Recover against the s'd Deft accordingly.

The State vs Ann Nevels. Bastardy. The said Ann Nevels came into Court & made oath that Martin Hughey is the father of a certain Bastard child begotten on her body. Ordered that she the said Ann Nevels pay a fine of £3 s11 d8 with cost. The court Gives her twelve months to pay the s'd fine in.

Robert Cooper vs Rich'd Carrol. S. Process. The Court after hearing the parties Decreed that the said Plft Recover against the s'd Deft the sum of £5 s10 together with his cost by him in this Behalf Expended.

Joseph Akins vs Philip Wells. In Trover. Dismist at Defts Cost.

Lewis Banton adm'r of P. Wood Decd vs Joseph Williams. In Trespass. Dismist at Defts Cost.

A Deed for the Conveyance of 150 acres of Land from Dan'l Wright to Lewis Akins acknowledged in open Court & ordered to be Recorded.

Lewis Banton adm'r of P. Wood Decd vs Thos Wood Sen'r & James Wood. In Trover. Dismist at Defts Cost.

On application of Jonathan Johnson he is admitted to sell & Retail all kinds of Spirituous Liquors at his house in this County in any Less Quantity than three Gallons for the term of one year.

Page 312: Reubin Pyles vs James McNees. James McNees vs Reubin Pyles. Same vs Same. On motion to the Court by Consent of all parties Concerned in these three actions. Ordered that all matters now in Controversy Touching the same be Refered to the Arbitratement of Thomas Wadsworth & And'w Rodgers Jun'r & case they cannot agree in their award that they Chose a

LAURENS COUNTY SC COURT MINUTES 1786-1789

Third person whose Judgem't shall be Conclusive on both parties. Ordered also that the award be Returned to next Court & that Judgem't be Entered upon the same & that in case of Refusal, neglect or any other cause, the award shall not be Return'd at next Court that then these Causes do posotively come on to Trial without further Delay or procrastination.

[10 June 1789]

On application of Bradford Camp he is hereby Licenced, allowed and admitted to Sell & Retail all kinds of Spirituous Liquors at the Cross Road near the Tumbling Shoals on Redy River for the Term of one whole year from the date hereof in any Less Quantity than three Gallons he paying the tax due thereon.

William Fleming vs Francis Cuningham. Att'a. The attachment being Return'd on sundry Articles the property of the said Defts on motion of James Yancey Plfts attorney. Ordered that the Sheriff Expose to sale so much of the property of the said Deft as shall be sufficient to satisfy the Pltf his Demand amounting to £11 s4 & cost of suit.

Robert Cooper vs Francis Cuningham. Att'a. The Constable Returned the Attachment into Court executed on sundry Articles of the property of the said Defts. Therefore on motion of the Plft Ordered that the Sheriff Expose to publick sale so much of the property attach'd in the hands of the Constable as shall be sufficient to satisfy the Pltf his Demand amounting to £5 s19 & cost of suit.

Wm Griffin vs John Jones. In Trover. The parties by their attorneys mutually submitted the Determination of this suit to the award of John Hunter Esq'r, Jacob Brown, and Joshua Teague, & agreed that their award thereupon should be made a Judgment of this Court. Ordered that the said Arbitrators Return their Award to next Court.

John Smith vs Wm Davis. In Trover. Refered to the award of Joshua Teague, Wm Cason, Cager Bennet & Thomas Ewing & agreed that their award thereupon should be made a Judgment of this Court. Ordered that the said Arbitrators Return their award to next court.

Ordered that all officers fees upon Estrays be hereafter paid them out of the price of s'd Estrays when sold.

Page 313: Ordered that the County Treasurer pay unto Lewis Saxon Clerk of the Court five pounds due him for his Extra Services for the Last Year.

Reubin Pyles vs Clement Davis. Att'a. Ordered that all the Property of the s'd Deft attached be by the Sheriff Exposed to Publick sale & The moneys arising from such sale pay unto the Plft to satisfy his Demand amounting to £13 s11 with Interest & Cost of suit.

[10 June 1789]

Ordered that the County Treasurer pay unto Sheriff Anderson what money shall appear on Settlement to be Due him for his Extra Services &c.

Ordered that the Sheriff cause the door of the Goal of this County to be Repaired & Return a bill of the Expence of the same to next court.

Richard Carrol vs Francis Cuningham. Att'a. The Constable Return'd the attachment Executed on sundry articles in the hands of Edward Gideon the property of the Deft. Ordered that the Sheriff Exposed to Publick sale so much of the said Property attach'd as will satisfy the Plfts Demand amounting to £5 s10 d3 & Cost of suit.

Ordered that the County Treasurer pay unto Thomas Ruly[?] a poor man of this County the sum of forty shillings when he shall [have] so much of the publick money in his hands.

Saml Boling is appointed overseer of the highway leading from the County Line to Crumbies mill & Kitt Smith Do from s'd mill at the Cross Road at Kemp's. Ordered that they cause the several free male Inhabitants & Slaves Contagious to & convenient to s'd Road to work thereon & keep the same in Good repair for one year from the date hereof.

Ordered that the Road Leading from Little River near the Courthouse to John McClintock's be Turned by Dan'l Martin's & Robert Culbertson's thence the way the same is Layd off to s'd McClintock's.

Court adjourn'd Till Court in Course. Minits sign'd by Angus Campbell, Geo: Anderson, James Montgomery, John Rodgers.

Page 314: At a Court held for the County of Laurens at the Courthouse on the 14th day of Sept'r 1789. Present Joseph Downs, Silvanus Walker, Geo: Anderson, Esq'rs.

The following persons were drawn to serve as Grand Jurours at next Decm'r Court (to wit)

1. Richard Griffin
2. Reubin Pyles
3. Charles Allen
4. Wm Hunter
5. Nehemiah Franks
6. Thomas Ewing
7. John McClintock
8. Edmond Learwood
9. James Saxon
10. Wm Teague
11. Robert Cooper
12. John Brown Jun'r
13. Robert Hunter
14. Robert Todd
15. Ezekiel Griffin
16. Zachariah Bailey
17. James Watts
18. And'w Rodgers Jun'r
19. Sam'l Fleming
20. Sam'l Saxon

LAURENS COUNTY SC COURT MINUTES 1786-1789

[14 September 1789]

The following persons were drawn as Pettit Jurours for next Court.

1. Robert Allison	11. Cornelius Dendy	21. Jonth'n Reed
2. Thomas Cason	12. Drury Smith	22. Dan'l South
3. John Manley Jun'r	13. Jesse Meeks	23. John Saxon Jun'r
4. John Miller	14. James Willson	24. John Copeland
5. Drury Boyce	15. Wm Hall	25. Wm Thomason Jun'r
6. John George	16. John Fowler	26. John Norris
7. Martin Martin Bg	17. Sam'l Scott	27. John Meek
8. John Medole	18. John Wigginton	28. Wm East
9. Sam'l Lemon	19. Elliott Clardy	29. Micheal Megee
10. Marmaduke Pinson	20. Wm Wadkins	30. Wm Martin

John Milam came into Court & Resigned the office of Constable whereupon it was ordered accordingly.

David Bailey vs Thomas Rodgers. Assault & Battery. By consent of the parties this suit mutually Submitted [to] the Determination of this suit to the award of Silvanus Walker Esq'r, Saml Wharton, James Abercrumbie, & Geo Hollingsworth as arbitrators & agreed their award Thereupon should be made a Judgment of this Court. The said Arbitrators now return their award in these words, to wit, we find for the [Page 315] Plft Cost of suit Whereupon it was ordered accordingly.

Hugh Crumbless vs Curtis Moore. In Slander. Ordered to be Dismist.

Thomas Elliott vs David Logan & John Richey. In Debt. Abated as to Logan.

Reubin Pyles vs Hugh Young. S. Process in Debt. The Deft Comes into Court & says that he cannot gainsay the Plfts action for the sum of £10 with interest whereupon it was considered by the Court that the s'd Plft Recover against the Deft the aforementioned sum of £10 with Interest & Cost.

An account of the estate of George Carter Dec'd was Returned into open Court by John Carter the adm'r & was ordered to be Recorded.

On application of David Madden, Ordered that Licence be granted him to Sell & Retail all kinds of Spirituous Liquors in any Less Quantity than three Gallons at or near the Cross Roads near James Sullivant's in this County for the term of one year from this date.

Ordered that the defaulters of the Jury be Cited to appear at next Court to shew Cause why they did not appear at this Court in order to serve as Jurours.

On application of Mary Murphey, Ordered that Letters of Adm'n be granted her on the estate of John Murphey Dec'd, she being first duly sworn according to Law. Ordered that a warrant of Appraisement Issue to four freeholders in This County authorising them to Value & Appraise the Estate of the said John Murphey Decd & Return an account of s'd appraisement to the Adm'r within the time prescribed by law. David Green & Daniel Wright Security £500 penalty.

Court adjourn'd till Tomorrow Morning 9 OClock. Minits signed by Silvanus Walker, Geo: Anderson, Joseph Downs, Esquires.

Court met according to Adjournment the 15th of Sep'r 1789. Present James Montgomery, John Rodgers, Wm Mitchusson, Esquires.

Charles Saxon vs Cornelius Cargill. Sum Process. The Court after hearing the parties decreed that the Plft Recover against the s'd Deft the sum of £2 s18 d4 with Cost of suit.

Page 316: A Deed for the Conveyance of 100 acres of land from Edward Pucket to Douglas Pucket was Acknowledged in open Court & Ordered to be Recorded.

Hugh Young vs James McNees & Robert McNees. S. Process. Debt. Nonsuit.

Charles Saxon vs Sam'l Neighbours & James Hulsey. S. Process. Debt. The Deft Sam'l Neighbours came into Court & sayed that he Could not Gainsay the Plfts Action for the sum of £3 s9 d11 with Cost whereupon it was Considered by the Court that the said Plft Recover against the Deft the afores'd sum of £3 s9 d11 with Cost of suit.

Wm Hill vs Ja's McNees. In Debt. The Deft came into Court & says that he Cannot Gainsay the Plfts Action for the sum of £16 s16 d10, according to Note, whereupon it was Considered by the Court that the said Plft Recover against the Deft the afores'd sum aforesaid with Interest & Cost of suit.

Ordered that Letters of adm'n of all and Singular the Goods & Chattles Rights & Credits of James Lindley Dec'd be granted to Tho's Lindley he being duly Sworn as the Law directs, whereupon he the said Thomas Lindley together with John Rodgers Esq'r & David Dunlap his Securities Entered into & acknowledged their bond in the sum of £500 with condition according to Law.

Ordered that a warrant of Appraisement Issue to four freeholders in This County to View & appraise the Estate of the s'd Ja's Lindley Dec'd & Return an account of their Appraisement to the s'd Adm'r within the time Prescribed by Law.

Reubin Pyles vs James McNees. Case in Assumpset. This day came the parties by their attorneys & thereupon came also a Jury (to wit) John Powel, Wm. Blackley, James Clardy, Wm. Rodgers, Charles Pucket, John Carter,

LAURENS COUNTY SC COURT MINUTES 1786-1789

Charles Jones, Hugh Abernath, George Madden, Sam'l Dunlap, James Miller & Benjamin Maddin, who being Elected Tried & sworn the truth to speak upon the Issue Join'd upon their oath do find for the Plft the sum of £5 s4 d8 with Interest & cost Whereupon it was Considered by the Court accordingly & the s'd Deft in Mercy &c.

Page 317: [15 September 1789]

John Boyd vs Thomas Springfield. Sum'r Process Debt. This day came the Parties by their Att'ys but the Plft's atto not bring the Action Lawfully it was ordered that the Plft be nonsuited & that the Deft Recover against Him the sum of 5/ for his Damages in said suit besides his Cost by him in this behalf Expended.

On application of John Langston on oath a witness in said suit, ordered that the Plft pay him the sum of 12/6 for 5 days attendance at 2/6 P'r day with Mileage for Going & Coming 30 Miles Twice at 2d P'r Mile.

Reubin Pyles vs Jas McNees. On application [of] John Martin Sen'r on oath a witness in s'd suit, Ordered that the Deft pay him the sum of £3 for 24 days attendance at 2/6 P'r day.

Also to Ambrose Hudgins the sum of 20/ for 8 days attendance at 2/6 P'r day.

Court adjourn'd till Tomorrow morning 9 OClock. Minits sign'd by John Hunter, James Montgomery, Dan'l Wright, Esq'rs.

Court met according to adjournment the 16th day of Sept'r 1789. Present John Hunter, James Montgomery, John Rodgers, William Mitchusson, Esq'rs.

On application of Robt H. Hughes, ordered that he be Licenced, allowed & Admitted to keep a publick Tavern & to Sell & Retail all kinds of Spirituous Liquors in any Less Quantity than three Gallons at his house on Duncan's Creek near Kern's store for the term of one year from this date. Whereupon he the s'd Robt H. Hughes together with Doct'r George Ross & John Willson entered into and acknowledged their bond in the sum of £500 with Condition according to Law.

James Adair vs Eliphaz Riley. S. Process Debt. Continued by Consent till next Court.

A. Rapley & Geo Anderson vs John Richey. Att'a. Dismist at Defts Cost.

Thomas Cahoon vs Wm Mitchusson. Sum'r Process. Dismist at Defts Cost.

Page 318: Robert Long is appointed Overseer of that part of the Highway leading from Dunkin's Creek to Hendrick's old place on the so fork of Dunkins' Creek in the place of Wm Boarling. Ordered that he cause the several free male Inhabitants & Slaves Contagious to & convenient to s'd Road to work thereon & keep the same in Good repair for one year from this date.

[16 September 1789]

David Pedan vs Holloway Power. Sum'r Process Debt. The Court after hearing the Parties by their Attorneys Decreed that the Plft Recover against the said Deft the sum of ---- according to Note with Interest & Cost.

Wadsworth & Turpin vs John Richey. Att'a. The Sheriff having Return'd the att'a Levyed on Sundry articles the property of the said John Richey & The Deft having come into Court by Cha's Goodwin his Att'o and Confessed Judgment for the sum of £38 s13 s6 sterling with Cost of suit. Ordered that the Property return'd in the Scedule by the Sheriff or so much thereof as is Necessary to satisfy the afores'd debt & Cost be by the Sheriff Exposed to Public sale & The moneys arising from such sale be paid into the hands of the Plft.

Wm Goodman & his wife vs John Richey. The Parties mutually submitted the Determination of the suit to the award of Doct'r Jacob Brown & Richard Griffin with Leave to Chose an umpire in case they cannot agree & agreed that their award thereupon should be made a Judgement of this Court. Ordered that the s'd Arbitrators Return their award to next Court.

Wm Goodman vs John Richey. Att'a. Refered to the award of Doctor Jacob Brown & Richard Griffin & that their award thereupon should be made a Judgem't of this Court. Ordered that they Return their award to next Court.

Page 319: State vs Martin Hughey. On a case of Bastardy. On the Examination of Ann Nevels on oath it appears that the said Martin Hughey is the father of a bastard Child begotten on her body. Whereupon it was Considered by the Court that the s'd Martin Hughey pay a fine of £10 proclamation money at next Court.

Ordered that the said Martin Hughey Pay unto the said Ann Nevels the sum of £3 p'r year for the term of Ten years for the Maintainance of the said bastard child.

The Last will and Testament of David Logan Dec'd was presented in open Court by Angus Campbell Esq'r one of the Ex'trs therein Named & proven in open court by the oath of Reubin Pyles one of the witnesses thereto & was ordered to be Recorded.

Ordered that Letters testamentary Issue him the said Angus Campbell on the estate of the said David Logan dec'd he being Duly qualified according to Law.

LAURENS COUNTY SC COURT MINUTES 1786-1789

[16 September 1789]

Ordered that a warrant of Appraisement Issue to four freeholders to wit Geo: Anderson, Richard Griffin, Jonth'n Johnson & Alex'r Snell to View & Appraise the Estate of the s'd David Logan Decd & Return an account of the said appraisement to the said Ext'r within the time prescribed by Law.

James McNees vs Reubin Pyles. In Detinue. This day Came the parties by their Attorneys & thereupon came also a Jury (to wit) John Powel, Wm Blackley, James Clardy, Wm. Rodgers, Charles Pucket, John Carter, Charles Jones, Hugh Abernath, George Madden, Saml Dunlap, James Miller & Ben Malden who being Elected, Tried, & sworn the Truth to speak upon the Issue Joined went out of Court to consult of their Verdict & being Return'd into Court to Render the same, The Plfts was solemnly called but came not is his suit further prosecuted; whereupon on motion of the Deft by his atty was Considered by the Court that the Jurours from Rendering their Verdict be Discharged & the said Pltf be nonsuited & that the said Deft go hence without day & recover against the s'd Plft five shillings Damages besides his cost by him in this Behalf Expended &C.

The Last will and Testament of And'w McNight Dec'd was presented in open Court by Abigail McNight & And'w McNight Jun'r the Ex'rs therein Named & was proven by the oath of Martin Hughey & ordered to be Recorded.

Page 320: Ordered that Letters testamentary be granted unto Abigail McNight & And'w McNight Junr on the estate of the said And'w McNight dec'd they being Duly sworn as the Law directs. Also ordered that a warrant of Appraisement Issue to four freeholders in this county to View & Appraise the Estate of the s'd Decd & Return an account of the same to the Ext'r within the time prescribed by Law.

Justices present Silvanus Walker, Angus Campbell, James Montgomery, Joseph Downs, John Hunter, Charles Saxon, Wm Mitchusson, Danl Wright, George Anderson, Esquires.

The Court proceeded to the Choice of a Sheriff when Wm Hunter was by a majority of the Justices chosen as Sheriff for the County of Laurens & The same was ordered to be Recorded & a certifyed copy thereof Given unto him.

John Rodgers Esq'r comes into court & Resigns his Commission as a Justice of the Peace for the County of Laurens, which was accordingly Received, ordered that the same be Recorded.

A Lease & Release for the Conveyance of 74 acres of land from John Hunter Esq'r to John Black acknowledged in open court & ordered to be Recorded.

James McNees vs Reubin Pyles. In Slander. This day Came the parties by their Attorneys & Thereupon came also a Jury (to wit) John Powell, Wm

Blackley, James Clardy, Wm. Rodgers, Charles Pucket, John Carter, Charles Jones, Hugh Abernath, Geo: Madden, Sam'l Dunlap, James Miller & Ben Malden who being Elected, Tried, & sworn the Truth to speak upon the Issue Join'd upon their oaths do say that the Deft is Guilty of the slander as in the Declaration mention & they do assess the Plfts damages by occation thereof to the amount o £19 s15, whereupon it was considered by the Court that the Plft Recover against the s'd Deft his Damages afores'd in form afores'd assest & his Cost by him in this behalf Expended & the s'd Deft in Mercy &c. The Deft moved for a new Tryall to be taken up in the morning.

[16 September 1789]

Page 321: Angus Campbell vs John Kellet. In Trover. Refer'd to the award of John Hunter & And'w Rodgers Ordered that they Return their award to next court.

Martin Williams vs Holloway Power. S. Process. Debt. Nonsuit.

Court adjourn'd till Tomorrow Morning 9 OClock. Minits signed by Joseph Downs, Dan'l Wright, John Hunter, Esquires.

Court met according to Adjournment the 17th day of Sept'r 1789. Present John Hunter, Cha's Saxon, Wm Mitchusson, Dan'l Wright, Esquires.

John Crabtree vs Thomas Hughes. S. Process in Debt. This day came the Deft into Court & the Plft tho Solemnly Called came not nor is his suit further prosecuted, therefore on Motion of the Deft it is Considered by the Court that he Recover against the s'd Plf't five shillings Damages besides his Cost by him in this behalf Expended.

This day John Milam came into Court & was sworn according to Law as Constable. Also Lewis Wells is appointed Constable & was duly sworn in open court.

Thomas Garner assinee of Daniel Brown vs Wm Jackson and Wm Gilbert. Sum'r Process. Debt. The Court after hearing the Parties Decreed that the Plft Recover against the Defts the sum of £10 with interest & cost of suit.

John Simpson vs John Richey. Att'a. Came the Deft into Court by Charles Goodwin his Attorney & Confessed Judgment for the sum of £42 s1 d1 with Interest from the dates of the Several Notes & Cost of suit, Whereupon it was ordered that the Sheriff expose to sale the property attach'd & the money arising from such sale pay unto the Plaintiff.

Page 322: The State vs Philip Wells. The Sheriff having Return'd the Fi Fa Executed on the property of the Deft & not sold, Wm. Mitchusson Esq'r comes into court & undertakes as security for the Deft that he will pay the fine dew by the Deft to the state of £10 at next Court. Whereupon it was ordered that the Sheriff stay the sale of the Defts Property till next court.

[17 September 1789]

James Adair vs Eliphaz Riley. By Consent of the Parties ordered that a Commission Issue directed to John Calloway Smith and Wm Robertson Esq'r or any other Justices of the County of Wintown [sic, for Winton] to take the Examination of John Wild a witness for the Deft he giving the adverse party Ten days Previous Notice of the Time & place of s'd Examination & Return a Certificate of the same to our next Court Together with this Commission.

John Cargill vs Wm Harris. Sum'r Process. Debt. This day Came into Court the deft & the Plft tho Solemnly Called came not but made Default Nor is his suit further Prosecuted, therefore on Motion of the Deft it is Considered by the Court that the Def't Recover against the s'd Plf't five shillings Damages Besides his Cost in This Behalf Expended.

Joel Burgess vs James Owens. Att'a. This day came the Parties by their attorneys, Whereupon it was Ordered by the Court that the Deft Enter into Special Bail. Wm Dandy came into Court & undertakes for the Deft James Owings that in case he the said James Owings Deft shall be cast in this Action that he the said Wm Dendy will satisfy & pay the Cost & Condemnation of the Court or Render the sd Owings's body in discharged thereof. The Parties by their Attorneys came forward to Try & after some debates on both sides it was Considered by the Court that the Plft Recover against the s'd Deft the sum of £5 with cost.

On Application of Roland Burgess a witness for the Pltf vs the s'd Deft, Ordered that the Deft: Pay him the sum of 5/ for 2 days attendance.

Also to Wm Ship the sum of 10/ for 4 days attendance at 2/6 P'r day.

Wm Dendy the Defts Special bail brought the Deft into Court & Delivered up his body in Discharge of his being his Special bail. Whereupon it was ordered that the s'd Wm Dendy be Discharged from being bail as afores'd & For want of other bail the Deft is ordered to [be] committed into the Custody of the Sheriff.

Page 323: A Renounciation from Ann Barksdale to wm. Barksdale proven in open Court & ordered to be Recorded.

Rosanna Glenn vs Reubin Flanagin. By Consent of the Parties by their Attorneys This suit is ordered to be Continued till next Court & the parties agrees in these words (to wit) we do hereby agree to Continue this suit by consent & to take Col'o Levy Casey's Deposition at next Newberry Court & Col'o Thomas Brandon's Deposition at the next Union Court to be read in Evidence in Chief on the Tryal of this Cause.

LAURENS COUNTY SC COURT MINUTES 1786-1789

[17 September 1789]

Robert Cooper vs Francis Cuningham. Att'a. The Constable having attached Divers articles which was afterwards proven by Susanna & Isabella Cuningham before John Hunter & Charles Saxon Esq'rs which They the s'd Susanna & Isabella Claims as their property, Ordered that a Jury thereupon be sworn & Thereupon they came to wit, John Powell, Wm Blackley, Ja's Clardy, Wm. Rodgers, Charles Pucket, John Carter, Charles Jones, Hugh Abernath, George Madden, Saml Dunlap, James Miller & Ben Malden who being Elected, Tried, & sworn to Try this cause do say that the s'd Susanna Cuningham & Isabella Cuningham's claim to the Property is Good. Whereupon it was ordered that the Property proven by the s'd young women be Delivered up to them.

Susanna Man vs Josiah Greer & James Greer. The Trial of this suit being Refer'd to the Award of John Hunter Esq'r, John Owings, & Joseph Adair, & the award being Return'd Sign'd by Two of the s'd Arbitrators but was objected against by the Plfts Att'o & the objection being agreed to by the attorneys on both sides of the Question it was ordered that the s'd Award be set aside; & the parties therefore by their attorneys came to trail & thereupon came also a Jury (to wit) John Powell, Wm Blackley, Ja's Clardy, Wm. Rodgers, Charles Pucket, John Carter Jun'r, Charles Jones, Hugh Abernath, George Madden, Saml Dunlap, Ja's Miller & Ben Malden who being Elected, Tried, & sworn well & Truly to Enquire of Damages in this suit upon their oath do say that the Plft hath Sustained Damages by occation of the Trover & Convertion in the Declaration Mentioned to the Amount of £19 besides her cost; therefore it is considered by the Court that the Plft Recover against the s'd Defts her Damages afores'd in form afores'd assest & her cost by her in said suit Expended & the s'd Defts in Mercy &c.

The Defts gave Notice that they Intended to move an arrest of Judgment. Ordered to be Taken on Saturday.

On motion made by Jane Nicks on oath a witness for the Plft vs the Defts in s'd Suit, Ordered that they the s'd Defts pay her the sum of ten shillings for 4 days attendance at 2/6 p'r day.

Page 324: James Saxon & Samuel Saxon vs Francis Cuningham. Att'a. Default. Ordered that the Deft appear either himself or by his atty & plead to the Plfts Declaration on or before the Second Monday in Septr in the year 1790, otherwise Judgment will then be Given & awarded against him.

Court adjourn'd till Tomorrow morning 9 OClock. Minits sign'd by Wm. Mitchusson, Dan'l Wright, John Hunter, Joseph Downs, Esq'rs.

Court met according to adjournment the 18th of Sept'r 1789. Present John Hunter, Wm Mitchusson, Dan'l Wright, Esquires.

LAURENS COUNTY SC COURT MINUTES 1786-1789

[18 September 1789]

The State vs Wm Dean. Bastardy. Ordered that an Execution Issue against the s'd Wm Dean for the Money which was adjudged to Ann Hall for the Maintainance of a bastard Child begotten on her body by the s'd Wm. Dean.

On Motion made by Ephraim Ramsey, ordered that the schedule of accounts with the Vouchers for the same Relative to the Estate of James Williams Dec'd be Lodged by the Executors in the Court of Ordinary for this County & that Joseph Downs, John Hunter & Lewis Saxon, Esq'r, be appointed to Examine the said Accounts & Report the amount of the same.

John Adair vs James Miller. In Slander. By Consent this suit is ordered to be Dismist at Deft's Cost.

John Simpson vs James Owings. S. Process. Debt. The deft came into court & says that he cannot Gainsay the Plfts action for the sum of £2 s1 d4 with Interest whereupon it was considered by the Court that the Plft Recover against the s'd Plft his debt afores'd & his cost by him in this behalf Expended.

Wm Moore & Sarah Moore vs Joseph Parsons. Special action on the Case. Dismist at Plfts Cost.

Thomas Elliot vs David Burns, Barnes Chandler & David Burns Jun'r. By consent this suit is ordered to be Dismist at Defts Cost.

Page 325: John Rainey vs Thomas Philpot. Att'a. John Philpot by James Yancey his Attorney Enters an Interpleader & Claims a Right to a bay horse that was attach'd ordered to be Tried at next Court. They deft being solemnly called came not whereupon it was ordered that Judgement by Default be Entered against him. Ordered that the other property of the Defts attach'd be by the Sheriff Exposed to Publick sale & the money arising from such sale to Remain in the hands of said Sheriff & that he make Return of the same to Next Court.

Thomas Elliott vs David Logan & John Richey. In Debt. Dismist at Plfts Cost. Ordered to be Renew'd vs Logan's Ext'rs & Richey.

Sam'l Eakins vs John Richey. Att'a. The Constable Return'd the Attachment Executed by Summoning George Anderson Esq'r as Garnishee. Ordered that a Sci: Fa: Issue against the s'd Garnishee to appear at next Court to shew cause why Judgement should not be Entered against him.

Ordered that all officers of the court & Major Millwee Produce on Wednesday in next court a fare & true settlement of all accounts they have against the County with all Due credits to s'd acct's to be Examined by John Hunter,

LAURENS COUNTY SC COURT MINUTES 1786-1789

Jonathan Downs, & Silvanus Walker, esquires, & that the s'd parties be served by a Copy of this order by the Sheriff.

[18 September 1789]

Susanna Man vs Josiah Greer & James Greer. This day the Defts attorney moved for an arest of Judgement but the same was overruled by the Court.

Ordered that all Estrays liable to be sold this court be by the Sheriff Exposed to Publick sale at a Credit of six months, the purchasers giving their notes with approved Security.

Court adjourn'd till Court in Course. Minits sign'd by John Hunter, Joseph Downs, Wm Mitchusson, Esquires.

Page 326: At a court held for the County of Laurens at the Court house on the 14th day of Decem'r 1789. Present Silvanus Walker, George Anderson, Jona'n Downs, Angus Campbell, Joseph Downs, Esquires.

The[n] Proceeded to draw the Petty Jury when the following Persons were drawn to wit

1. John Shirley
2. Sam'l Eakins
3. Steven Emery
4. Isaac Carter
5. Francis Lester
6. Wm Taylor
7. Jas Obryant
8. Alex'r Hamilton
9. George Berry
10. John Wells
11. Frederick Little
12. Wm Thompson
13. Willeby Pugh
14. Moses Pinson
15. Wm Goodman
16. Joseph Gallagly
17. Rob't Carter
18. Joseph Patterson
19. James White
20. Nathaniel Neiles
21. Sam'l Williams
22. James Adair
23. Andrew Burnsides
24. Nathan Granshaw
25. Ja's Sullivants
26. Edward Garret
27. John Riverland
28. John Carter
29. Wm Elliott
30. John Sadler

On application of Mary Murphey adm'r of John Murphey Dec'd Ordered that time be Given her till next court to make Return of the Inventory of said Estate.

On application of Edw'd Box, Ordered that Letters of adm'n of all & singular the goods & chattles Right & Credits of James Williams Dec'd be granted to him the said Edward Box, he being first duly sworn as the Law directs.
Ordered that a warrant of appraisement Issue to four freeholders in this county to view and appraise the estate of the s'd Dec'd, Return an account of the same to the adm'r with the time Prescribed by Law. Duke Pinson & John Box Security, £500 penalty.

An account of the appraisement of the Estate of James Lindley dec'd was Return'd in open court by Thos Lindley the adm'r & was ordered to be recorded.

LAURENS COUNTY SC COURT MINUTES 1786-1789

[14 December 1789]

Ordered that a Citation Issue to Francis Johnson to appear at our Next court to shew cause why Letters of Adm'n with the will annexed should not be granted to Peter Smith on the estate of Rob't Johnson Dec'd.

The Court Proceeded to Chose a County attorney for this county Whereupon William Shaw Esq'r was appointed county attorney temporary.

The State vs Peter Smith. Rescous. On the oath of Timothy Goodman a constable that Peter Smith on Thursday the 24th of Sept'r Last forceably took out of his custody Property which he had Legally Executed & Assaulted him in the Execution of his office. Ordered that the s'd Peter Smith Enter into Recognizance with Two Good Securities in the sum of £20 not to depart this court till he is Discharged from the same by a Due course of Law.

Page 327: The said Peter Smith together with John Smith his Security came into court and acknowledged themselves Indebted to the Justices of the County court of Laurens in the sum of £20 to be levyed of their Respective goods & Chattles, Lands & Tenements yet upon condition that if the s'd Peter Smith shall not Depart this court untill Discharg'd therefrom by a Due course of Law.

Thomas Cargill vs Cornelius Cargill. Appeal from the Judgment of Esq'r Walker. The court after hearing the Parties confirm'd the Judgement for the sum of £ 1 17 4 together with cost of suit. John Martin comes into court & undertakes as security for the s'd Cornelius Cargill that in case the s'd Cornelius Cargill does not Pay the afores'd Judgement & Cost that he will; the Plft agrees to stay Execution Three months.

Ben: Rainey vs Wm Jackson. Att'a. Ordered to be Dismist.

Ordered that the Appearance Docket & Trial Docket be both called over which was accordingly done.

Watson & Guess vs Robt H. Hughes. Atta. Dismist at Defts Cost.

The State vs Peter Smith. Timothy Goodman the Prosecutor comes into court and acknowledged himself Indebted to the Justices of this County in the sum of £20 be Levyed of his Respective Goods and chattles, Lands & Tenements yet upon condition that if he the said Timothy Goodman shall appear & Prosecute this Indictment against the said Peter Smith.

Ordered that the children of Grace Bailey, orphan Children of Thos Bailey, Dec'd, be by Wm Dendy constable brought to court in order to be bound out at the Law Directs.

LAURENS COUNTY SC COURT MINUTES 1786-1789

Court adjourn'd till Tomorrow morning Nine OClock. Minits sign'd by Jonth'n Downs, Geo: Anderson, Joseph Downs, Esquires.

Court met according to Adjournment the 15th day of Decem'r 1789. Present Jonth'n Downs, Geo: Anderson, Charles Saxon, James Montgomery, Esquires.

The last will and Testament of John Cuningham Dec'd was brought into open court by the Ext'r therein named & was proven by the oath of David Dunlap and ordered to be Recorded. Orderd that Probate thereof Issue in Due Form.

Page 327 [there are two pages numbered 327: Ordered that Letters of adm'n of all and Singular the Goods, Chattles & Credits of John Sullivant Dec'd be granted unto Fanney Sullivant (widow of the s'd John Sullivant Dec'd) & James Sullivant they being duly Sworn as the Law directs. Whereupon they the said Fanney Sullivant & James Sullivant Together with David Green their securities Entered into and acknowledged their Bond in the sum of £100 as the law directs.

Ordered that a warrant of Appraisement Issue to four freeholders to View & appraise the Estate of the s'd John Sullivant Decd & Return an account of the said Appraisement to the s'd Adm'r within the Time Prescribed by Law.

The Last will & Testament of Ellenor Lewis Dec'd was presented in open Court by John Dalrymple & George Dalrymple the Executors therein name & was proven by the oath of Joshua Teague one of the witnesses thereunto & Ordered to be Recorded & that Probate thereof Issue in due from.

Ordered that a warrant of Appraisement Issue to four freeholders to View & appraise the Estate of the s'd Ellenor Lewis & Return an account of s'd Appraisement to the s'd Ext'r within the Time Prescribed by Law.

Ordered that Letters of Adm'n with the will annexed on the Estate of Barnet Kernall Dec'd be Granted to Grace Kernall & Thomas Cason they being duly sworn as the Law Directs. Patrick Kernall being Dead & John Turner the other Ex'tr having Resign'd their Executorship. Whereupon the s'd Grace Kernall & Thos Cason Together with ---- their Security Entered Into and acknowledged their bond in the sum of £250 as the Law Directs.

Ordered that a warrant of Appraisement Issue to four freeholders to view & appraise the Estate of the said Barnet Kernall Dec'd, Return an account of s'd Appraisement to the s'd adm'r within the Time Prescribed by Law.

William Hunter Produced a Commission in open Court signed by his Excellency Charles Pinckney Esq'r Gov'r and Commander in chief in & over the state of So Carolina Bearing date the 21st day of Nov'r 1789 Commissioning him the said Wm Hunter Esq'r to be Sheriff for the County of Laurens & he took the oaths of office as the Law Directs, whereupon he the said Wm Hunter together with Jonathan Downs & James Montgomery, Esqrs, his

LAURENS COUNTY SC COURT MINUTES 1786-1789

Securities in open Court acknowledged their Bonds in the penal sum of £1500 with Condition according to law.

[15 December 1789]

Page 328: Commission from Gov. Charles Pinckney to Wm Hunter appointing him as Sheriff, 21 Nov 1789.

John Archer Elmore by Wm Hunter & the approbation of the Court is hereby appointed Deputy Sheriff for the County, Whereupon he the s'd John Archer Elmore came into Court & took the oath of Allegiance Together with the oath of Office as the Law Directs.

Page 329: Wm Goodman & Mary Goodman vs John Richey. Att'a. The parties mutually Submitted The Determination of This suit to the award of Jacob Brown & Rich'd Griffin & agreed that their award thereupon should be made a Judgement of this Court which s'd Arbitrators now return'd their award in these words (To wit) that the Deft John Ritchey Pay unto the s'd Plfts the sum of £7 s2 d7 with Cost of suit, Whereupon it was ordered accordingly.

Same vs Same. Att'a. The parties mutually Submitted The Determination of This suit to the award of Jacob Brown & Rich'd Griffin & agreed that their award thereupon should be made a Judgement of this Court which s'd Arbitrators now return'd their award in these words (To wit) that the s'd Goodman Pay all the Cost accrued on This suit, Whereupon it was ordered accordingly.

The Last will & Testament of Nehemiah Ferguson being presented in open Court by James Ferguson one of the Ex'trs therein Named & was proved by John Dalrymple a witness thereto and Ordered to be Recorded & that Probate [**Page 330**] thereof Issue in Due Form, he the s'd James Ferguson being duly sworn as the Law Directs.

Ordered that a warrant of appraisement Issue to four freeholders To View & appraise the Estate of the s'd Nehemiah Ferguson & Return an Account of the s'd Ext'r within the term prescribed by Law.

John Simpson assinee of Tho's Cuningham vs David Bailey. S. Process in Debt. The Deft. came into court & Confessed Judgement according to Note with Interest & Cost the Pltf allowing him 4/8 P'r hundred weight it being a Tobacco Note, Whereupon it was ordered accordingly.

John Simpson vs Josiah East. S. Process. Debt. The Deft comes into Court & says that he cannot Gainsay the Plfts action for the sum of ----- according to Note with Interest & Cost, Whereupon it was ordered accordingly.

LAURENS COUNTY SC COURT MINUTES 1786-1789

[15 December 1789]

Ordered that the Sheriff Put Wm Rodgers in Joal for Contempt of Authority & Misbehaviour in Court.

On application of Ben Stone The court Granted that the s'd Ben Stone could turn the Road that Leads from Laurens Courthouse to Swancey's ferry where it passes his house.

James Owings is appointed overseer of that part of The highway Leading from Micheal Waldrop's to Hugh Oneal's mill in the place of Hugh Young. Ordered that he the s'd James Owings cause all & singular the free male Inhabitants & Slaves Contagious to & convenient to s'd Road to work thereon & keep the same in Good repair for one year from this date.

On application of Thomas Lindley adm'r of Ja's Lindley Dec'd, Ordered that the s'd Tho's Lindley Expose to publick sale all the Estate of the s'd dec'd.

On application of Esq'r Mitchusson, ordered that James Satterfield be appointed Constable for s'd Wm Mitchusson, Esq'r.

The State vs Abbey Dorsett. Recognizance. Continued till next court.

John Simpson vs Micheal Gaffort & Francis Lester. Sum'r Process in Debt. Dismist at Defts Cost.

Ordered that the Sheriff Summon Twelve men as Guard to set over & Guard the Goal.

Page 331: Ben: Adair Jun'r, Joseph Adair, Martha Adair, Hezekiah Adair & Isaac Adair, Infants orphans of John Adair Dec'd came into Court Chose Ben: Adair Senr as their Guardian; Whereupon he the s'd Benjamin Adair Sen'r Together with Joseph Adair his Security Entered into & acknowledged their Bond according to Law.

Court adjourned Till Tomorrow Morning Nine OClock. Minits signed by Silvanus Walker, George Anderson, William Mitchusson, Esquires.

Court met according to Adjournment the 16th day of Decm'r AD 1789. Present Jona'n Downs, Ja's Montgomery, Wm Mitchusson, Silv's Walker.

John Simpson vs Benj'n Stone. S. Process. Debt. The Deft comes into court & says that he cannot Gainsay The Plfts action for the sum of ---- according to Note with Interest & Cost Whereupon it was Considered by the Court that the s'd Plft Recover against the s'd Deft his debt & Cost afores'd.

LAURENS COUNTY SC COURT MINUTES 1786-1789

[16 December 1789]

John Simpson vs Ayres Goley. Sum'r Process in Debt. The Court after hearing the Parties Decreed that the Plft Recover against the s'd Deft the sum of £6 s15 together with Interest & Cost.

James Adair vs Eliphaz Riley. S. Process debt. This day came the Parties by their attorneys & thereupon came also a Jury (To wit) John Meeks, Drury Boyce, Martin Martin, John Medole, Sam'l Lemon, Marmaduke Pinson, Jesse Meeks, John Wigginton, James Willson, Elliott Clardy & John Norris who being Elected Tried & Sworn the Truth to spa upon the Issue Join'd upon their oaths do say that the Plft take nothing by his bill but for his false Clamour be in Mercy &C & that the Deft Go hence without day & recover against the s'd Pft his cost by him in this behalf Expended &C.

On appl. of John Willson a witness in s'd suit for the s'd Deft against the s'd Plft, Ordered that the Plft pay him the sum of Twelve shillings six pence for 5 days attendance at 2/6 P'r day.

Also to Sam'l McConathy the sum of 17/6 for 7 days attendance at 2/6 P'r day.

Page 332: The State vs Mary Babb. Indictm't Larceny. The Grand Jury Return'd a true bill.

The state vs Peter Smith. Indictm't, Rescous. No bill found. Ordered that the s'd Peter Smith be Discharg'd from his Recognizance on Payment of Cost of the Prosecution.

Where there was yesterday an order made for the Sheriff to put Wm Rodgers in confinement for contempt of authority & the Wm Rodgers this day comes into court & submitted himself to the mercy of the s'd court & Asked Pardon for said offence, whereupon the court forgave him. Ordered that he be discharged from the custody of the Sheriff.

John Lard vs Wm Neil. Assault & Battery. Dismist at Plfts Cost.

John Lard vs Ishem East. Assault & Battery. Dismist at Plfts Cost.

John Simpson assinee of Rich'd Jowell vs Rich'd Carol. Sum'r Process. Debt. Judgem't for the Plfts for 1100 weight of Tobacco at Eleven shillings & Eight pence p'r C Wt with Interest & Cost.

John Simpson vs Micheal Waldrop. In Debt. The Deft comes into court & says that he cannot Gainsay the Plfts action for the sum of £13 s16 d6, Whereupon it was considered by the court that the Plft Recover against the s'd Deft the s'd sum of £13 s16 d6 with Interest & cost.

LAURENS COUNTY SC COURT MINUTES 1786-1789

[16 December 1789]

On application of Charles Simmons & Robt Ross securities for Nancy Simmons administratrix of the Estate of John Simmons dec'd, Ordered that the said Charles Simmons & Robt Ross be Discharged from their being Security as afores'd & that Charles Simmons Jun'r & Wm Simmons Enter into bond as Security for the s'd Nancy Simmons adm'x as aforesaid.

Hugh Young vs James McNees & Robt McNees. S. Process in Debt. The Deft came into court & says that they cannot Gainsay the Plfts action for the sum of £10 with interest, Whereupon it was considered by the court that the Plft Recover against the s'd Defts the s'd sum of £10 with Interest & cost.

Page 333: And'w Rodgers forman, Nehemiah Franks, Zachariah Bailey, Reubin Pyles, Charles Allen, Edmond Learwood, Sam'l Saxon, John McClintock, Sam'l Fleming, Rob't Cooper, Rob't Todd, Rob't Hunter, Wm. Teague, Being sworn as Grand Jurours of Inquest for the body of This County having Rec'd their charge Return'd from the bar to Consult of their Verdict & after some time Return'd into Court & Present as follows, To wit:

The State vs Ben Rainey. Indictm't. The Grand Jury Return'd a True bill. Ordered that the Recognizance be continued till next Court.

The State vs James Rains. Indictm't. Grand Jury Return'd no bill found. Whereupon it was ordered that the s'd James Rains be Discharg'd on payment of cost.

Mary Griffin Adm'r of Anthony Griffin vs. Joseph Griffin Ext'r of Jas Williams Decd. Attachment. Judgment for the Plft for the sum of £8 d18 d1½ with Interest from the first day of Jan'y 1789 And Cost of Suit.

Page 334: Mary Griffin Adm'r of Anthony Griffin vs. Joseph Griffin Ext'r of Jas Williams Decd. Ordered that a Sciri facias Issue against Thos Carter, John Copeland & Robt Taylor to appear at next court to shew cause why Judgment may not be Entered then in This suit.

David Anderson former Sheriff of This county Exhibited his a/c against This County which was rec'd. Ordered that the County Treasurer pay unto the said David Anderson what shall appear to be due him by said bill.

Elizabeth Briggs vs Robt H. Hughes. Att'a. This day came the parties by their attorneys & the Court after hearing the parties by their attorneys & Examining several Witnesses upon the Occation decreed that the Plft recover against the s'd Deft The sum of £4 with Cost of suit.

Court adjourn'd till Tomorrow morning 9 OClock. Minits sign'd by Jonth'n Downs, Silv's Walker, John Hunter, Esquires.

LAURENS COUNTY SC COURT MINUTES 1786-1789

Court met according to adjournment the 17th day of Decm'r 1789. Present John Hunter, Charles Saxon, Ja's Montgomery, Esquires.

The last will and testament of Joseph Adair Dec'd was presented in open Court by James Adair the Ex'r & proven by the oath of James Montgomery & Ordered to be Recorded. Ordered that a Probate thereof Issue in due form &c.

Ordered that a warrant of Appraisement Issue to four freeholders of this county to View and appraise the Estate of the s'd Jo's Adair Decd & Return an account of the same to the Ext'r within the Time Prescribed by Law.

And'w Rodgers Senr vs John Filpot. In Debt. Continued by Consent till next Court.

Page 335: On application of John F. Wolf who obtained Licence at last Decm'r Court to sell & retail all kinds of Spirituous Liquors at his store in the County for the term of one year, Ordered that said Licence be continued of force till next Court.

Wm Harris vs Eliphaz Riley. The plaintiff by Wm Shaw his Att'o moved for a new Trial & the parties being heard by their attorneys, it was ordered that anew Trial be Granted at next court.

John Simpson vs James McNees. By Consent of the Parties the Plft & Deft it was Ordered that the Trial by Charles Saxon Esq'r in this Case should be retried at next Court.

John Rodgers Esq'r came into court & undertakes for James Mcnees the Deft in this action that in case he shall be cast in this action that he wil pay the Cost & Condemnation of the Court or render his body in Discharge thereof to prison.

The State vs Mary Babb. Indictm't. Larceny. This day came the parties by their attorneys & thereupon came also a Jury to wit, John Meek, John Miller, Drury Boyce, Martin Martin, John Medole, Sam'l Lemon, Marmaduke Pinson, Jesse Meeks, James Willson, Wm Hall, Elliott Clardy & John Norris who being Elected Tried & Sworn the Truth to speak upon the Issue Join'd upon their oaths do say that the Deft is not Guilty of charge in the Indictment alledged. Whereupon it was ordered that she be Discharg'd from her Recognizance on payment of Cost of Prosecution. The Deft made oath in open court that she was not able to pay the cost of the above Suit & that she has no property except her cloaths, Whereupon she was Discharged from the paym't of the same. by him in this behalf Expended &C.

Ordered that all the Estrays liable to be sold This court be by the Sheriff Exposed to public sale at a Credit of six months Giving notes with such Security as shall be approved of.

LAURENS COUNTY SC COURT MINUTES 1786-1789

[17 December 1789]

Sam'l Neighbors is appointed overseer of that part of the highway leading from the Tumbling shoals on Redy river to Rutledge's ford on Salluda in the place of Mr. Mitchusson. Ordered that **[Page 336]** he cause the several free male Inhabitants & Slaves Contagious to & convenient to s'd Road to work thereon & keep the same in Good repair for one year from this Date.

Whereas there was an order made that the Children of Thos Bailey should be bound out, but it appears to the Court that the said Children were provided for by their uncle, it was ordered that said order be set aside.

Mary Griffin Adm'r of Anthony Griffin Dec'd vs. Joseph Griffin Ext'r of Jas Williams Decd. Ordered that the Sciri facias ordered to be Issued against Elizabeth Owings & Thomas Carter in this suit be set aside.

David Pedan vs Holloway Power. There being an Execution Issued in This case against the property of the Deft Holloway Power, which Execution the Sheriff has return'd Levyed on the property of the said Deft & the property not sold for the want of Bidders, Whereupon it is ordered that a writ of Venditione Exponas Issue.

On application of Nancy Simmons adm'rx of the Estate of John Simmons Decd it is ordered that she sell & Dispose of the Principal property of the s'd John Simmons dec'd at a Credit of Twelve months after duly advertising the same.

Whereas John Rodgers Esquire has resign'd the office of a Justice of the peace for This County by which means a Vacancy on the bench has been occasioned. The Court in pursuance of the law in such case made & provided proceeded to the Recommendation of a magistrate in his room & upon Taking the --- of the Justices present, Joshua Saxon, Esquire, was deemed by them unanimously to be the Person so Recommended.

John Hunter Esquire having present the court with a court seal as a present from Henry Laurens Esqr, Ordered that ---- to write a letter to that Gentleman in the name of the --- Returning him their thanks for his polite & friendship to the County.

Page 337: Jacob Manor is appointed overseer of that part of the highway leading from the Durbins Creek to the beaverdam Creek in the place of Martin Williams. Ordered that he cause the several free male Inhabitants & Slaves Contagious to & convenient to s'd Road to work thereon & keep the same in Good repair for one year from this Date.

A probate taken before John Hunter Esq'r by Jeremiah Searcy Respecting a set of title deeds from Micheal Willson to Saml Henderson presented in open Court & ordered to be Recorded.

LAURENS COUNTY SC COURT MINUTES 1786-1789

[17 December 1789]

Ordered that the County Treasurer Give up to Hugh Middleton a Certain Note of hand which he hath against him the s'd Middleton which note of hand he Gave for a certain stray hog that he Purchased.

Court Adjourn'd till Court in Course. Minits sign'd by Jonth'n Downs, John Hunter, Joseph Downs, Wm Mitchusson, Esquires.

At a Court held for the County of Laurens at the Courthouse of s'd County on the Eighth day of March 1790. Present Joseph Downs, John Hunter, Dan'l Wright, Ja's Montgomery, Angus Campbell, Esquires.

INDEX

Prepared by James D. McKain

Abbercrumbie, Daniel 50
Abbercrumbie, James 30
Abbercrumbie, John 54
Abercrumbie, James 3, 15, 21, 22, 38, 79, 113, 152
Abercrumbie, John 79
Abercrumby, James 114
Abernath, Hugh 145, 154, 156, 157, 159
Abernathy, Hugh 57
Ackley, Bazaleel 63
Adair, Alex'd 17, 18
Adair, Benjamin 6, 70, 73, 74, 77, 165
Adair, Hezekiah 165
Adair, Isaac 165
Adair, James 6, 9, 10, 12, 20, 24, 25, 32, 42, 44, 49, 53, 85, 87, 141, 154, 158, 161, 166, 168
Adair, John 56, 98, 160, 165
Adair, Joseph 6, 23, 74, 79, 88, 92, 98, 100, 110, 126, 130, 141, 147, 159, 165, 168
Adair, Martha 165
Adair, Ruth 62
Adams, Abraham 141
Adams, George 56, 89
Adams, John 69, 124
Adams, Sarah 89
Akins, George 105
Akins, Joseph 124, 149
Akins, Lewis 149
Akins, Saml 120
Alexander, David 1, 4, 65, 76
Allen, Charles 79, 90, 104, 145, 151, 167
Allen, Lidall 90
Allin, Charles 3-5, 8, 20
Allin, Susannah 20
Allison's Mill 129
Allison, David 10, 30, 31, 43, 47, 79, 93, 97, 100-104, 109, 111, 114
Allison, Elizabeth 132
Allison, Francis 32
Allison, James 9, 14, 29, 34, 43, 64, 70, 72, 130, 132, 138, 146
Allison, Joseph 95, 106, 123, 126, 129, 132
Allison, Mary 132
Allison, Nancy 132
Allison, Robert 67, 152
Allison, Susannah 9, 14, 29, 34, 43
Allison, Thomas 87, 113, 144
And'w Rodgers's Mill 127
Anderson, 151
Anderson, Amus 134
Anderson, Andrew 85
Anderson, David 15, 38, 53, 57, 62, 71, 129, 167
Anderson, George 3, 14-16, 19, 21, 22, 27, 32, 35, 37-40, 43, 45, 46, 50, 51, 57, 58, 62, 64, 68-70, 72, 77-79, 81, 86, 88, 90, 93-95, 101, 106, 115, 118, 119, 130, 131, 133, 135, 136, 140, 141, 144, 146, 148, 151, 153, 154, 156, 160, 161, 163, 165
Anderson, James 87, 91-93, 119
Anderson, Molley 38
Anderson, William 24, 34, 38, 58, 71, 89, 148
Antiant boundry Line 26
Armstrong, Jo's 107
Armstrong, Lancelot 112, 149
Arnald, Edward 36, 37
Arnald, Hendrix 37
Arnald, John 93, 115
Arnald, Joshua 34, 63, 69, 120, 134-136, 138, 140-143, 149
Arnold, Joshua 9, 10
Arnold, Leanna 149
Arnold, Wm 53
Arthur, Hargrove 116
Attaway, Elisha 137
Attaway, John 137
Atteway, Elisha 82
Atteway, Jesse 82
Atteway, Joseph 82
Attoway, Harley 120, 137, 145
Attoway, John 131, 147
Austin, Dickason 144
Austin, Nathaniel 3, 35, 49, 71, 75, 76, 108
Austin, William 10, 13, 90, 103
Babb, Abner 79, 104, 119
Babb, Joseph 57
Babb, Mary 57, 108, 137, 166, 168
Babb, Mercer 80
Babb, Messer 38
Babb, Nancy 16
Bailey, Charity 109
Bailey, David 79, 85, 97, 104, 137, 152, 164
Bailey, Grace 162
Bailey, Gracy 109
Bailey, James 59, 66, 67
Bailey, John 59
Bailey, Thos 162, 169
Bailey, William 55, 63-67, 77, 89, 120
Bailey, Zachariah 50, 54, 73, 79, 82, 104, 151, 167
Bald, William 60, 64
Banton, Lewis 3-5, 8, 30, 33, 34, 54, 81, 92, 93, 96, 106, 124, 125, 129, 131, 137, 138, 142, 146, 149
Barksdale, Ann 158
Barksdale, Nathan 32, 71, 130, 145
Barksdale, Wm 80, 86, 130, 158
Barnes, George 84-86
Barnet, John 14, 32, 33, 35
Barns, George 66
Barton, Beverly 67
Barton, James 39
Batey, Wallace 87
Baugh, Wm 51
Beaverdam Creek 28, 97, 169
Bell, Adam 70, 73, 74, 77
Bell, Robert 144

Bennet, Cager 86, 150
Bennet, Micajah 98
Benson, John 144
Benson, Wm 130
Berry, George 18, 19, 23, 76, 103, 161
Berry, Jean 3
Berry, Wm 103
Bevin, David 60
Bishop-- see also Byshop
Bishop, Boling 89, 140-143
Bishop, Rebecca (Brown) 65
Bishop, Roling 100
Black, John 156
Black, Robt 73
Black, Thomas 102
Blackley, James 123, 126, 129, 145
Blackley, John 120, 134-136, 140-143
Blackley, Thos 20, 50, 120, 138
Blackley, Wm 144, 153, 156, 157, 159
Blackwell, John 30, 42, 89
Blakely, Joseph 106
Blakely, Thos 16, 17
Blalock, John 13, 71, 91, 108
Boarling, Wm 154
Boatman, Waterman 61, 64-67
Bobo, Absolam 104
Bobo, Absolem 50, 79
Bobo, Spencer 97
Boling, Abel 33, 43, 61, 79, 100-104
Boling, John 64
Boling, Saml 21, 22, 26, 42, 58, 103, 151
Boling, William 60
Bowen, Jacob 148
Bowen, Rolley 132
Bowin, Rolley 72
Bowles, John 108
Bowman, Jacob 69, 107, 114
Bowman, John 69
Box, Abraham 101, 106, 123, 126
Box, Edward 53, 135, 161
Box, John 11, 79, 161
Box, Joseph 1, 2
Box, Micheal 107, 123, 126, 129
Box, Phillis 4
Box, Robert 129, 143
Boyce, Drury 51, 120, 134-136, 138, 140-143, 152, 166, 168
Boyce, Thomas 69, 79, 85, 104, 131, 137
Boyce, William 80, 98, 121
Boyd, Abraham 45, 100
Boyd, Jas 72
Boyd, John 30, 47, 54, 69, 88, 99, 132, 154
Boyd, Martha 100, 101
Boyd, Mary 116
Boyd, Saml 47, 72
Boyd, Wm 40, 45, 107
Bradey, Ch'as 113
Brady, Charles 144
Brady, Owen 137
Bramblet, Enoch 41, 81
Brandon, Thomas 4, 158
Bratcher, William 22
Braudy, Chas 79

Bridge over little river 63, 145, 146
Briggs, Elizabeth 71, 167
Briggs, John 32, 71
Briggs, Wm 9
Brigs, Elizabeth 117
Brigs, John 38
Brock, Elias 50
Brock, James 76, 77, 89, 110
Brodey, Charles 100-104, 113
Brooks, Elisha 55
Brooks, George 35
Brotherton, John 6
Brown, Bartlet 58
Brown, Benjamin 19, 58, 137
Brown, D. 33, 34, 36, 48, 147
Brown, Daniel 1, 2, 4, 9, 10-13, 17, 84, 95, 157
Brown, David 143
Brown, Hugh 89, 143
Brown, J. 5, 8-11
Brown, Jacob 2-4, 21, 24, 150, 155, 164
Brown, Jacob R. 90, 98, 139
Brown, John 16, 17, 20, 43, 59, 61, 70, 96, 124, 125, 130, 151
Brown, Joseph 123, 127, 128, 139
Brown, Nicholas 76, 131, 141
Brown, Rebecca (Bishop) 65
Brown, Roger 6, 54, 65, 96, 100, 109, 111, 113, 115, 117
Brown, Saml 14
Brown, Vinson 37
Brown, William 69, 117, 137, 145
Browster, Ann 41
Bryan, Edwerd 66
Bryan, Francis 53
Bucks[?], William 30
Bull, John 81
Bullock, Richard 88, 138
Burchfield, James 42
Burchfield, Joseph 26, 54
Burges, Joel 3-5, 8
Burgess, Elener 80
Burgess, Joel 31, 74, 79, 80, 100-104, 119, 158
Burgess, Richard 32, 38
Burgess, Roland 158
Burk, Aedanus 120
Burk, Edanus 14
Burk, Wm 106
Burke, 21
Burke, Edanus 27, 80, 96
Burn, David 28, 45, 54, 61, 62, 89
Burn, John 82
Burn/s, Ann 125
Burns, David 144, 160
Burns, James 111
Burns, John 111
Burns, Mary 93, 111, 114
Burnsides, Andrew 161
Burnsides, James 50, 55
Burton, Hutchings 79
Burton, Joseph 83, 145
Burton, Wm 54, 106

Bush River 16, 21, 23, 46, 53, 125
Bush, George 29, 31, 33, 34, 36
Bush, John 93
Bydston, Samuel 36, 89
Byshop, Boling 100, 120, 134-136, 138, 140, 142
Cahoon, Thomas 59, 94, 154
Cain Creek 54
Caldwell, Elizabeth 58
Caldwell, George 10, 144
Caldwell, John 13, 16, 39, 40, 89
Caldwell, William 28, 58
Cambridge 116
Cammel, John 20, 80
Cammock, John 96, 109, 111, 113, 115
Camp, Bradford 150
Camp, Nathan 76, 89, 93, 103, 104, 108, 110
Campbell, Anguish 50, 51, 65, 79
Campbell, Angus 86, 87, 94, 96-98, 101, 102, 106-108, 110, 112, 115, 119-122, 126, 128, 129, 133, 135, 141, 144, 146, 151, 155-157, 161, 170
Campbell, Dunkin 121
Campbell, John 119, 145
Campbell, Mary 121
Canant, Hardy 107
Cane Creek 125
Cannon, James 92, 126
Capias, 36
Cargill's Path 97
Cargill, Cornelius 72, 153, 162
Cargill, John 7, 12, 66, 76, 77, 89, 107, 120, 158
Cargill, Sarah 15, 29, 72, 77, 88, 101, 102, 117
Cargill, Thomas 107, 162
Carnes, P. 124
Carnes, Peter 27, 35, 83, 84, 99, 110, 122, 127, 133
Carnes, T. H. P. 101
Carnes, Thomas P. 27, 104, 134
Carns, Peter 122
Carol, Rich'd 166
Carral, Richard 74
Carrol, Richard 102, 149, 151
Carsey, Charity 74
Carsey, Randolph 74
Carter, Benj'n 54, 58, 123, 131, 147
Carter, Elisha 124, 127, 128, 134
Carter, George 147, 152
Carter, Isaac 161
Carter, John 54, 57, 61, 64-67, 79, 104, 128, 130, 144, 147, 152, 153, 156, 157, 159, 161
Carter, Joseph 54
Carter, Rob't 161
Carter, Theoderick 124
Carter, Thomas 81, 124, 131, 146, 167, 169
Carters old fields, 51
Casey, Levy 158
Cason's Ferry 125, 127
Cason's Road 54
Cason, John 58
Cason, Thomas 30, 52, 94, 152, 163

Cason, William 28, 40, 80, 150
Cates, Joseph 81
Cates, Joshua 81, 131
Chandler, Barnes 144, 160
Chandler, King 50
Chapman, John 43, 110, 119, 124
Chapman, Thomas 106, 123, 126, 129
Chappell, Thomas 112
Charleston 16, 116
Charleston Road 28, 97
Chesnut, John 120
Chesser, John 117
Chew, D. 142
Childers, David 68
Childers, John 38
Childers, Richard 38
Childres, David 123
Childres, Richard 132, 140
Childs, Jonathan 35, 65, 131
Choice, Tully 3, 30
Choice, Wm. 112
Chumney, Joseph 63
Chumney, Mary 63
Chumney, William 63
Clarday, Benj'n 110
Clardy, Elliott 152, 166, 168
Clardy, James 62, 144, 153, 156, 157, 159
Clardy, John 59
Clark, Thos 40
Cleaton, James 16
Clinton, Mary 80
Clinton, Pamela 80
Clinton, Robt 80
Clinton, Wm 80
Coal, John 94, 139
Cob, Samuel 10, 14, 22, 29, 34, 39, 43
Coker, John 30, 57, 76, 94, 107
Coker, Rob't 94
Collens, Richard 76
Collins, Richard 32, 36, 37, 72, 110, 148
Conner, John 109
Cook, James 3, 30, 39, 118
Cook, John 52
Cooper, Robert 5, 37, 45, 84, 91, 92, 102, 149-151, 159, 167
Cooper, Wm. 145
Copeland, 130
Copeland, John 134-136, 138, 140-143, 152, 167
Copelin, John 120
Couch, Agnes 145
Couch, Isaac 43
Couch, Millinton 81
Cox, Elizebeth 67
Cox, John 67
Crabtree, John 157
Craddock, Bartholomew 11, 103
Craddock, Bat 116
Craddock, Edmond 37, 54, 57, 67
Craddock, John 13, 17
Craddock, Mary 116
Craddock, Sarah 17, 103
Craig, James 60, 96, 113

3Craig, William 72, 85, 97
Cregg, James 6
Crips, Mansel 82
Crisp, Manuel 135
Criswell, James 40, 45
Crooks, James 28
Cross Road 42, 120, 150, 151
Cross Roads near James Sullivant 152
Crowther, Isaac 99
Crumbies mill 151
Crumbless, Hugh 123, 152
Crumpton, John 6
Culberton, Robert 82
Culbertson, James 142
Culbertson, Robert 8-10, 142, 144, 151
Culpepper County, Virginia 52
Cummins, Wm 139
Cuningham, And'w 97
Cuningham, David 60
Cuningham, Elizabeth 97
Cuningham, Francis 150, 151, 159
Cuningham, Isabella 159
Cuningham, James 97, 140
Cuningham, John 107, 163
Cuningham, P. 134
Cuningham, Patrick 98, 131
Cuningham, Robert 96, 124, 125
Cuningham, Susanna 159
Cuningham, Tho's 164
Cunnigham, Andrew 12
Cunningham, Andrew 24, 58, 82, 85
Cunningham, James 34, 122
Cunningham, Thos 30, 85, 86, 130
Dalrymple--see also Dilrumple
Dalrymple, George 163
Dalrymple, John 163, 164
Daly, Rich'd 135
Dandy, Wm 158
Daniel, Jeremiah 145
Davis, Clement 7, 20, 22, 23, 42, 43, 48, 54, 59-62, 75, 91, 103, 104, 111, 112, 122, 133, 135, 136, 139, 140, 144, 148, 150
Davis, Daniel 22, 80, 104, 136
Davis, Henry 81
Davis, Jonathan 90
Davis, Tho's 127
Davis, William 46, 107, 143, 150
Day, Amry 84
Day, Philip 130
Deal, Clement 29, 31, 33, 34, 36, 52, 67, 129, 130
Dean, Wm 98, 126, 146, 148, 160
Deen, Susannah 41, 44
Defts, John Martin 11
Dendy, Clary 66
Dendy, Cornelius 152
Dendy, Curnelius 64, 70
Dendy, John 87, 91, 93
Dendy, Mary 28
Dendy, Thomas 28, 43-49, 54, 66, 79, 82, 116, 120
Dendy, William 43-49, 66, 79, 82, 104, 146, 162

Denny, John 40
Devall, Lewis 3, 6, 15, 130
Devall, Terry 6
Devenport, 124
Dial-- see also Doyal, Doyall
Dial, Clement 115, 134, 145
Dial, Hasting 98
Dial, Rebekah 98
Dickes, Edmond 104
Dillard, Agness 40
Dillard, James 16, 31, 40, 52, 54, 60, 61, 75, 104, 111, 112, 135
Dillard, Saml 40, 61, 141
Dilrumple, Samuel 36, 89
Dirbins Creek, 26
Dixon, Rich'd 107
Dobson, Wm 126
Docherty, Jas 38
Dodd, Wm. 67
Dohertie, James 120, 124
Dollar, Reubin 31
Donnahoe, Cornelius 122
Donnahoe, Wm 100, 103, 104, 122
Donnahow, John 142, 143
Donnahow, Wm 142, 143
Donnohow, Wm 134
Donohoe, John 13, 36, 74, 77, 79, 80
Dorough, James 29, 31, 33, 34, 36, 61, 64-67
Dorsett, Abbey 165
Dossett, Joseph 139
Dourough, James 84
Downen, James 8, 22, 26, 29, 31, 33, 34, 36, 58, 146
Downs's Shoals 129
Downs, Jonathan 14-16, 19-22, 27, 30, 50, 51, 53, 55, 57, 58, 62, 65-67, 72, 74, 77-79, 86, 90, 92-95, 106, 108, 110, 112, 118, 119, 130, 133, 137, 140, 146, 161, 163, 165, 167, 170
Downs, Joseph 6, 8, 14, 15, 19, 20, 21, 26, 37, 39, 43, 45, 46, 50, 51, 55, 57, 66-68, 77, 79, 81, 94-97, 101, 106, 118, 119, 121, 130, 133, 137, 138, 140, 141, 144, 151, 153, 156, 157, 159-161, 163, 170
Downs, Joshua 118
Doyal, Haisten 40
Doyal, Haisting 52
Doyal, Martin 145
Doyal, Rebecca 52
Doyall, Haisten 40, 45
Doyall, Haisting 50, 59
Doyall, Hasting 114
Doyall, Martin 29, 31, 33, 34, 36
Drake, Edm'd 40
Drew, William 82, 107
Ducket, Thos 131
Duckett, Jacob 25
Dug(g)an, Thomas 93, 94, 104
Duggin, Thos 109
Duke, Elizabeth 3
Dukes, William 105
Duncan's Creek 14, 16, 23, 51, 60, 154
Duncan, James 135

Dunkin's Creek 141, 154
Dunklin, Joseph 143
Dunklin, Mary 143
Dunklin, Sarah 142, 143
Dunlap, David 42, 130, 153, 163
Dunlap, Elizebeth 50
Dunlap, Robert 50
Dunlap, Samuel 73, 145, 154, 156, 157, 159
Dunlap, William 8, 79, 124
Durbin's Creek 97, 129, 148, 169
Durham, Arthur 96, 124, 125, 127
Durham, Mary 77
Durrum, Margaret 57
Durrum, Mary 57
Duty, Rich'd 118
Duvall, Lewis 43, 53, 59, 70, 77, 105, 114, 117
Duvall, Terisy 53
Dyson, Daniel 72
Eakin, Jean 40
Eakin, Saml 40
Eakins, Samuel 3-5, 43, 127, 160, 161
East, Ishem 166
East, Josiah 3, 4, 22, 44, 51, 62, 104, 140, 164
East, Shadrach 108
East, Thos 43
East, Wm 108, 152
Edg(e)hill, Thomas 8, 9, 16, 40, 67, 93, 115, 129, 134
Edwards, Cha's 97
Edwards, James 97
Edwards, John 41, 62, 97
Edwards, Mary 97
Edwards, Stokes 96, 108, 110, 112, 113, 115, 117
Edwerds, Charles 72, 85
Edwerds, James 81
Edwerds, John 81
Edwerds, Mary 81
Elliott, George 78
Elliott, Thomas 84, 89, 131, 144, 152, 160
Elliott, Wm 161
Elmore, John 68, 90, 92, 121
Elmore, John A. 82, 139
Elmore, John Archer 109, 164
Emery, Steven 161
Endsley, Andrew 37
England, Charles 30, 31
Enoree River 16, 23, 28, 32, 63, 141
Entrekin, Elizebeth 41
Entrekin, John 21, 41, 94, 97, 105
Entrekin, Thomas 47
Entrikin, John 139
Evans, Benjamin 4
Evans, Thomas 31, 59, 135
Ewing, Samuel 18, 51, 70, 86, 89, 98, 100, 111, 124, 139, 140, 147, 148
Ewing, Thomas 6, 23, 53, 54, 96, 110, 113, 123, 135, 141, 150, 151
Fakes, Thomas 96
Fakes, Thomas W. 42, 65
Fakes, Thomas Wm. 40, 57

Falkner, John 68
Farbarn, James 76
Faris/s, Robert 13, 103, 107, 108, 123, 126, 129
Faris/s, Wm. 51, 103
Farris, Robert 90
Farrow, John 37
Farrow, Landon 114
Farrow, Saml 113, 114, 116
Farrow, Thomas 37
Ferguson, James 78, 164
Ferguson, John 78, 135
Ferguson, Mary 135
Ferguson, Nehemiah 164
Fields, John 81, 120, 121, 131, 134-136, 140-143
Filbay, Absolem 60
Filpot, James 143
Filpot, John 79, 168
Findley, Charles 117
Finney, Jas 9, 30
Finney, Robt 61, 64
fishdam Road 125
Flack, 58
Flanagan, George 90
Flanagan, Mary 134
Flanagan, Reuben 81
Flanagan, Reubin 110
Flanagen, Mary 136
Flanagin, Mary 139
Flanagin, Reubin 158
Fleming, Samuel 16, 17, 20, 151, 167
Fleming, William 150
Floyd, James 26, 47, 55, 68, 118
Floyd, Wm 123
Ford, Elisha 37, 38, 80
Ford, John 26, 61
Fowler, John 152
Fowler, Joshua 29, 63
Fowler, Wm 28
Frank, Saml 10
Franks, Marshall 14, 51, 63, 79, 149
Franks, Marshel/l 3, 42
Franks, Nehemiah 3, 21, 24, 42, 47, 52, 63, 69, 95, 96, 124, 125, 151, 167
Franks, Patty 149
Franks, Robert 30, 39, 46, 47, 79
Franks, Samuel 69, 87, 91-93
Freeman, Rob't 120
Freemon, Mary 17
Freemon, William 17
Freneau, Peter 16
Fuller, Winney 33
Furgurson, John 83
Furguson, James 58, 83
Furguson, John 57, 83
Furguson, Mary 58
Gafford, Michl 79
Gafford, Thomas 20
Gaffort, Micheal 165
Gaigee, Joseph 106
Gallagla, Wm 96
Gallagly, Joseph 161

175

Gamel, James 96
Gammel, James 109, 121
Gammel, John 47, 121
Gammell, James 111
Gant, Nebo 92
Garner, John 63, 67, 73, 75, 78, 137, 148
Garner, Thomas 128, 138, 157
Garrat, John 54
Garrat, Silas 54
Garret, Edward 149, 161
Garret, John 95, 107, 126, 129
Garret, Silas 96, 108, 110, 112, 113, 115, 117
Garrett, Edwerd 89
Gary, Elizebeth 60, 66
George, John 152
Georgia, State of 92
Gibson, Goyn 71, 83, 136
Gibson, Jacob 60, 66
Gibson, Mary 60, 66
Gideon, Edward 59, 151
Gidien, Edw'd 94
Gilbert, James 117
Gilbert, Jonathan 24, 89
Gilbert, William 63, 84, 87, 90, 65, 115, 117, 145, 157
Gill(i)am, Robt 28, 42, 111
Glass, Vinson 47
Glen/n, John 37
Glen/n, Joseph 29, 31, 33, 34, 36, 69
Glen/n, Rosanna 110, 158
Glidewell, Wm 47, 78
Gocher, John 2, 65, 143
Golden, Anthon(e)y 46, 90
Golden, Richard 17
Golding, Anthony 135, 137
Goley, Ayres 166
Gooden, Theophiless 16, 17
Goodman, James 110
Goodman, Joseph 36, 45, 72, 90, 104, 108, 109, 121
Goodman, Mary 136, 142, 164
Goodman, Meriah 38
Goodman, Moriah 109
Goodman, Samuel 80
Goodman, Timothy 162
Goodman, William 83, 91, 93, 94, 110, 127, 136, 142, 147, 155, 161, 164
Goodwin, 15
Goodwin, C. 34-36
Goodwin, Charles 1-3, 5, 7, 8, 10, 12, 39, 75, 91, 155, 157
Goodwin, Jesse 39
Goodwin, John 21, 22, 54, 88, 125, 127
Goodwin, Rachel 88
Goodwin, Robt 17, 63, 76
Goodwin, Theophiless 20, 54, 81
Goodwin, Theopholis 144
Gorden, Adam 73
Gorden, Elizabeth 82
Gorden, Thomas 82
Gorely, Ayres 13, 15, 23, 92, 93
Gorely, John 69, 117, 142
Gorman, Thomas 54, 80

Granshaw, Nathan 161
Grant, Alex'd 11, 12, 48
Grant, Jane 11, 12
Grant, Jean 11, 48
Graves ford 21
Graves, Lewis 38, 87, 91-93, 144
Gray, Abraham 19, 58, 85
Gray, John 29, 31, 33, 34, 36, 61, 86, 96, 98, 108, 110, 112-115, 117
Gray, Wm 105
Green, David 147, 153, 163
Green, Wm. 43-49
Greenville County 112
Greer, 99, 138
Greer, Isia 112
Greer, James 112, 159, 161
Greer, Josiah 159, 161
Greir, John 126, 129
Grier, James 29, 31, 33, 34, 36, 62, 147
Grier, John 62, 106
Grier, Joseph 42
Grier, Josiah 147
Griffen, Anthony 42
Griffen, Ezekiel 16, 17, 20
Griffen, Joseph 93
Griffen, Mary 37, 51, 93
Griffen, Richard 42, 73
Griffeth, Benjamin 64
Griffin, Abia 139
Griffin, Anthony 98, 145, 167, 169
Griffin, Benj'n 120
Griffin, Chas 99
Griffin, Ezekiel 12, 151
Griffin, Jo's 98
Griffin, John 139
Griffin, Joseph 99, 106, 109, 144, 145, 167, 169
Griffin, Mary 98, 99, 167, 169
Griffin, Peter 133
Griffin, Richard 130, 151, 155, 156, 164
Griffin, Wm 96, 124, 125, 143, 150
Griffith, Benjamin 70, 72
Grimkey, John F. 14, 80
Grims, Wm 122
Grubbs, Benj'n 107
Guess, 162
Gunter, John 120
Hain, 21
Haisten, Thomas 41
Hall, Acquilla 95
Hall, Ann 146, 148, 160
Hall, John 41, 61, 63-67, 96, 100, 108, 110, 112, 113, 115, 117, 119, 120
Hall, Nathaniel 68
Hall, Robt 131
Hall, Saml 79, 100-104
Hall, Wm 95, 141, 152, 168
Hambleton, Alexander 16, 17, 20
Hambleton, Henry 19, 85
Hambleton, Rob't 120
Hambleton, Temperance 68
Hambleton, Thomas 68
Hamilton, Alex'r 161

Hammond, 16
Hammonds old Store, 16
Hammons's old store 146
Hampton, Nathan 16
Hancock, Esabella 112
Hancock, Richard 35, 43
Hanna, James 82
Hanna, Robert 70, 89, 100, 113
Hanna, William 44, 82, 91, 100
Hannah, (Slave) 21
Hannah, Robert 54, 82
Hardy, Jean 24
Harison, Robert 26
Harlan, Aaron 82
Harper, Alexander 3, 70, 130
Harper, Rich'd 87
Harper, Robert 15
Harper, Robert Goodloe 60
Harris, Catharina 74
Harris, Clough 72
Harris, William 3, 38, 50, 54, 87, 96, 117, 129, 138, 158, 168
Harvey, Charles 93, 94, 110, 123
Harvey, John 50
Harvey, Littleberry 17
Harvey, Phillip 50
Hatter, Richard 64
Haward, Thomas 27, 80
Head, John 68
Head, William 68, 121, 123, 124
Heads ford on Enoree 42
Hearvey, John 73
Hellams, John 132, 145
Hellams, Wm 130, 132, 145, 147
Helloms, Constant 57
Helloms, John 57
Helloms, William 57
Henderson, Charles 67
Henderson, James 80, 111, 130
Henderson, John 107, 128, 145
Henderson, Mary 107
Henderson, Mary Ann 45
Henderson, Nathaniel 16
Henderson, Richard 45
Henderson, Samuel 21, 45, 73, 80, 130, 169
Henderson, Thos 67
Hendrick's old place 154
Hendrix's old place 23, 60
Hendrix, Ann 9, 55
Hendrix, Margaret 61
Hendrix, Micajah 61
Heyward, Tho's 120
Hia, Rich'd 126
Hicks, Richard 12, 17, 22
Higgins, James 96, 108, 110, 112, 113, 115, 117
Higgins, Newton 127
Higgins, Thomas 81
Higgins, William 106, 123, 126, 129
Hill, Nathaniel 116
Hill, Wm 153
Hillon, John 20
Hillon, Mary 20

Histelo, John 32
Hitt, Peter 40, 127, 131
Hix, Richard 29, 30
Hogan, Silvester 93
Holcome, Joseph 120
Hollen, Bazel 62, 77
Hollingsworth, George 96, 107, 113, 152
Hollingsworth, Isaac 86
Hollingsworth, Jo's 109
Hollingsworth, John 96, 131
Hollingsworth, Jonathan 147
Hollingsworth, Joseph 96, 106, 111, 115
Hollon, Bazel 70, 73, 74
Honeycut, John 66, 69
House, John 124
Hubbs, Wm. 52, 69
Huddleston, Ja's 69
Huddleston, Jane 69
Huddleston, William 29, 31, 33, 34, 36, 69
Hudgins, Ambrose 67, 87, 105, 106, 154
Hudson, Caner 114
Hudson, John 126, 128
Hudson, Richard 60
Hudson, Sarah 114
Huggins, David 52
Huggins, Mary 27
Huggins, Susannah 52
Huggins, Wm. 27
Hugh Neal's Mill 120
Hugh Oneal's Mill 90, 125, 127, 146
Hughes's mill on Enoree, 53
Hughes, John 63, 79, 100-104
Hughes, Robert H. 32, 38, 57, 68, 69, 109, 154, 162, 167
Hughes, Thomas 12, 55, 157
Hughes, Wm 120
Hughey, Martin 149, 155, 156
Hugins, Ambrose 120
Hulsey, James 52, 153
Hunt, Charles 75
Hunter, 75
Hunter, John 14-17, 19, 21, 22, 28, 30, 51, 53, 55, 57, 58, 62, 65-68, 70, 73, 74, 88-90, 92, 93, 100, 101, 106, 108, 110, 112, 119, 127, 131, 146, 147, 150, 154, 156, 157, 159-161, 167-170
Hunter, Matthew 3-5, 69, 79
Hunter, Robert 46, 47, 151, 167
Hunter, William 3-5, 111, 130, 151, 156, 163, 164
Huston, John 132
Hutcheson, William 71, 83
Hutching, Tho's 116
Hutchings, Charles 16, 28, 68-70, 73, 74, 77, 92, 121, 141, 144
Hutchings, Elizebeth 68, 69
Hutchins, Charles 31
Hutson, John 80, 103, 104, 131
Hutson, Mary 52
Hutson, Richard 27
Indian Creek 46
Irwin, 76
Irwin, Agness 41

Irwin, Alex'd 41
Irwin, James 41
Island ford 28, 146
Island ford on Salluda River 52, 63, 145
Jackson, Daniel 2, 74, 112
Jackson, William 44, 66, 70, 84, 87, 94, 132, 137, 138, 157, 162
Jett, James 60
Johnson, Francis 162
Johnson, Jas 141
Johnson, Jonathan 123, 149, 156
Johnson, Rob't 162
Johnston, Absolem 114
Johnston, Henry 44
Johnston, Jonathan 31, 44, 86, 107
Jones's old mill 16, 23
Jones, 73, 84, 106
Jones, Benjamin 79
Jones, Charles 61, 118, 135, 144, 154, 156, 157, 159
Jones, James 25, 91, 101
Jones, John 98, 112, 119, 122, 127, 140, 143, 144, 147, 150
Jones, Margaret 141
Jones, Saml. P. 20
Jones, Sarah 98
Jones, Thomas 12, 22, 30, 42, 145
Journey, John 56, 136
Jowel/l, Rich'd 87, 91, 93, 166
Kellet/t, Hanna 63
Kellet/t, Jane 53
Kellet/t, Jean 8, 50
Kellet/t, John 53, 63, 102, 128, 157
Kellet/t, Joseph 51, 53
Kellet/t, Susannah 53
Kellet/t, William 53
Kelley, Saml 38
Kellogh, Robt 23
Kemp, 151
Kemp, Nathan 12, 46, 54, 58, 67
Kennedy, Eliz'a 142
Kern's store 154
Kern, John D. 38, 54, 65, 70, 88, 92, 116, 121, 141
Kern, John Danl 137, 144
Kernall, Barnet 163
Kernall, Grace 163
Kernall, Patrick 163
Kil(l)gore, Benjamin 14, 63, 66, 93, 105, 112, 114-116, 138, 149
Kil(l)gore, Jas 10
King, Benjamin 84
King, John 71
Koewin, John 76
Lang, Rich'd 13, 16, 39
Langston, Christian 62, 76
Langston, John 154
Langston, Solomon 96, 97, 108, 110, 112, 113, 115, 117, 145
Lard, John 166
Lard, Ludwick 46
Lard, Robert 42, 130
Lard, Saml 96

Laurens, Henry 169
Learwood, Edmond 79, 104, 151, 167
Lemon, Sam'l 73, 83, 152, 166, 168
Lester, Francis 50, 161, 165
Lethes, Elizebeth 64
Lethes, Margaret 64
Leveston, George 69
Lewis, Ellenor 75, 163
Lewis, Ellinor 163
Lewis, John 28
Lewis, Presilla 28
Lewis, Thos 28, 112, 128
Lexington County 116
Linch, Aaron 28
Linch, John 119
Lincoln County, N. Carolina 71
Lindley, James 153, 161, 165
Lindley, Thomas 153, 161, 165
Lindsey, John 19, 58, 71, 85, 96, 109, 111, 113, 115, 146
Lindsey, Thos 131
Little River 14, 28, 42, 46, 47, 51, 54, 59, 81, 91, 127, 132, 144, 146, 151
Little River Bridge 90, 98
Little, Frederick 69, 161
Little, James 17, 112, 127, 130
Loften, Thomas 147
Loftin, John 124, 148
Lofton, John 140, 147
Logan, David 152, 155, 156, 160
Logan, Francis 58
Logan, Tho's 107
Long, Richard 16
Long, Robert 70, 73, 74, 77, 154
Love, Matthew 80
Lowery, Thomas 54
Lowery, William 110, 124
Loyn, Joseph 132
Lucust, John 50, 55
Lucust, Sarah 50, 52, 55
Lynch, Aron 97
Madden, Ann 140
Madden, David 152
Madden, George 145, 154, 156, 157, 159
Madden, John 104
Maddin, Benjamin 154
Maddin, George 121
Madding, Ann 7
Madding, John 93, 94
Mading, John 21, 34
Magness, Saml 84, 87
Magniss, Saml 117
Mahon, Joseph 104, 108, 110
Mahorn, Joseph 147
Malden, Benj'n 144, 156, 157, 159
Man, Susanna 112, 113, 123, 147, 159, 161
Manley, John 152
Manly, John 3-5, 8, 67
Manor, Jacob 97, 169
Mars, Thomas 45, 63-65, 143
Martin, Dan'l 82, 151
Martin, Dycey 15
Martin, George 24, 112

Martin, John 7, 9, 15, 22, 30, 39, 43, 50, 55, 63, 115, 116, 118, 135, 138, 154, 162
Martin, L. Martin 145
Martin, Lumpy John 17
Martin, Martin 17, 43-49, 52, 109, 124, 141, 152, 166, 168
Martin, Shadrach 2, 15, 71, 84, 96, 99, 113, 114, 116, 124, 125, 148
Martin, William 3-5, 8, 35, 41, 50, 16, 148, 152
Martindale, Joseph 60
Mason, Joseph 130
Masse, Ann 125
Mastes, Noltey 59
Mastes, Notley 25, 36
Maxwell, Robert 3, 87
Mayhon, Dickson 30
Mayhon, Joseph 7, 12, 46, 66, 69, 76, 89
McBee, Vardry 63
McCaa, David 38, 63, 67
McCain, Elizabeth 96, 107
McCain, James 96, 97, 107
McCarty, Bryan 10, 15
McCarty, Daniel 136, 140
McCelvey, John 61
McClain, Daniel 52, 80
McClain, James 144
McClintick, James 28
McClintick, John 28
McClintock, James 136
McClintock, John 71, 96, 124, 125, 130, 151, 167
McCluer, Ann 18
McClure, Wm 144
McClurkin, Sam'l 40, 45, 103, 104, 126, 128, 131, 147
McClurkin, Thomas 11, 12, 37, 47, 48
McConathy, Sam'l 166
McCrary, Jean 28
McCrary, John 16, 28, 37
McCrary, Robert 16, 22, 25, 28, 30, 38, 46, 61, 86, 91, 98, 101, 105
McCrary, Thomas 96
McCrery, Robert 130
McDanald, James 127
McDanald, Joseph 73
McDanald, Mary 77
McDanald, Rich'd 130
McDanald, Thomas 16, 40, 71, 91, 108
McDavid, David 17
McDavid, Jane 105
McDole, Wm 120
McDonald, Thos 13
McDowall, Alexander 23, 72
McDowalls Store 21
McDowell, Patrick 80, 127
McElory, John 15
McElroy, John 8-10, 83, 122
McFagin, Mary 142
McFarson, Wm. 61, 63-67
Mcgee, John 44
Mcgin, Daniel 42
Mcglathery, David 57

Mcgregory, Thomas 31
McGrigger, Thomas 19
McLain, Danl 131, 132
McLaughlin, James 93
McLaughlin, James 66, 115
Mcloklin, Jas 3
McMahan, Cornelius 145
McMahon, Curnelius 53, 58
McMillian, Alex'r 115
McMillion, Matthew 115
McNees, 47, 54, 55, 68, 69, 88
McNees, James 7, 26, 29, 46, 64, 71-74, 83, 91, 93, 99, 103, 104, 107, 108, 113, 114, 118, 121, 123, 124, 128, 134, 136, 149, 153, 154, 156, 167, 168
McNees, John 103, 118
McNees, Mary 61
McNees, Robert 6, 7, 9, 16, 17, 20, 21, 24, 29, 61, 70, 74, 77, 153, 167
McNess, James 99
McNight, Abiga(i)l 148, 156
McNight, And'w 148, 156
McVay, David 5, 8
McVay, Hugh 3, 14, 30, 33, 34, 82, 87, 142
McVay, Martha 82
McWilliams, Andrew 91
McWilliams, Hugh 78
Medole, John 152, 166, 168
Medole, Wm 145
Meek, John 145, 152, 168
Meeks, Jesse 152, 166, 168
Meeks, John 166
Megaffey, Charles 67
Megaffie, Chas 69
Megee, John 26
Megee, Micheal 152
Megin, Daniel 59, 66, 80, 135
Meglathery, David 86
Mehaffy, Martin 53, 63
Mehaffy, Mary 103, 104, 109, 113
Menary, Alex'd 17
Menary, Gilbert 23, 76
Meredith, Henry 56
Merill, Chas 131
Methany, Dan'l 120
Michusson, Wm. 110
Middleton, Hugh 78, 170
Midole, Wm 137
Milam, John 89, 94, 97, 152, 157
Mill Creek 42, 46, 52, 54, 90, 98, 145
Miller, Haunce 110
Miller, James 144, 154, 156, 157, 159, 160
Miller, John 152, 168
Millwee, James 23
Millwee, John 72
Millwee, Major 160
Millwee, William 13, 58, 61, 111, 126
Mitchell, Isaac 35, 65
Mitchell, John 143
Mitchell, Mary 142
Mitchell, William 83, 136, 146
Mitchuson, Edward 9, 14, 26
Mitchuson, William 6, 14, 15, 22

Mitchusson, 169
Mitchusson, Edm'd 138
Mitchusson, Edward 29, 75, 93, 77, 96, 112, 115, 117, 130, 142
Mitchusson, Edwerd 8, 10
Mitchusson, William 4, 5, 8, 14, 15, 30, 32, 50, 51, 74, 75, 77, 90, 93, 115, 118, 128, 130, 141, 143, 144, 153, 154, 156, 157, 159, 161, 165, 170
Molden, 54
Monary, Gilbert 130
Mondith, Henry 136
Montgomery, 75
Montgomery, James 4, 6, 8, 14, 15, 19-22, 24, 27, 28, 30, 32, 35, 37, 39, 43, 45-47, 49-51, 55, 57, 58, 61, 62, 65-69, 78, 79, 81, 86, 89, 90, 93-95, 97, 98, 100, 101, 106, 110, 112, 114, 115, 119, 130, 133, 137, 140, 141, 144, 146, 148, 151, 153, 154, 156, 163, 165, 168, 170
Montgomery, John 121, 124
Moor, George 48
Moor, Mark 22
Moore, Curtis 109, 121, 123, 152
Moore, George 11, 12, 48, 76, 145
Moore, James 131
Moore, John 2, 65
Moore, Joshua 52, 53
Moore, Mark 47, 130
Moore, Martha 52
Moore, Sarah 160
Moore, William 88, 160
Morgan, George 131, 136, 146, 147
Morison, Alex'd 43
Moss, Ebenezer 26
Mosse, Ann 125
Motes, Joseph 127
Motley, John 44
Moultrie, William 15
Mudlick Creek 73, 90
Murphey, Ebenezer 121
Murphey, John 145, 152, 153, 161
Murphey, Mary 152, 161
Murphey, Roger 79, 100-104
Murphey, Thomas 99, 107, 138
Murphey, Wm 112, 128
Murphy, Roger 121
Murrey, John 56
Musgrove, Edward 2, 70, 71
Mutchuson, Wm. 27
Myers, Henry 22, 89, 91, 103, 104
N. Carolina, State of 58, 89
Neal's Mill 59
Neal, Charles 94
Neal, Hugh 120
Nealy, John 81
Nealy, Joseph 97
Neeley, George 131
Neighbors, Sam'l 169
Neighbours, Abraham 34, 51, 75, 79, 81, 89, 101, 102, 116, 129
Neighbours, Sam'l 101, 120, 134-136, 138, 140-143, 153

Neil, Charles 73
Neil, Jacob 68
Neil, Samuel 82
Neil, William 8, 82, 166
Neiles, Nathaniel 161
Neiley, James 120
Neiley, John 90, 123, 128
Neily, John 97, 139
Nevels, Ann 149, 155
Newberry County 46, 48, 55, 105, 139
Newberry Court 158
Newman, Jacob 91
Newman, John 32, 38, 57
Niblet, Solomon 37
Niccles, Wm 120
Nickalls, Charles 79
Nickels, Nath'l 67
Nickols, Nathaniel 62, 64-66
Nicks, Jane 159
Niel, Saml 22, 79
Niel, Wm 3-5, 79
Ninety Six 114
Ninety Six Road 54
Nobles, Joshua 79, 100-104
Norris, John 82, 152, 166, 168
Norris, William 16, 17, 20, 120
Norwood, George 28
Norwood, Nathaniel 20
Nun/n, Joshua 25, 56, 64
Obannion, Wm 132
Obennian, Wm. 80
Obryan, Duncan 42, 58, 65, 85
Obryan, Elizebeth 22, 24
Obryan, John 7
Obryan, Patrick 15, 43-49, 79, 85
Obryant, Jas 161
Odels ford 28
ONeal's Mill 73 -- see also Hugh Oneal's mill
Oneal, Abijah 37, 107
Oneal, Hugh 16, 37, 38, 40, 42, 59, 67, 71, 73, 80, 90, 125, 127, 146, 165
Oneal, John 51
Owens, James 158
Owens, Rich'd 132
Owin, John 43-49
Owing, John 144
Owings, Elizabeth 169
Owings, James 160, 165
Owings, John 159
Owins, And'w 107
Owins, Ann 103, 104, 109, 113
Owins, Archebald 80
Owins, John 57, 94, 97, 147
Ozborn, William 16
Ozburn, Daniel 6, 79, 82, 104
Ozburn, John 17, 39, 59
Ozburn, Wm. 45
Page, Robert 86
Palmore, Thomas 51, 97
Palmour, Thomas 43
Pamplin, 107
Pamplin, John 38

Parker, Andrew 130
Parker, Charity 15, 34
Parker, Wm 148
Parkes, And'w 130
Parks, Andrew 87, 91-93
Parks, James 87, 91-93, 105
Parrot, Danl 131
Parsons, Joseph 16, 17, 20, 26, 54, 71, 88, 106, 109, 111, 113, 115, 127, 160
Parsons, Saml 94, 106, 107, 113, 129
Pate, Jeremiah 124
Patterson, Joseph 29, 31, 32, 161
Pearson, John 50
Pearson, Joseph 28
Pearson, Samuel 38
Pearson, Thomas 49, 70
Pedan, David 149, 155, 169
Pendleton, Henry 14, 60, 96, 120
Pendleton, James 60
Penington, Jacob 76
Penington, John 105, 106, 128
Pennington, John 113
Pennsylvania, 41
Perkins, Thomas 143
Perry, John 27
Persons, Thomas 24, 25
Peterson, James 112
Philpot, John 160
Philpot, Thomas 160
Phindley, John 43
Phindley, Paul 126
Phindly, John 35
Pinckney, Charles 163, 164
Pinckney, Thomas 57
Pinson, Duke 161
Pinson, John 57
Pinson, Joseph 16, 106, 129
Pinson, Marmaduke 15, 152, 166, 168
Pinson, Mary 16
Pinson, Moses 161
Pitts, John 133
Pitts, William 68
Plant, Stephen 107, 123, 126, 129
Plunkett, Robert 37
Polard, Richard 28
Pollard, James 126
Pollard, Richard 44, 52
Pollard, Robert 119
Pollock, James 44
Polock, John 51
Pool, Seth P. 56
Pool, Seth Petty 107
Poole, James 131
Portswood, Thomas 48, 115, 134
Potter, Stephen 7, 9, 10, 18, 34
Powel, John 153, 156
Powel, Saml 59, 82
Powell, John 37, 144, 156, 159
Powell, Saml 43-49, 55, 96, 109, 111, 115
Power, Holloway 72, 88, 131, 133, 143, 147, 149, 155, 157, 169
Power, Holoway 16, 17, 20
Power, Howloway 102

Powers, John 6, 87, 91-93
Prater, Josiah 64
Prater, Midleton 79
Prather, Wm 146
Prator, Bazel 29, 31, 33, 34, 36
Prator, Bazzle 113
Prator, Josiah 29, 31, 33, 34, 36
Prator, Mary 37
Prator, Wm 37
Price, Isaac 77
Price, Jane 77
Price, Margaret 73
Price, Mary 77
Price, Ruth 77
Price, Sarah 77
Price, William 13, 23, 43, 66, 70, 73, 74, 77, 123
Proctor, Margaret 111
Prude, John 38, 145
Pucket, Charles 78, 145, 153, 156, 157, 159
Pucket, Douglas 153
Pucket, Edward 153
Pucket, James 74, 79, 88, 92, 96, 100, 108, 110, 112, 113, 115, 117, 144
Pucket, Jonathan 61, 63, 64, 79
Puckett, Charles 89, 149
Puckett, James 146
Pugh, Edwerd 5, 91
Pugh, Martin 122, 133
Pugh, Rich'd 96, 124, 124, 137
Pugh, Willeby 161
Pugh, William 99, 116
Pyles, 47, 54, 55, 68, 69, 88
Pyles, Reuben 11, 36, 93, 124, 125, 134, 139, 148
Pyles, Reubin 2, 23, 24, 37, 46, 59, 72, 83, 84, 88, 95, 96, 99, 113, 114, 128, 144, 149-156, 167
Quin, John 133
Raburn, Elizebeth 19
Ragsdale, William 120, 134-136, 138, 140-143
Rainey, Benjamin 3, 20, 44, 70, 76, 91, 100, 114, 123, 124, 134, 136-139, 142, 162, 167
Rainey, John 3, 4, 107, 160
Rainey, William 3, 106
Rains, James 167
Ramage, Joseph 42, 126, 129
Rammage, John 113, 123
Rammage, Joseph 107
Ramsey, Ephraim 145, 160
Rapley, A. 154
Ray, William 40
Reaburns Creek 4, 26, 58, 71, 127, 129
Redman, John 39
Redy River & Saluda 125
Redy River 125, 129, 150
Reed, George 26
Reed, Jonth'n 152
Reed, Joseph 59
Reede, George 44
Retherford, Robert 109
Revill, Thos 119

Reyley, Ferrell 40
Reyley, Patrick 11, 21, 22, 36, 51
Richey, John 129, 130, 142, 144, 152, 154, 155, 157, 160, 164
Richey, Margaret 17
Richey, Robert 136, 147
Ridgeaway, John 67
Ridgeway, David 67
Ridgeway, Henry 59
Ridgeway, John 47
Ridgeway, Saml 59
Riding, Joseph 86
Rieley, Patrick 70
Right, Jacob 100
Right, Sarah 114
Riley-- see also Reyley
Riley, Charles 134
Riley, Eliphaz 154, 158, 166, 168
Riley, P. 130
Riley, Patrick 90, 103
Ripley, Ambrose 56, 139
Ripley, John 56-58, 138
Ritchey, John 1, 3, 15, 30, 31, 45, 52, 59, 64, 66, 93, 94, 164
Ritchey, Robert 91, 93
Riverland, John 161
Road from County Line to Crumbies mill 151
Roberts, Sarah 82
Roberts, Walter 143
Robertson, John 32
Robertson, Rich'd 134
Robertson, Wm 158
Robinson, Richard 74, 131, 134
Robison, John 60
Robison, Richard 74
Rodgers, Andrew 7, 9, 10, 15, 23, 24, 30, 36, 42, 46, 52, 54, 55, 62, 73, 79, 88, 100, 101, 104, 107, 127, 129, 131, 149, 151, 157, 167, 168
Rodgers, Dan'l 130
Rodgers, Isaac 16, 17, 20
Rodgers, John 4, 6, 8-11, 14, 20, 21, 27, 30, 32, 50, 57, 58, 62, 67-69, 72, 74, 77-79, 81, 86, 94, 95, 106, 108, 110, 112, 114, 115, 118-122, 126, 128, 130, 131, 133, 137, 140, 144, 148, 151, 153, 154, 156, 168, 169
Rodgers, Letty 62
Rodgers, Margaret 14
Rodgers, Thomas 42, 108, 131, 137, 147, 152
Rodgers, William 73, 94, 104, 107, 145, 153, 156, 157, 159, 165, 166
Rodgers, William Thos 131, 142
Rogers, And'w 22, 122
Rogers, John 6, 42, 118, 120
Roland, Ezekiel 126
Roland, John 86
Roland, Reubin 98
Roland, Richard 16, 17
Rooks, Nathl 86
Rooks, Wm 86
Roseman, James 38
Ross, David 59
Ross, George 20, 111, 154
Ross, Robert 3, 11, 30, 33, 61, 81-83, 92, 144, 167
Ruble, Peter 108
Ruly[?], Thomas 151
Russell, James 4, 41, 50, 70, 90, 149
Russell, John 63
Rutherford County, N. Carolina 14, 76, 87
Rutledge's ford 129
Rutledge's ford on Saluda 143, 169
Rutledge, John 27, 60, 75, 84, 85, 96
Rutledge, Reason 75, 84
Rutledge, Russel 85
Sadler, John 60, 161
Salmon, Wm. 27
Saluda river 21, 28, 125, 129, 143, 146, 169
Sample, James 87, 91-93
Sanders, John 52, 60
Satterfield, James 165
Satterwhite, John 55
Saturwhite, Bartlet 48
Saxon, Charles 4, 6, 8, 12, 14, 15, 25, 27, 37-39, 50-52, 57, 58, 62, 65, 67-70, 79, 90, 96, 97, 101, 107, 108, 112, 121, 122, 126, 133, 137, 141, 153, 156, 157, 159, 163, 168
Saxon, James 9, 22, 25, 37, 73, 79, 83, 104, 133, 151, 159
Saxon, John 45, 73, 96, 108-111, 113, 115, 152
Saxon, Joshua 37, 61, 63, 90, 96, 124, 125, 169
Saxon, Lewis 14, 19, 21, 27, 51, 57, 63, 67, 90, 105, 106, 118, 119, 131, 145, 147, 149, 150, 160
Saxon, Robt 66
Saxon, Salley 67
Saxon, Samuel 37, 50, 56, 57, 61, 64, 68, 71, 83, 86, 88, 89, 100, 104, 106, 116, 130, 151, 159, 167
Scott, Robert 51, 70, 73, 74, 77, 96
Scott, Samuel 1, 3, 4, 8, 29, 45, 46, 63, 64, 122, 152
Scrugs, James 74
Scrugs, Pamela 74
Scrugs, Sarah 74
Searcy, Jeremiah 169
Shaw, W. 25, 36
Shaw, William 2, 4, 5, 7-9, 13, 23, 24, 26, 39, 40, 44, 75, 87, 88, 103, 111, 116, 132, 162, 168
Ship, Thomas 47, 79, 80, 131
Ship, Wm 158
Shirley, Argile 120
Shirley, John 59, 83, 161
Shirley, Lidia 7
Shirley, Rebecca 83
Shirly, John 53
Simmons, Charles 15, 32, 42, 79, 92, 104, 145, 167
Simmons, John 92, 99, 167, 169
Simmons, Nancy 92, 99, 167, 169
Simmons, Wm 167
Simms, Charles 3

Simpson, Alex'r 127
Simpson, David 44
Simpson, James 127
Simpson, John 41, 53, 82, 88, 102, 127, 137, 157, 160, 164-166, 168
Simpson, John 137
Simpson, Robert 127
Simpson, Wm. 58
Sims, Clabourn 108, 120, 147
Sims, Claburn 24, 34, 87, 91-93, 135
Sims, Danl 127
Sims, John 51, 79, 81, 100, 103, 104
Sims, Micajah 66
Sims, Robert 51, 66, 76
Sims, Wm 79, 87, 99-104, 108, 120, 131, 135, 147
Sims, Zachariah 79, 91-93
Singleton, Tho's 116
Smart, Rob't 96
Smith, 73, 84, 106
Smith, Charles 52, 83
Smith, David 143
Smith, Drury 152
Smith, Ezekiel 28, 44, 52
Smith, Job 4
Smith, John 35, 92, 126, 143, 150, 162
Smith, John Calloway 158
Smith, Joseph 29, 31, 71
Smith, Kitt 42, 130, 151
Smith, Luther 73
Smith, Peter 162, 166
Snell, Alex'd 64, 156
Solmon, Matthew 124
South fork of Dunkins' Creek 154
South, Dan'l 152
South, Joseph 31, 32, 99, 106, 110, 115, 129
South, Wm 120
Spartanburgh County 32, 35
Spence, David 57
Spence, Robert 43-49, 57
Springfield, Thomas 131, 147, 154
Starnes, Aaron 51
Starns, Aron 61, 63-67
Starns, Ebenezer 107
Stean, Martha 109
Steen, James 19
Stephens, Elijah 94
Stephens, John 30
Stewart, Alse 3
Stewart, John 92, 126
Stewart, Wm 3
Stinson, James 21, 22, 30, 34, 59
Stone, Benj'n 131, 147, 165
Stone, Reubin 32, 148
Stone, William 42, 120, 134-136, 138, 140-143
Strain, James 96, 108, 110, 112, 113, 115, 117
Stroud, John 60
Stubblefield, John 10
Sullivan-- see also Swillivant
Sullivan, Charles 43, 103, 142
Sullivant, Charles 33, 34, 38, 39, 48, 61, 83, 84, 147, 149
Sullivant, Fanney 163
Sullivant, Harrison 74
Sullivant, James 29, 39, 42, 48, 71, 74, 115, 127, 131, 134, 152, 163
Sullivant, John 163
Sullivant, Stephen 143
Sullivants, James 51, 81, 161
Sulton, Robert 73
Suter, Wm. 96, 109, 111, 113, 115
Swancey's Ferry 129, 146, 165
Swancey's ferry on Saluda 81
Swearings, John 98, 120, 134-136, 138, 140-143
Swillivant, Charles 4, 5, 9, 10, 15, 21, 22
Swillivant, James 15
Tate, William 80
Taverns 4, 16, 21, 37, 45, 54, 71, 75 (3), 78 (2), 82, 85, 90, 115 (2), 131, 139, 154
Tavern rates 7
Taylor's path 97
Taylor, Elijah 91, 132
Taylor, George 120
Taylor, James 145
Taylor, Jean 21
Taylor, Robert 12, 61, 96, 111, 113, 115, 167
Taylor, William 20, 57, 61, 64-67, 161
Teague, Abner 120
Teague, Joshua 28, 150, 163
Teague, Wm. 151, 167
Templeton, David 131
Templeton, James 58, 85, 145
Templeton, John 81
Templeton, Rob't 120
Tenney, Patience 58
Terry, Nancy 18
Terry, William 18, 117
Thomas Carter's old place 81, 131, 146
Thomas, John 129
Thomason's Mill 26, 58, 122, 145
Thomason, John 129, 142
Thomason, William 4, 5, 14, 21, 22, 35, 36, 41, 42, 73, 84, 94, 103, 106, 107, 129, 138, 142, 152
Thompson, Flanders 84
Thompson, Wm 161
Thurston, James 100, 139
Tiber, 47
Tindsley, Ann 10
Tindsley, Elizebeth 29, 77
Tindsly, Ann 15
Tindsly, Elizabeth 6
Tinker, James 21
Tinsley, Elizabeth 99
Tirpin, 102
To(o)mbs, Robert 48, 72, 91, 108, 122, 133, 135
Tod/d, John 52, 96, 108, 110, 112, 113, 115, 117
Tod/d, Robert 52, 67, 69, 151, 167
Tod/d, Thomas 16
Tolds, Jean 36, 72, 90, 108, 121
Trotter, John 69

183

Tue, Drury 112
Tumbling shoal on Redy River 143, 169
Tumbling Shoals 129, 150
Tune, John 24
Turner, Asa 87, 91-93
Turner, Gilbert 40
Turner, John 163
Turner, Richard 56, 89, 131
Turpin, 39, 40, 59, 74, 88, 89, 101, 114, 135, 155
Tweedy, William 43-49, 79, 91, 104
Underwood, James 3-5, 43-49, 85
Union County 124
Union Court 158
Vance, John 61
Varford, Benjamin 68
Vines, Isia 119
Virginia, State of 60, 83, 124
Waddleton, James 63
Wadkins, Wm 152
Wadsworth, 40, 59, 74, 88, 89, 101, 102, 114, 135, 155
Wadsworth, Thomas 39, 73, 89, 127, 128, 149
Wafer, Frances 84, 87, 117
Waldrop, James 55, 99
Waldrop, Jo's 108
Waldrop, John 55, 107
Waldrop, Joseph 96, 108, 110, 112, 113, 115, 117
Waldrop, Luke 70, 73, 74, 77, 108
Waldrop, Mary 108
Waldrop, Michael 3, 4, 10, 24, 43, 46-49, 53-55, 71, 84, 87, 91, 96, 99, 111, 109, 113, 115, 124, 132, 165, 166
Waldroup, James 9, 10, 21, 37, 43
Waldroup, Luke 45
Waldroup, Michael 5, 10, 38, 40, 43, 44, 47, 48
Waldroup, Shadrach 43
Walker, 15, 162
Walker, George 96
Walker, John 70, 73, 74, 77, 84, 86, 98, 107, 111
Walker, Mansfield 42
Walker, Memk'n 107
Walker, Memucan 89, 129
Walker, Sarah 50
Walker, Silvanus 14, 20-22, 27, 28, 30, 32, 35, 37, 39, 43, 45, 46, 50, 53, 59, 66, 68, 77, 96-98, 106, 112-114, 119-121, 127, 128, 130, 144, 146, 151-153, 156, 161, 165, 167
Walker, Tandy 17, 82, 96, 127, 129
Wallace, John 48, 55, 109, 115, 116
Wallace, Michael 33, 61, 64-67, 73
Ward, Jeremiah 65
Ward, Sarah 65, 98
Ward, Thos 71
Ward, Widow 71
Warren, Simpson 96
Watson, 162
Watson, Elijah 19
Watson, James 9, 10, 120

Watson, John 29, 31-34, 36, 68, 79, 138
Watson, William 19, 32
Watts, George 130
Watts, James 151
Watts, John 98
Watts, Richard 27, 53, 56, 89
Weathers, Martha 57
Weathers, Samuel 57, 61, 63-67, 125, 126
Web, Susannah 47, 54
Webb, Jeremiah 73, 94
Weir, David 45
Weir, George 28
Weir, Jean 45
Weir, John 40
Weir, Mary 28
Welch, David 14, 32, 33, 35
Wells, James 79, 101, 102
Wells, John 161
Wells, Lewis 68, 157
Wells, Philip 124, 142, 149, 157
Westmoreland, John 54
Westmoreland, Lenoir 68
Wharton, Samuel 38, 62, 69, 152
Whealer, Wm 80
White, Henry 5, 14
White, James 161
White, Jean 21
White, Nicholas 20
Whitmore, George 81, 120, 134-136, 138, 140-143
Whitmore, Joseph 96
Whitton, Rob't 135
Whorton, Saml 3, 30, 51, 97, 113, 114
Widowman, Barbery 68
Widowman, John 68
Wigginton, George 106
Wigginton, John 152, 166
Wild, John 158
Wilkes, Thomas 142
Wilks, Thomas 120, 134-136, 138, 140, 141, 143
Willard, John 79
Williams, 46
Williams, Duke 45, 85, 139
Williams, Hester 53
Williams, Isaac 37, 51
Williams, J. 109, 122
Williams, James 48, 99, 106, 109, 160, 161, 167, 169
Williams, Jo's 109
Williams, John 13, 36, 45, 50, 57, 80, 85, 99, 106, 121, 123, 126, 127, 129, 136, 139
Williams, Joseph 96, 113, 137, 149
Williams, M. 123
Williams, Martin 4, 8, 63, 72, 76, 88, 90, 97, 102, 117, 133, 138, 143, 157, 167
Williams, Mary 8, 9, 29, 45, 46, 48, 72, 90, 91, 99, 104, 108, 109, 122, 133, 135
Williams, Mastin 65
Williams, Sam'l 57, 161
Williams, Stephen 16
Williams, Washington 99
Williamson, Thomas 85

Williamson, Wm 87
Willson, Charles 51
Willson, James 119, 152, 166, 168
Willson, John 36, 96, 108, 110, 112, 113, 115, 117, 154, 166
Willson, Micheal 169
Willson, William 63, 67, 96, 108, 110, 112, 113, 115, 117
Winn, Jones 59
Winters, George 35
Winton, County of 158
Wolf, John F. 122, 168
Wolf, M. 129
Wood, 137
Wood, Elizabeth 121, 124-127, 134
Wood, James 138, 149
Wood, Mary 125, 126
Wood, P. 138, 149
Wood, Peter 92, 93, 129, 130, 142
Wood, Stephen 16, 59, 61, 83, 94
Wood, Thos 138, 149
Wood, Wm 21, 22
Woodard, Thos 87
Woodroof, Fielding 84, 94, 99
Woods, Hugh 24
Word, Thomas 6
Wright, Daniel 7, 20, 50, 51, 53, 55, 57, 58, 62, 63, 65, 68, 69, 72-74, 77, 79, 86, 93, 95, 118, 119, 121, 122, 126, 140, 141, 144, 148, 149, 153, 154, 156, 157, 159, 170
Wright, Elizabeth 140
Wright, Jacob 79, 101-104
Wright, John 94, 144
Yanc(e)y, 32, 63, 99
Yanc(e)y, J. 5, 7, 9, 10, 12, 23-25, 66
Yanc(e)y, James 2-4, 10-14, 21, 37, 91, 102, 106, 111, 132, 137, 148, 150, 160
Yancey, Y. 8
York, John 29, 34, 70, 130
Young, Archibald 40
Young, George 42, 96, 124, 125, 135
Young, Hugh 29, 64, 73, 74, 91, 97, 104, 108, 113, 123, 124, 152, 153, 165, 167
Young, James 17, 23, 38, 40, 53, 78, 79, 87, 96, 115, 118, 124, 125, 131, 141, 147
Young, John 40
Young, Joseph 70, 74, 77
Young, Mary 40
Young, Robert 38, 39, 55, 68, 71, 127, 147
Young, William 29, 44-49, 64, 70, 73, 74, 77, 91, 104, 108, 123, 124

Heritage Books by Brent H. Holcomb:

Bute County, North Carolina Land Grant Plats and Land Entries

CD: Early Records of Fishing Creek Presbyterian Church, Chester County, South Carolina, 1799–1859

CD: Kershaw County, South Carolina Minutes of the County Court, 1791–1799

CD: Marriage and Death Notices from The Charleston [S.C.] Observer, *1827–1845*

CD: South Carolina, Volume 1

CD: Winton (Barnwell) County, South Carolina Minutes of County Court and Will Book 1, 1785–1791

Early Records of Fishing Creek Presbyterian Church, Chester County, South Carolina, 1799–1859, with Appendices of the Visitation List of Rev. John Simpson, 1774–1776 and the Cemetery Roster, 1762–1979
Brent H. Holcomb and Elmer O. Parker

Kershaw County, South Carolina Minutes of the County Court, 1791–1799

Laurens County, South Carolina, Minutes of the County Court, 1786–1789

Marriage and Death Notices from Columbia, South Carolina Newspapers, 1838–1860; Including Legal Notices from Burnt Counties

Marriage and Death Notices from The Charleston Observer, *1827–1845*

Memorialized Records of Lexington District, South Carolina, 1814–1825

Winton (Barnwell) County, South Carolina Minutes of County Court and Will Book 1, 1785–1791

South Carolina Deed Abstracts, 1773–1778, Books F-4 through X-4

South Carolina Deed Abstracts, 1776–1783, Books Y-4 through H-5

South Carolina Deed Abstracts, 1783–1788, Books I-5 through Z-5

York County, South Carolina Will Abstracts, 1787–1862 [1770–1862]

www.ingramcontent.com/pod-product-compliance
Lightning Source LLC
Chambersburg PA
CBHW060818190426
43197CB00038B/2076